EARLY AMERICAN SPORT

EARLY
AMERICAN
SPORT

A Checklist of Books by American
and Foreign Authors Published in
America Prior to 1860
including
Sporting Songs

Third Edition
Revised and Enlarged

Compiled by
Robert W. Henderson

RUTHERFORD • MADISON • TEANECK
FAIRLEIGH DICKINSON UNIVERSITY PRESS
LONDON: ASSOCIATED UNIVERSITY PRESSES

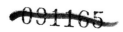

Associated University Presses, Inc.
Cranbury, New Jersey 08512

Associated University Presses
Magdalen House
136-148 Tooley Street
London SE1 2TT, England

Library of Congress Cataloging in Publication Data

Henderson, Robert William, 1888–
Early American sport.

Bibliography: p.
Includes index.
1. Sports—United States—Bibliography. I. Title.
Z7511.H49 1976   [GV583] 016.796′0973   74-30537
ISBN 0-8386-1677-1

PRINTED IN THE UNITED STATES OF AMERICA

CONTENTS

ACKNOWLEDGMENTS
FOR THE
THIRD EDITION

This checklist was first published in 1937, in a limited edition, by the Grolier Club. A second edition was published by A. S. Barnes and Company in 1953.

The compiler's interest in the bibliography of early American sport arose out of his duties for sixty years as Librarian of the Racquet and Tennis Club of New York. The library of the Club probably has more of the books included in the list than any other library. Appreciation is once more expressed to the Board of Governors, and especially to those members who served on the Committee on Library and Art, for their splendid interest and continuing support.

Acknowledgement is also given to the many friends who helped in previous editions. For valuable assistance in the preparation of this third edition, I gratefully thank Warder H. Cadbury, whose interest in the Adirondacks produced many related items, and Herm David, who suggested several books on dogs.

INTRODUCTION

The primary purpose of this checklist is to provide a guide to collectors of early American sporting books. It includes books relating to sports, by both American and foreign authors, published in the United States or Canada prior to the year 1860. Efforts have been made to make the list as complete as possible, but of course rarities will continue to appear, to the delight of the fortunate collector.

A secondary purpose is to contribute to the growing interest in the study of sport as social history, and to provide materials for those students who wish to know how the American character is reflected in the changing interest in sports and pastimes. For this purpose an index has been provided. It is arranged by subject, but within each subject books are arranged chronologically, thus giving a brief conspectus of each topic. Of course, the index will be useful to the sports historian who may be interested in a particular game or sport.

Children's books and works on gymnastics and exercises are included because they are invaluable sources of information on early games and recreation. Students of physical education have found these to be of special interest. The number of sporting songs has been considerably increased in this edition. Lithographs on their covers are an excellent source for illustrations of early American sports and pastimes.

It should be understood that this book is intended to be a checklist only. Full bibliographical details are not given except in a few special cases: it has not been possible to do this, because the compiler has not been able to see all the titles culled from many sources. Indeed, some of them are known only by advertisements. It has been the intention to give enough information to identify the title and scope of each book. All editions are grouped chronologically under the first, but only variation in title are given for succeeding editions.

What is "sport?" For the purposes of this checklist are included books on the major field sports, hunting, shooting, fishing, dogs, horsemanship, and such robust, athletic sports and pastimes as golf, baseball, racquets, court tennis (lawn tennis was not invented until 1873), fencing, swimming, and mountaineering. Not included are the indoor games and diversions: card playing, billiards, chess, checkers, and the like. Devotees of croquet will be disappointed not to find their game listed. Although croquet has an ancient lineage, it did not become popular either in England or America until the 1860s, and no reference to the game in America before 1860 has been found.

One might also have expected to find references to lacrosse, but it was not until the year 1860 that W. G. Beers, a Canadian lawyer, attempted to reduce the ancient Indian folk custom to the rules of an orderly game. Because of our formula there can not be included such early references to the Indian primitive "lacrosse" as the account of Gideon Lincecum, who in 1829 organized the first ball-team tour, when he took forty Choctaw Indians of Mississippi on an eight-month itinerary to exhibit "their ball plays and war dances." Lincecum's autobiography was published in volume 8 of the *Publications* of the Mississippi Historical Society, 1904, and the author is indebted to Miss Mary H. Clay of the Mississippi State College Library for the reference. Many early references to Indian ball games will be found in Stewart Culin's *Games of the North American Indians.*

The location of only one copy of each book is indicated by a symbol. Since the checklist is based on the collection in the Racquet and Tennis Club of New York City, that Club is given preference. In other cases, copies in public institutions are noted in preference to those held by private collectors.

There may be differences of opinion as to what constitutes a "sporting book," and objection may be made to the inclusion of certain titles. The principle followed has been to list those books that private collectors have found to be of sufficient interest to add to their collections. In general, works on natural history, ichthyology, and zoology are not included, but there are exceptions when the above principle is applied. For instance, C. S. Rafinesque's *Ichthyologia Ohiensis* (1820), or Joseph Seccombe's sermon in praise of fishing, *Business and Diversion Inoffensive to God* (1739), are both keenly sought by collectors. A few nonsporting books have been included because they contain early references to sports and pastimes of interest to historians. An example of this is Alexander Graydon's *Memoirs of a Life* (1811), which has a description of a game of racquets played in New York City in the year 1770. All books of this type, however, are also published before 1860. Further references of this type may be found in Foster Rhea Dulles's *America Learns to Play* (1940), which is excellently documented, and a fruitful source of information on early American sports.

It is of special interest to note the large number of books pertaining to the horse and horsemanship in this list, but it is not surprising when the importance of the horse is considered, both for business and for pleasure, before the day of the automobile. Hence, books of farriery, training, breeding, and general care of the horse sold in large numbers, and when an exceptionally good book came along, such as John Solomon Rarey's *The Modern Art of Taming Wild Horses*, it was pirated and imitated in wholesale fashion. Although the breeding of horses for racing began quite early, with the importation of thoroughbreds, it was comparatively limited until after the middle of the nineteenth century, and racing was not confined to race horses as known today.

The number of farriers published before 1860 is impressive, evidence of their great need, if not of their popularity. It has been thought desirable to list all so-called farriers, that is, when "farrier" or "farriery" occurs in the title, under the heading "Farriers" in the subject index.

11

BIBLIOGRAPHIES

CULIN, Stewart. *Games of the North American Indians.* Extracts from the Twenty-fourth Annual Report of the Bureau of American Ethnology. Washington, D. C.: Government Printing Office, 1907.

DULLES, Foster Rhea. *America Learns to Play: A History of Popular Recreation, 1607–1940.* New York: D. Appleton-Century Company, 1940. *Bibliography,* pp. 391–423.

EVANS, Charles. *American Bibliography: A Chronological Dictionary of All Books, Pamphlets, . . . Printed in the United States of America from . . . 1639 down to . . . 1820.* Vols. 1–12. Chicago: Privately Printed for the Author, 1903–1934.

GEE, Ernest R. *Early American Sporting Books, 1734–1844: A Few Brief Notes, With Portraits and Facsimilies.* New York: The Derrydale Press, 1928.

GOODSPEED, Charles Eliot. *Angling in America: Its Early History and Literature.* (With illustrations.) Boston: Houghton Mifflin Company, 1939.

HARRISON, Fairfax. *The Background of the American Stud*

Book. Richmond, Va.: Privately Printed, 1933. *Bibliography,* pp. 98–112.

HEYL, Edgar. *A Contribution to Conjuring Bibliography. . . .* Mimeographed. Baltimore: [1963].

HOLLIMAN, Jennie. *American Sports (1785–1835).* Durham, N.C.: The Seeman Press, 1931. *Bibliography,* pp. 193–211.

JILLSON, Willard Rouse. *The Boone Narrative. . . .* Louisville, Ky.: The Standard Printing Company, 1932.

MACLAY, Alfred B. *Five Centuries of Sport. . . . Rare American Sporting Periodicals. . . . The Distinguished Collection Formed by the Late Alfred B. Maclay. . . . Public Auction Sale April 10 and 11. . . .* New York: Parke-Bernet Galleries, Inc. 1945.

MAGRIEL, Paul. *Bibliography of Boxing: A Chronological Checklist of Books in English Published before 1900.* New York: The New York Public Library, 1948.

MASSACHUSETTS INLAND FISHERIES, COMMISSION-ERS. *A Collection of the Laws of Massachusetts Relating to Inland Fisheries, from the Year 1623 through the Year 1871.* In its Sixth Annual Report for the Year Ending 1 January 1872. Boston: Wright and Potter, 1872.

OLIVER, Peter. *A New Chronicle of The Complete Angler.* New York: The Paisley Press, Inc., 1936.

PHILLIPS, John C. *American Game Mammals and Birds: A Catalogue of Books 1582–1925. Sport, Natural History, and Conservation. With the Approval of the Boone and Crockett Club.* Boston: Houghton Mifflin Company, 1930.

RACQUET AND TENNIS CLUB, NEW YORK. *A Dictionary Catalogue of the Library of Sports, with Special Collections on Tennis, Lawn Tennis, and Early American Sport.* [Edited by Robert W. Henderson.] 2 vols. Boston: G. K. Hall and Company, 1970.

RILING, Ray. *Guns and Shooting: A Selected Chronological Bibliography. . . .* New York: Greenberg, [1951].

SABIN, Joseph. *Bibliotheca Americana: A Dictionary of Books Relating to America. . . . Begun by Joseph Sabin, Continued by Wilberforce Eames, Completed by R. W. G. Vail for the*

Bibliographical Society of America. Vols. 1–29. New York: 1868–1936.

VAN WINKLE, William Mitchell. *Henry William Herbert [Frank Forester]: A Bibliography of His Writings, 1832–1858.* Compiled by William Mitchell Van Winkle, with the Bibliographical Assistance of David A. Randall. Portland, Me.: The Southworth-Anthœsen Press, 1936.

VAN WINKLE, William Mitchell. *Hunting. Shooting. Angling. Ornithology. Racing. . . . The Renowned Library on American Sport. . . . Public Sale December 4, 5. . . .* New York: Parke-Bernet Galleries, Inc., 1940.

WEGELIN, Oscar. *Early American Poetry; a Compilation of the Titles of Volumes of Verse and Broadsides by Authors Born and Residing in North America, North of the Mexican Border.* Second edition, revised and enlarged. New York: P. Smith, 1930.

WESSEN, Ernest J. *American Sporting Books.* [Midland Notes, no. 13.] Mansfield, Ohio: Midland Rare Book Company, [1940].

WESSEN, Ernest J. *Sports.* [Midland Notes, no. 60.] Mansfield, Ohio: Midland Rare Book Company, [1955].

WRIGHT, Lyle H. *American Fiction: 1774–1850. A Contribution toward a Bibliography.* Revised edition. San Marino, Calif.: Henry E. Huntington Library and Art Gallery, 1948.

LIST OF ABBREVIATIONS

AAS	American Antiquarian Society, Worcester, Mass.
B	Boston Public Library, Boston, Mass.
BA	Boston Athenaeum, Boston, Mass.
BM	British Museum, London, England.
CU	Columbia University, New York.
DCL	Dartmouth College Library, Hanover, N.H.
H	Henry E. Huntington Library, San Marino, Cal.
HCL	Harvard College Library, Cambridge, Mass.
HPL	Haverhill Public Library, Haverhill, Mass.
HSP	Historical Society of Pennsylvania, Philadelphia.
HTP	Harry T. Peters, Jr., New York.
JLO	John L. O'Connor, Schuylerville, N.Y.
LC	Library of Congress, Washington, D.C.
N	The New York Public Library, New York.
P	Philadelphia Library Company, Philadelphia.
RT	Racquet and Tennis Club, New York.
UP	University of Pennsylvania, Philadelphia.
VW	William Mitchell Van Winkle, New York.
Y	Yale University, New Haven, Conn.
W&M	College of William and Mary, Williamsburg, Va.

AMHERST EXPRESS.

EXTRA.

WILLIAMS AND AMHERST
BASE BALL AND CHESS!
MUSCLE AND MIND!!

July 1st and 2d, 1859.

AMHERST Express. July 1st and 2d, 1859.

PLAYING BALL

With bat and ball some boys we find,
T' amuse themselves are much inclin'd.

From CHILDREN'S Amusements. Baltimore, 1820.

THE

ART

OF

SWIMMING,

CONTAINING

INSTRUCTIONS

RELATIVE TO

THE PROPER MANNER OF GOING
INTO THE WATER; HOW TO
LEARN TO SWIM; CAUTIONS
TO LEARNERS, &c. &c.

WITH

AN ENGRAVING

REPRESENTING

TWELVE DIFFERENT ATTITUDES

TO WHICH ARE ADDED,

Dr. FRANKLIN's Advice to Swimmers;

Dr. BUCHAN's Remarks on River and Sea
Bathing;

An Account of Mr. Mallison's Invention,
called "The Seaman's Friend, or
Bather's Companion;" AND

The Rules and Directions of THE HUMANE
SOCIETY, for restoring to life persons
apparently drowned.

BALTIMORE:

PRINTED AND SOLD BY W. TURNER.

The ART of Swimming. Baltimore, 1821.

THE

ARCHER'S MANUAL:

OR

The Art of Shooting with the Long Bow,

AS PRACTISED BY

THE UNITED BOWMEN OF PHILADELPHIA.

Philadelphia:

R. H. HOBSON, 147 CHESTNUT STREET.

1830.

The ARCHER'S Manual. Philadelphia, 1830.

THE

CABINET

OF

NATURAL HISTORY

AND

AMERICAN RURAL SPORTS.

WITH ILLUSTRATIONS.

A MONTHLY PUBLICATION.

VOL. I.

Philadelphia:
PUBLISHED BY J. & T. DOUGHTY, S. E. CORNER WALNUT & FOURTH STREETS.
Russell & Martien, Printers.
1830.

The Cabinet of Natural History. Vol. 1, no. 1. Philadelphia, 1930.

THE

BOOK OF SPORTS.

BY ROBIN CARVER.

BOSTON:

LILLY, WAIT, COLMAN, AND HOLDEN.

1834.

CARVER, Robin. The Book of Sports. Boston, 1834.

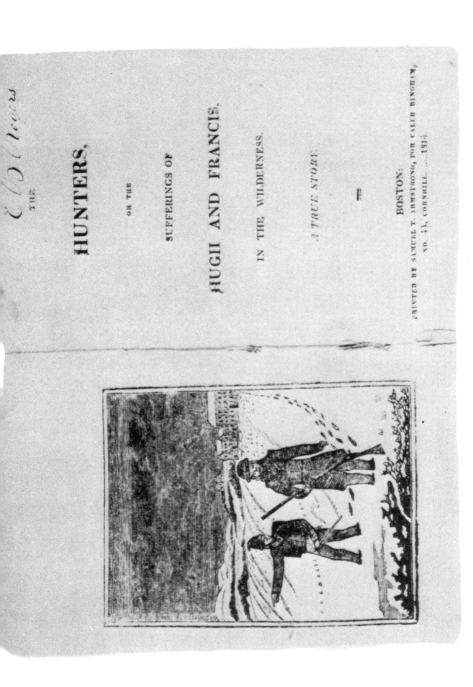

THE

HUNTERS.

OR THE

SUFFERINGS OF

HUGH AND FRANCIS,

IN THE WILDERNESS.

A TRUE STORY.

BOSTON:

PRINTED BY SAMUEL T. ARMSTRONG, FOR CALEB BINGHAM,
NO. 44, CORNHILL.......1814.

The Hunters, or The Sufferings of Hugh and Francis in the Wilderness.
Boston, 1814.

John G. Deans
Petersburg

Thos *Nichol...*

THE
GENTLEMAN's NEW

POCKET COMPANION,

COMPRISING

A GENERAL DESCRIPTION

OF THE

NOBLE AND USEFUL ANIMAL

THE HORSE;

TOGETHER

WITH THE QUICKEST

AND

SIMPLEST MODE

OF

FATTENING;

NECESSARY TREATMENT WHILE UNDERGOING
EXCESSIVE FATIGUE, OR ON A
JOURNEY ;

THE CONSTRUCTION

AND

MANAGEMENT OF STABLES;

DIFFERENT MARKS

FOR ASCERTAINING THE AGE OF A HORSE,
FROM THREE TO NINE YEARS OLD.
With a concise account of the Diseases, to which the
Horse is most subject; with such remedies as long
experience has proven to be effectual.

BY RICHARD MASON,
OF SURRY COUNTY, VIRGINIA.

PETERSBURG :......
PRINTED BY JOHN DICKSON,
BOLLINGBROOK STREET.

1811.

MASON, Richard. The Gentleman's New Pocket Companion. Petersburg,
Va., 1811.

ARTICLES AND RULES

OF THE

NEW-YORK ASSOCIATION

FOR THE

IMPROVEMENT

OF THE

BREED OF HORSES.

NEW-YORK :

PRINTED BY J. SEYMOUR,

No. 49 John-street.

1823.

NEW-YORK Association for the Improvement of the Breed of Horses.
Articles and Rules. New York, 1823.

THE

MODERN ART

OF

TAMING WILD HORSES.

BY J. S. RAREY.

COLUMBUS:
PRINTED BY THE STATE JOURNAL COMPANY.
1856.

RAREY, John Solomon. The Modern Art of Taming Wild Horses. Columbus, 1856.

The Hill Tops, a New Hunting Song. In: The Royal American Magazine. Boston, April, 1774.

THE
SPORTSMAN'S COMPANION;
OR, AN
Essay on Shooting,

Illustriously shewing in what Manner to fire at Birds of Game, in various Directions and Situations;

AND,

Directions to Gentlemen for the Treatment and breaking their own Pointers and Spaniels, and the necessary Precautions to guard against many Accidents that attend this pleasant Diversion;

WITH

Several other useful and interesting Particulars relative thereto.

[*Never before Published.*]

By a GENTLEMAN,

Who has made shooting his favourite Amusement upwards of Twenty-six Years, in Great-Britain, Ireland, and North-America.

NEW-YORK:

PRINTED by ROBERTSONS, MILLS and HICKS.

M,DCC,LXXXIII.

The Sportsman's Companion; or, An Essay on Shooting. By a Gentleman. New York, 1783.

THE

Sportsman's Dictionary;

OR,

CYCLOPEDIA.

Vol. 1.]   FEBRUARY, 1833.   [No. 1.

THE HORSE.

Beautiful as is the Horse, and identified so much with our pleasure and
our profit, he has been the object of almost universal regard; and there
are few persons who do not pretend to be somewhat competent judges of his
form, qualities, and worth. From the sportsman with his numerous and
valuable stud, to the meanest helper in the stable, there is scarcely a man
who would not be offended if he were thought altogether ignorant of horse-
flesh. There is no subject on which he is so positive, there is no subject on
which, generally speaking, he is so deficient, and there are few horses, on
some points of which these pretended and self-sufficient judges would not
give a totally opposite opinion.

The noblest conquest that was ever made by man is that of this spirited
and haughty animal, which shares with him the fatigues of war and the glory
of the combat. Equally intrepid as his master, the Horse sees the danger,
and braves it; inspired at the clash of arms, he loves it, he seeks it, and is
animated with the same ardor. He feels pleasure also in the chase, in tour-
naments, in the course: he is all fire, but, equally tractable as courageous;
does not give way to his impetuosity, and knows how to check his inclina-
tions: he not only submits to the arm which guides him, but even seems to
consult the desires of his rider; and, always obedient to the impressions
which he receives from him, presses on, moves gently, or stops, and only
acts as his rider pleases. The Horse is a creature which renounces his being,
to exist only by the will of another, which he knows how to anticipate, and
even express, and execute by the promptitude and exactness of his movements: he feels as much as we desire, does only what we wish, giving himself up without reserve, and refuses nothing, makes use of all his strength,
exerts himself beyond it, and even dies the better to obey us.

Such is the Horse, whose natural qualities art has improved. His education commences with the loss of his liberty, and by constraint it is finished.
The slavery or servitude of these creatures is universal, and so ancient that

EARLY AMERICAN SPORT

CHECKLIST

CHECKLIST

A., S. A. The song of the S. I. B. Sung at the celebration of their 99th anniversary, June 17th, 1840. Composed & adapted to the air, "In the days when we went gipseying." By S. A. A., and devotedly dedicated to the skipper of that association. Boston: Parker & Ditson [ca. 1840].   RT

Words and music. A fishing song. Lithograph of small yacht off Egg Rock on cover, by R. Cooke.

[ABBOTT, Jacob.] Prank; or, The philosophy of tricks and mischief. New York: Harper & Brothers, publishers, [cop. 1855.]
                                                                          N

Title from engraved title-page. Series title page: Harper's story books. A series of narratives, dialogues, biographies, and tales, for the instruction and entertainment of the young, by Jacob Abbott. Embellished with numerous and beautiful engravings. Chapters on *Minnow-fishing, Pickerel-fishing, Whaling*.

ADANCOURT, Frances, publisher. *See:* BRACKEN, Henry.

ADELAIDE. Original poems; calculated to improve the mind of youth, and allure it to virtue. By Adelaide. Part II. Ornamented with elegant engravings. Philadelphia: Published by Benjamin Warner . . . 1821.   N

Contains poems and woodcuts: *The hoop, The battledoor*. Stiff gilt paper wrappers, with frontispiece pasted down.

The ADVENTURES of Daniel Boone . . . See: HAWKS, Francis Lister.

ADVENTURES of hunters and travellers, and narratives of border warfare. By an Old Hunter. Philadelphia: H. C. Peck & Theo. Bliss, 1852.   LC

Frontispiece, plates, illustrations.

1854: Philadelphia, H. C. Peck & Theo. Bliss.   N

1855: Philadelphia, H. C. Peck & Theo. Bliss.   N

1857: Philadelphia, H. C. Peck & Theo. Bliss.   RT

1858: Philadelphia, H. C. Peck & Theo. Bliss.   N

1859: Philadelphia, H. C. Peck & Theo. Bliss.   N

AIKEN, Jesse. The citizen's tutor, containing a variety of recipes for the cure of the different diseases of man and beast, also, for colouring wool, cotton, and hats. Printed in Mountpleasant, [Ohio,] 1831.   RT

ALFONCE, J. E. d'. Instructions in gymnastics, containing a full description of more than eight hundred exercises, and illustrated by five hundred engravings. By J. E. d'Alfonce, late professor in the Military School in St. Petersburgh, and in Paris. New-York: George F. Nesbitt & Co., Publishers and printers, Corner of Wall and Walter Streets, 1851.   N

13 double-page plates. Plates in N copy in incorrect order.

[ALKEN, Henry.] The beauties & defects in the figure of the horse, comparatively delineated in a series of engravings. Boston: Published by Carter & Hendee, 1830.   RT

Engraved frontispiece, 1 unnumbered and 18 numbered plates. First published London, 1816, with colored plates. Boston 1830 edition not colored. Paper label, with circular design as on title-page, on front cover. Plates lithographed by Pendleton's.

ALLEN, R[ichard] L[amb]. Domestic animals. History and description of the horse, mule, cattle, sheep, swine, poultry, and farm dogs. With directions for their management, breeding, crossing, rearing, feeding, and preparation for a profitable market. Also, their diseases, and remedies. Together with full directions for the management of the dairy. By R. L. Allen . . . New York: O. Judd Company [ca. 1847].

Frontispiece and illustrations.

1848: New York, Published for the author, by C. M. Saxton, 205 Broadway.   RT

ALTOWAN; or, Incidents of life and adventure in the Rocky Mountains: *See:* STEWART, Sir William Drummond.

AMATEUR. Crayon sketches. *See:* COX, William.

The AMERICAN angler's guide. *See:* BROWN, John J.

The AMERICAN comic almanac for 1831. With whims, scraps and oddities . . . Boston: Published by Charles Ellms, (proprietor of the copy right) . . . [1830.]   RT

Sporting jokes and caricatures.

[1831:] . . . for 1832 . . . Philadelphia, John Grigg, North 4th Street.   RT

[1832:] . . . for 1833 . . . Boston, Charles Ellms & Willard Felt & Co. Vol. 1, no. 3.   RT

Other editions of Vol. 1, no. 3: Philadelphia, Sold by Grigg and Elliot. Published by Charles Ellms, Boston, in N; New York, David Felt, 245 Pearl St. Published by Charles Ellms, Boston, in Oneida Historical Society.

[1833:] for 1834 . . . New York, Wm. Minns, 116 Water Street. Published by Charles Ellms, agent, Boston. Vol. 1, no. 4.
                                                                                          N

Other edition of vol. 1, no. 5: Boston, Sold by Allen & Co., 72 State St. Published by Charles Ellms, agent, Boston.   RT

[1834:] . . . for 1835 . . . New York, Sold by D. Felt & Co. Published by Charles Ellms, agent, Boston. Vol. 1, no. 5.   N

Other edition of vol. 1, no. 5: Boston, Sold by Allen & Co., 72 State St. Published by Charles Ellms, agent, Boston.   RT

[1835:] . . . for 1836 . . . Boston, Sold by Lemuel Gulliver, State St. Boston, published by Cha's Ellms, agent, Boston. Vol. 1, no. 6.   RT

[1836:] . . . for 1837 . . . Boston, Sold by Thomas Groom, at Stationers Hall . . . Published by Charles Ellms, agent, Boston. [Whole no. VII.] Vol. 2, no. 1   RT

[1837:] . . . for 1838 . . . Boston, Sold by Thomas Groom, State Street. [Whole no.] VIII. Vol. 2, no. 2.   RT

[1838:] . . . The old American comic almanac for 1839 . . . Boston, Printed and published by S. N. Dickinson . . . Whole no. IX. New series No. 1.   RT

[1839:] . . . The old American comic almanac for 1840 . . . Boston, Printed and published by S. N. Dickinson . . . Whole no. X. New series No. 2.   RT

The AMERICAN farmer, containing original essays and selections . . . [Edited by] John S. Skinner. Baltimore, 1819–1834.
N

A weekly magazine. *The Sporting Olio* first apeared in the issue of January 21, 1825. It printed turf news, and eventually led to the foundation of *The American Turf Register* in 1829. *See: Gee.*

The AMERICAN farrier, or New-York horse doctor . . . *See:* BRACKEN, Henry. Farriery improved. 1826.

The AMERICAN keepsake for 1851. Edited by Anna Wilmot. New York: Cornish, Lamport and Company. [Cop. 1850.]   RT

17 engraved plates. Gilt edges, gilt tooled binding.
A Virginia fox-hunt, by A. Roland. pp. 63–73. Also contains, "The Sphinx," by Edgar Allen Poe.

AMERICAN monthly magazine. New York, April, 1838.   RT

Contains: *Duelling* [An essay], and *The lost hunter* [A poem] by A. B Street.

The AMERICAN race turf-register. *See:* EDGAR, Patrick Nisbett.

AMERICAN racing calendar and trotting record from September 1, 1856 to January 1, 1858. Compiled from Porter's Spirit of the times. New York: Published at the office of Porter's Spirit of the times, 1858.   LC

[Vol. 2.] . . . From January 1, 1858 to January 1, 1859. New York: Published at the office of Porter's Spirit of the times, 1859.
LC

The AMERICAN shooter's manual, comprising such plain and simple rules, as are necessary to introduce the inexperienced into a full knowledge of all that relates to the dog, and the correct use of the gun; also a description of the game of this country. By a gentleman of Philadelphia County. Philadelphia: Carey, Lea & Carey, 1827.   RT

Three engraved plates by F. Kearney, 1 p. errata, 3 pp. advertisements at end. Attributed to Dr. Jesse Y. Kester.

[1828:] Second edition. Philadelphia, E. L. Carey & A. Hart.
RT

Errata and advertisements same as 1st edition. *See: Gee.* AAS has a copy without title-page, in which the plate opposite p. 173, *Rail shooting,* is not signed. In both RT copies it is signed by both artist and engraver. This plate originally appeared in *The American turf register,* Vol. 2, where it is signed by both artist and engraver, and also has an additional line: *Engraved for the American turf register and sporting magazine.* RT copy of the second edition is identical with the RT first edition as to paper, etc., except that the title-page appears to have been printed on inferior paper, and perhaps, substituted for the original title-page. The composition of the title-page, and copyright notice on verso of title-page varies.

The AMERICAN sporting chronicle. Published by John Richards and edited by William T. Porter. Vol. 1. New York, 1843.

Only known copy in Brown University Library, which has nos. 1-30, 21 March 1842 [i.e. 1843]—10 October 1843. The second leaf of the October 24th issue is bound in, but there is no indication that this is the final issue.

AMERICAN sports, for the amusement of children. New York [ca. 1820].

Title only noted in a chapbook in the Harris Collection, Brown University Library.

AMERICAN turf register and racing & trotting calendar. Containing complete and correct reports of all the races and trots in the United States and Canada during the year . . . Also alphabetical lists of winning horses, in racing and trotting. New York, 1845–1860.   N

Issued annually. A continuation of: *American Turf Register and Sporting Magazine*, which was issued monthly.
1845–1857 published: New York: John Richards.
1858–1859 published: New York: Jones, Thorpe and Hays.
1845–1855 edited by William T. Porter.
1856–1860 edited by Edward E. Jones.

AMERICAN turf register and sporting magazine. Baltimore and New York, 1829–1844. 15 vols.   RT

Vols. 1–6 (1829–1835) edited by J. S. Skinner.
Vol. 7 (1836) edited by Allen J. Davie.
Vols. 8–9 (1837–1839) edited by Gideon B. Smith.
Vols. 10–15 (1840–1844) edited by William T. Porter.
A development of *The Sporting Olio*, which started in *The American Farmer*, 1825. Issued in monthly numbers, beginning September 1829, and ending December 1844. Continued by the annual publication: *American Turf Register and Racing & Trotting Calendar. See: Gee.*

The AMERICAN veterinary journal. Devoted to the diffusion of veterinary knowledge. Edited by Geo. H. Dadd. Boston, 1851–1859.

Vol. 1: Sept. 1851–Aug. 1852. N.S. Vol. 1–4 no. 3: Oct. 1855–March 1859. Copy in Army Medical Library, Washington, D.C.

Der AMERIKANISCHE Pferdearzt . . . *See:* TOWAR, Alexander.

AMHERST express. Extra. Williams and Amherst base ball and chess! Muscle and mind!! July 1st and 2d, 1859.   RT

Broadsheet, 2 pp. Only 2 copies known: RT and Amherst College. *See* p. xvii.

ANECDOTES of the dog. [Woodcut and verse.] Dayton, O.: Published and sold by B. F. Ells. [ca. 1853].   RT

At head of title: *No. 12. Price 3 cts.* Woodcuts through text. RT copy has no covers. No. 12 of *The golden treasury for my little friends by Lady Lovelace,* published with a series title-page bearing the imprint, Dayton: L. F. Graflin, 1853. One of 2 known copies.

ANGLER'S almanac. *See:* BROWN, J. J.

The ANNUAL visitor; or almanac, for the year of Our Lord,— 1799—Being the third after leap year. Calculated for the meridian of Baltimore . . . Baltimore: printed by W. Pechin . . . 1798.   AAS

Contains: *Directions for the Management of Horses when Travelling.* Evans: 33306.

[APPERLEY, Charles James.] Nimrod's hunting tours, interspersed with characteristic anecdotes, sayings and doings of sporting men, including notices of the principal crack riders of England . . . To which are added Nimrod's Letters on riding to hounds . . . In two volumes. Philadelphia: Carey, Lea and Blanchard, 1836.   RT

Paper labels. First published London, 1835.

The ARABIAN art of taming and training wild & vicious horses. *See:* RAREY, John Solomon.

The ARCHER'S manual: or, The art of shooting with the long bow, as practised by The United Bowmen of Philadelphia. Philadelphia: R. H. Hobson . . . 1830.   RT

Frontispiece, plates. Based on Thomas Waring's *A Treatise on Archery* . . . London, 1814.

[ARMSTRONG, John.] The art of preserving health: a poem. London, Printed: Philadelphia, Reprinted and sold by B. Franklin, 1745.   N

First published London, 1744. Book 3: *Exercise.* Evans: 5532.

1757: The fourth edition. London, Printed. Boston: New England, Reprinted and sold by Green & Russell.   N

Evans: 7836.

1786: Philadelphia, Printed for Thomas Dobson . . .   AAS

Not in Evans, but probably intended for 20204.

1802: *In:* Poems of established reputation . . . Baltimore, Warner & Hanna.   N

1803: *In:* Poems of established reputation . . . Baltimore, Warner & Hanna.   N

41

ARMSTRONG, John. *Continued:*

1804: *In:* Poems of established reputation . . . Baltimore, Warner & Hanna.　　　　N

1804: The art of preserving health. By John Armstrong, M.D. To which is prefixed A critical essay on the poem, by J. Aikin, M.D. Philadelphia, Printed for Benjamin Johnson . . .　　RT

Engraved title-page. With this is bound: Green, Mathew. *The Spleen, and other poems* . . . Philadelphia: Printed for Benjamin Johnson . . . 1804.

ARNOLD, J. The wolf is out. Sung by Mr. Russell & Mr. Morley. Words by J. Arnold. Music composed by T. Cook. New York: Atwill [ca. 1835].

Noted in: Dichter, Harry. *Handbook of American sheet music.* Philadelphia, 1947. Reprinted by Albert Saifer, West Orange, N. J.

The ART of swimming, containing instructions relative to the proper manner of going into the water; how to learn to swim; cautions to learners, &c. &c. With an engraving representing twelve different attitudes, to which are added, Dr. Franklin's Advice to swimmers; Dr. Buchan's Remarks on river and sea bathing; an account of Mr. Mallinson's invention, called "The seaman's friend, or bather's companion;" and The rules and directions of The Humane Society for restoring to life persons apparently drowned. Baltimore: Printed and sold by W. Turner. [1821].

Frontispiece and 12 folded engravings.　　RT

The ART of Taming Horses . . . *See:* RAREY, John Solomon.

ASHLAND Jockey Club. Rules and regulations of the Ashland Jockey Club. March 1, 1859. Richmond, 1859.　　H

ASPIN, Jehoshaphat. A picture of the manners, customs, sports and pastimes of the inhabitants of England . . . New York: Harper, 1832.

In: Heyl, Edgar. *Contribution to conjuring bibliography.*

ASTLEY, Philip. The modern riding-master: or, A key to the knowledge of the horse and horsemanship . . . Adorned with various engravings. Philadelphia: Printed and sold by Robert Aitken, 1776.　　AAS

Paper covers. Small wood engravings in text. First published London, 1774. Evans: 14653.

ATALL, Peter, *pseud. See:* WALN, Robert.

ATKINSON, Joseph. See our bark. A boat glee written by Joseph Atkinson, Esqr. Composed by Sir J. Stevenson. Boston: Published by C. Bradlee, Washington Street [ca. 1835].   RT

Words and music. A rowing song.

The ATLANTIC souvenir; a Christmas and New Year's offering. 1828. Philadelphia: Carey, Lea & Carey. Sold in Boston by Hilliard, Gray, & Co.   RT

Tinted engraved presentation plate and 13 engraved plates. Contains: *Hunting song, A visit to the Catskills, The rifle.*

The ATLANTIC souvenir for MDCCCXXX. Philadelphia: Carey, Lea & Carey, Ches[t]nut Street, 1830.   RT

Gift book, gilt edges, 12 plates. Contains: *Love's falconric*, a story of Tudor England, with background of falconry.

AUDUBON, John James. The birds of America, from drawings made in the United States and its Territories. New York: Published by J. J. Audubon; Philadelphia: J. B. Chevalier, 1840–1844.   N

Referred to as: *"Birds* in Miniature." Seven volumes in 100 parts, 500 plates, large octavo. Each volume concludes with *List of Subscribers,* the original list in Vol. 1, and supplementary lists in Vols. 2-7. Vols. 6-7: New York, Philadelphia: J. J. Audubon, 1843-1844. Plates first issued in Edinburgh and London 1826-1837, in 87 parts, or 4 folio volumes, with 438 plates, daated 1827-1838.

1856: New York, Published by V. G. Audubon. 7 vols.

A re-issue of the 1840-1844 octavo edition, but the 500 plates have tinted backgrounds. Vol. 1 has added steel engravings of J. J. Audubon by H. B. Hall, after Henry Inman.

1856: New York, Published by V. G. Audubon. 7 vols.

Same as 1856 edition, above, but without the plates. Doubt exists as to the publication of Vol. 5.

1859: New York, V. G. Audubon, Roe Lockwood & Son. 7 vols., octavo.

AUDUBON, John James. Ornithological biography: or, An account of the habits of the birds of the United States of Amarica; accompanied by descriptions of the objects represented in the work entitled The birds of America, and interspersed with de-

AUDUBON, John James. *Continued:*

lineations of American scenery and manners. Philadelphia: Judah
Dobson, Agent . . . 1831. [Vol. I only.]   N

The original Edinburgh edition of 1831-1839, in 5 volumes, was the letterpress to the elephant folio *Birds of America*. There were no American
reprints of vols. 3, 4, and 5.

1835: Philadelphia, E. L. Carey and A. Hart. [Vol. I only.]

1835: Boston, Hilliard, Gray and Company. Vol. II [only].   N

AUDUBON, John James The viviparous quadrupeds of North
America, by John James Audubon . . . and the Rev. John
Bachman . . . New York: Published by J. J. Audubon, 1845–
1848. 3 vols.   N

Issued in imperial folio, without text, 150 hand colored lithographic plates,
30 parts, paper covered, 5 plates each. Bound in 3 volumes. Each volume
contains 2 preliminary pages and 50 colored plates. Vol. 1: 1845. Vol. 2:
1846. Vol. 3: 1848.

1846: The viviparous quadrupeds of North America . . . New
York: Published by J. J. Audubon, 1846–1854.   N

Text to the 1845-1848 edition, in 3 volumes royal octavo. Vols. 2-3 have
imprint: New York: Published by V. G. Audubon, 1851 and 1854, respectively. Herrick lists volume 3 as: New York, 1853, Pp. i-vi, 1-257. N copy
runs to p. 348. Herrick states: A supplement of 93 pages and 6 colored
plates, added in 1854, and apparently issued to all previous subscribers to
this and the large folio, is sometimes bound up with the third volume of the
present edition, when the date of which is usually quoted as "1854." Title-
page of volume 3 reads: *The quadrupeds of North America*. Vol. 1 has
List of subscribers. Vol. 2 has *List of subscribers, continued*. Volume 3 ends
with unnumbered leaf: *Table of Genera described in this volume*.

1851: The quadrupeds of North America . . . New York, Published by V. G. Audubon, 1851–1854. 3 vols.   LC

Text and 155 colored plates, royal octavo. Vol. 1:1852. Vol. 2: 1851. First
octavo edition with text and plates combined. Title-page of volume 2
reads: *The viviparous quadrupeds of North America*.

1854: The quadrupeds of North America . . . New York, Published by V. G. Audubon, 1854–1855. 3 vols.   LC

Practically identical with the 1851-1854 edition.

1855: The viviparous quadrupeds of North America . . . New
York, Roe, Lockwood & Sons.   N

AUDUBON, John James. *Continued:*

Plates: 2 vols., folio. Text: 3 vols., royal octavo. Publisher claims "precisely the same, in every respect" as the 1845-1848 edition. But Sabin says: "I cannot endorse this statement." *See: Sabin. See also:* Herrick, Francis H. *Audubon's bibliography.* In: *The Auk.* Cambridge, Mass. 1919. Vol. O.S. 44, N.S. 36, pp. 372-380.

AUDUBON, The, magazine, published in the interest of the Audubon Society for the Protection of Birds. C. W. Webber, editor. New York, 1847.

AWAKE ye dull sluggards. [Anonymous]. A favorite hunting song sung by Mrs. Mills. Philadelphia: Printed for G. Willig & sold at his Musical Magazine, no. 12 South 4th St. [ca. 1805–1809].   N

Words and Music.

B, T. W. H. B., composer. *See:* BAILEY, Johanna. O swiftly glides the bonny boat.

BABCOCK, S. *See:*
  The SPORTS of childhood.
  The BOY'S book of sports.

BACON, M. A. Winged thoughts. [New York,] 1851.   H

Illustrated.

[BADCOCK, John.] The groom's oracle, and Pocket stable directory . . . By John Hinds [*Pseud.*] . . . From the second London edition . . . Philadelphia: E. L. Carey and A. Hart . . . 1831.   AAS

Colored folding frontispiece is reprint of Henry Alken plate as in London edition. First published London, 1829.

[BADCOCK, John.] The veterinary surgeon: or, Farriery taught on a new and easy plan; being a treatise on all the diseases and accidents to which the horse is liable; the causes and symptoms of each, and the most approved remedies employed for the cure in every case; with instructions to the shoeing-smith, farrier, and groom, how to acquire knowledge in the art of farriery, and the prevention of diseases. Preceded by a popular description of the animal functions in health, and showing the principles on which these are to be restored when disordered. By John Hinds, Veterinary Surgeon. With considerable additions and improvements, particularly adapted to this country. By Thomas M. Smith . . . Philadelphia: John Grigg . . . 1830.   RT

Illustrations and 4 folding plates. Title partly open-face type, 224 pp., 1 l. advertisements.

1830: Philadelphia, John Grigg . . .   RT

Illustrations and 4 folding plates. Title-page solid type, 284 pp.

1832: Philadelphia, John Grigg . . .   RT

1833: Philadelphia, John Grigg.   DCL

1834: Philadelphia

Noted in E. C. Fales Catalogue, 1965.

1836: Philadelphia, John Grigg.   RT

1841: Philadelphia, Grigg & Elliot.   CU

1843: Philadelphia, Grigg & Elliot.   RT

1845: Philadelphia, Grigg & Elliot.

1848: Hinds' Farriery and stud book. Farriery taught on a new and easy plan . . . With a Supplement . . . Trotting and racing stables . . . pedigrees of winning horses since 1838 . . . by J. S. Skinner . . . Philadelphia, Grigg, Elliot & Co.   RT

1850: Hinds' Farrier and stud book . . . Philadelphia, Lippincott, Grambo & Co. . . .   JLO

1852: Hinds' Farrier and stud book . . . Philadelphia, Lippincott, Grambo & Co. . . .   RT

1854: Hinds' Farrier and stud book . . . Philadelphia, Lippincott, Grambo & Co. . . .   RT

1857: Hinds' Farrier and stud book . . . Philadelphia, Lippincott, Grambo & Co. . . .

1858: Hinds' Farrier and stud book . . . Philadelphia, J. B. Lippincott & Co.   N

BAILEY, F. W. N. The Newfoundland dog, a descriptive ballad. New York, 1843.   W & M

Music and words, with picture.

BAILEY, Johanna. O swiftly glides the bonny boat. A Scotch song, written by Johanna Bailey with an accompaniment for the pianoforte by T. W. H. B. B. Philadelphia: Published and sold by Geo. Willig, 171 Chestnut Street, [ca. 1835].   RT

Words and music. A fishing song. Printed on verso and recto pages of folded pink paper.

BAIRD, Samuel A., *pseud. See:* SQUIER, Ephraim George.

The BAKED head, and other tales. Now first collected, and forming the second volume of "Putnam's story library." New York: G. P. Putnam & Co., 321 Broadway, 1856.   RT

At head of title: *Putnam's library of choice stories. A cock-fight in the Havana,* pp. 172-187.

BAKER, N. B. Regattas on Lake Winnipissiogee! The boat races between the clubs of Harvard and Yale Colleges! . . . N. B. Baker for the Committee of Arrangements. July 28, 1852.

Broadside. Noted in *The Month at Goodspeed's.* Vol. 27, nos. 6-7, pp. 119-120, which mentions the date as July 26, 1852. Boston, 1956.

BALDWIN, Justice. The opinion of the Circuit Court of New Jersey . . . *See:* United States. Circuit Court. (3rd Circuit).

BALL, B[enjamin] L[incoln]. Three days on the White Mountains; being the perilous adventure of Dr. B. L. Ball on Mount Washington, during October 25, 26, and 27, 1855. Written by himself. Boston: Published by N. Noyes, 1856.   RT

Paper covers.

BALL, T. "When we were out a fishing!" A comic song, as sung with rapturous applause, Mr. W. F. Johnson, at the National Theatre. Music by J. C. White, words by T. Ball. New York: Published by Endicott, 359 Broadway [ca. 1836].   RT

Words and music. Fishing lithograph on cover. On p. 2 the statement: *Words by Tom Moody.*

47

BALL, William. The hunter boy, a ballad. The poetry & music by William Ball. New York: Published by J. L. Hewitt [ca. 1832]. RT

Words and music. First line: Oh! the song of the merry, merry hunter boy. From *The Songs of the Mountains* by William Ball. Lithograph of shepherd boy playing horn on cover.

BALL, W[illiam]. Hunter boy, or, "Mine alone!" Written by W. Ball. Music by C. de Beriot. Boston: Published by C. Bradlee, 107 Washington Street [ca. 1835–1836]. RT

Words and music. First line: Where is my hunter boy? Tra la ra la!

BALLMER, Daniel, Eine Sammlung von neuen Recepten und bewährten Curen, für Menschen und Vieh. Zusamengetragen und zum Druck befördert von Daniel Ballmer, bey Chämbersburg, Anno 1826. Schellsburg: Gedruckt bey Friedrich Goeb, 1827. RT

Paper covers. Title on cover: *Neue Recepte und bewährte Curen, für Menschen und Vieh . . .*

1842: Eine Sammlung von neuen Recepten und erprobten Kuren für Menschen und Thiere. Von Paul Bolmer. Harrisburg, Pa., Gedruckt für den Käufer, 1842. RT

Paper covers. Cover title: *Neue Recepte, und vortressliche Curen für Menschen und Vieh . . .* Woodcut on back cover. A non copyright rewrite of the above.

1843: A collection of new receipts and approved cures for man and beast. Made by Daniel Ballmer, near Chambersburg, Pa., A.D. 1826. Dayton, Ohio: Republished by Simon Snavely. RT

Lettering on cover same as on title-page, including vignette. This translation probably made by Gabriel Meisse.

BARCLAY, B. S. The merry sleigh bells, written and composed by B. S. Barclay. Philadelphia: Osbourn's Music Saloon . . . [1844]. RT

Words and music. Sleighing lithograph by T. Sinclair on cover.

BARNUM, H. L. The American farrier; containing a minute account of the formation of every part of the horse, from the extremity of the head to the hoof. With a description of all the diseases to which each part is liable; the best remedies to be applied in effecting a cure; and the most approved mode of treatment for preventing disorders: accompanied with a copious alphabetical list of medicines . . . Compiled chiefly from the celebrated "Library of useful knowledge," just published by a committee of one hundred and fifty eminent agriculturists . . . Illustrated by engravings, and arranged on a new plan. By H. L. Barnum. Editor of the "Farmer's reporter." Philadelphia: Uriah Hunt, 19 North Third Street; H. L. Barnum, at the Farmer's Reporter Office, Cincinnati, and booksellers generally throughout the United States, 1832. RT

Frontispiece: *Anatomy of the horse.* Copyright notice on verso title-page reads: District of Ohio, to wit: Be it remembered, That on the 21st day of October, Anno Domini, 1831, H. L. Barnum, of the said District, hath deposited in this office the title of a book, the title of which is in the words following, to wit: "The American Farrier . . ." Attest, William Miner, Clerk of the District. Leaf of advertisements at end. Line engravings pp. 9, 12.

1832: Title and book identical with above except note on verso of title-page, which reads: Entered according to the Act of Congress, in the year 1832, by Uriah Hunt, in the Clerk's Office of the District Court of the Eastern District of Pennsylvania, and does not have leaf of advertisements at end. RT

1832: Title and book as above.
Variations-illustrated with numerous engravings, and arranged on a new improved plan.
Editor of the "Farmers' Reporter" omitted after "By H. L. Barnum."
Philadelphia: Printed for the compiler. And for sale by the principal Booksellers in the city. Verso title-page: Anatomy of the horse. [Frontispiece in other editions.] Entered according to the Act of Congress, in the year one thousand eight hundred and thirty-one, by H. L. Barnum, in the clerk's office of the Distruct [sic.] of Ohio. Verso last page of index, and following leaf, 3 plates of trotters: Top Gallant, Whalebone, Tom Thumb.

1845: Title as above. Philadelphia: Uriah Hunt & Son, No. 44 North Fourth Street. And for sale by booksellers generally throughout the United States. RT

No frontispiece, leaf of advertisements at end.
Copyright notice as in second title above.

1856: Identical with 1845 copy, except for date.   RT

No frontispiece, leaf of advertisements at end.

BARNUM, H. L. Farmer's farrier, illustrating the peculiar nature and characteristic of the horse, and the diseases to which he is liable, with the symptoms and remedies familiarly explained; accompanied with the pedigree of the blooded horses in the west. With several elegant engravings. By H. L. Barnum, Editor of the United States Agriculturist, and Farmer's Reporter. Cincinnati: Published by A. B. Roff, and sold by Luke Loomis . . . Robinson and Fairbank, Printers, 1831.   RT

Frontispiece and 2 folded plates, small cuts in text. Contains: *Blooded horses in the West*, by D. Gano, which appeared earlier in *The Western Agriculturist* . . . Cincinnati, 1830, which see.

BARRETT, Samuel. "Thou shalt not kill." A sermon, preached in The Twelfth Congregational Church, Boston, Sunday, March 4, 1838, in consequence of the late duel in Washington. By Samuel Barrett, Minister of that Church. Boston: Printed [Not published] by request. I. R. Butts, Printer, 1838.   RT

Paper wrappers with title: *Mr. Barrett's Sermon on duelling.*

BARRINGTON, G[eorge]. The London spy; or The frauds of London detected: containing also a sketch of night scenes and notorious characters, in a ramble through the Metropolis . . . Also, A treatise on boxing, by John Belcher. Boston, 1827.   RT

Frontispiece. First published, London, 1802: *The Frauds and Cheats of London Detected.*

1832: Boston   RT

BARTLET, J. The gentleman farrier's repository, of elegant and approved remedies for the diseases of horses; in two books . . . The third edition. Philadelphia: Printed and sold by Joseph Crukshank . . . 1775.   RT

First published London, 1764: *Pharmacopœia Hippiatrica.* Evans: 13826.

1787: Philadelphia, Printed and sold by Joseph Crukshank.   AAS

Evans: 20222.

BARTLET, J. The gentleman's pocket farrier. *See:* BURDON, William.

The BASE BALL player's pocket companion . . . *See:* MANUAL of cricket and base ball.

BATES, Elisha. The moral advocate, a monthly publication, on war, duelling, capital punishment and prison discipline. By Elisha Bates. Mt. Pleasant, O.: Printed by the editor, 1821–1822.   N

BAUCHER, F[rancois]. New method of horsemanship, including the breaking and training of horses, with instructions for obtaining a good seat. Illustrated. Translated from the ninth Paris edition. New York: Albert Cogswell [ca. 1850?].

First published Paris, 1842: *Méthode d'Équitation Basée sur de Nouveau Principes.*

1851: A new method of horsemanship, founded upon new principles: including the breaking and training of horses: with instructions for obtaining a good seat. Illustrated with engravings. Translated from the ninth Paris edition. Philadelphia, A. Hart, late Carey and Hart.   RT

Errata: 1 leaf inserted after p. 38.

1852: Philadelphia, A. Hart . . .   AAS

1856: Third edition. Philadelphia, Parry and McMillan.   HPL

BEARDSLEY, Levi. Reminiscences; personal and other incidents; early settlement of Otsego County; notices and anecdotes of public men; judicial, legal and legislative matters; field sports; dissertations and discussions. By Levi Beardsley, Esq. late of the New-York Senate, and President thereof. New-York: Printed by Charles Vinten . . . 1852.   RT

Portrait frontispiece.

BEASLEY, Frederick. A sermon on duelling, delivered in Christchurch, Baltimore, April 28, 1811 . . . Baltimore: J. Robinson, 1811.   HCL

1822: A sermon upon duelling: delivered to the Senior Class in the University of Pennsylvania . . . July 21st, 1822. Philadelphia, S. Potter & Co.   LC

BEAUFORT, James. *See:* HOYLE, Edmond.

BECKELL, J[ames] C[ox]. Old Rosin the Beau. Favourite comic song dedicated with much respect to the members of the Falcon Barge, by the publisher. Arranged by J. C. Beckell. Philadelphia [cop. 1838]. RT

Words and music. Lithograph of eight-oar boat on cover.

BEECHER, Henry Ward. Seven lectures to young men, on various important subjects; delivered before the young men of Indianapolis, Indiana, during the winter of 1843–4. Indianapolis: Published by Thomas B. Cutler; Charles B. Davis, bookseller and stationer: Cincinnati, Wm. H. Moore & Co., 1844. RT

Lecture V: *Gamblers and gambling.* Lecture VII: *Popular amusements.*

1845: Lectures to young men, on various important subjects. Second edition. Salem: Published by John P. Jewett & Co. . . . 1845. RT

1846: Sixth thousand. Salem, J. P. Jewett & Co. N

1846: Thirteenth thousand. New York, Jewett & Co. LC

1849: Sixteenth thousand. Boston, J. P. Jewett & Co. N

1851: Nineteenth thousand. Boston, J. P. Jewett & Co. LC

1852: Twenty-third thousand. Boston, J. P. Jewett & Co. N

1853: Twenty-fifth thousand. Boston, J. P. Jewett & Co. N

BEECHER, Henry Ward. Star papers; or, Experiences of art and nature. New York: J. C. Derby; Boston: Phillips, Sampson & Co. . . . 1855. RT

Contains chapters: *Trouting, A ride, The morals of fishing,* etc.

1859: New York, Derby & Jackson, 119 Nassau St.

BEECHER, Lyman. The remedy for duelling. A sermon, delivered before the Presbytery of Long-Island, at the opening of their session, at Aquebogue, April 16, 1806 . . . Sag Harbor, N.Y.: Printed by Alden Spooner, 1807. RT

Paper covers.

BEECHER, Lyman. *Continued:*

1809: . . . To which is annexed, the Resolutions and Address of the Anti-Duelling Association of New York. New-York, Sold at . . . Williams and Whiting . . .   RT

Paper covers.

[1828:] No. 11. Remedy for duelling. A sermon delivered before the Presbytery of Long Island, at the opening of their session at Aquebogue, April 16, 1806. By Lyman Beecher, D.D. [Boston, Printed by Leavitt & Alden, 7 Cornhill, ca. 1828]. RT

No title page.

BEERS'S Almanac and ephemeris . . . For the year of Our Lord 1795 . . . Hartford: Printed by Hudson and Goodwin, [1794].

Should have 18 l. Contains: *Adventures of Col. Daniel Boon[e]* . . . RT
Evans: 26632. Probably lifted from Trumbull's 1786 plagiarization of Filson.

BELCHER, J. A treatise on boxing *See:* BARRINGTON, George. The London spy.

BELL, Wm. H., & Co. RACES! Pioneer Race Course. Sunday, June 12th. Purse $500. Free for all Trotting and Pacing Horses in California—three mile and repeat in Harness. Weight 145 lbs. To be governed by the Rules of UNION COURSE, Long Island. D. S. CAMPBELL, enters— DOMINICK BURNETT, pacer. JOHN CROOKS, enters—b.g. NEW YORK, trotter. Entrance to the Gate and Public Stand,——$2.00. Horses to start at half-past 2 o'clock, precisely. WM. H. BELL & CO., PROPRIETORS.

Broadside 12¼" by 7¼". Engraving in center of two horses racing, grandstand in background. Race recorded in: Chester, Walter T. *Complete trotting and racing guide.* New York, 1884. p. 540. NEW YORK won. Owned by Edward Morrill & Son, Boston. Quoted in letter, November 22, 1954.

BELLAMY, W. H. Philip the falconer. Song written by W. H. Bellamy, Esqre. Composed by Edward J[ames] Loder. New York: Published by Atwill, 201 Broadway [ca. 1834].

Words and music. Tinted lithograph of falconer, by E. Brown, Jr., on cover.

BEMENT, C[aleb] N. The American poulterer's companion: a practical treatise . . . New York: Saxton and Miles . . . 1845.

VW

Frontispiece, and illustrations throughout text. Chapter IX treats on the wild turkey.

1847: Fifth edition. The American poulterer's companion: a practical treatise on the breeding, rearing, fattening, and general management of the various species of domestic poultry, with illustrations, and portraits of fowls taken from life. New York: Harper & Brothers, publishers, 82 Cliff Street.

RT

Frontispiece and illustrations throughout text.

1856: New York, Harper & Brothers.

RT

[BENHAM, Asahel.] Hunting song. Entered according to act of Congress the 20th(?) Day of October, 1834 . . . of the State of Connecticut.

A sheet of engraved music, with words, five bars of music alternating with a panoramic hunting scene. Date may be 1815, "the thirty-ninth year of independence." Quoted, with illustration and opening words of the song. In: *Antiques*. Boston. Vol. 27, no. 3, March 1935, pp. 116–117.

BENNET, James Arlington. The art of swimming, exemplified by diagrams, from which both sexes may learn to swim and float on the water; and, Rules for all kinds of bathing . . . New York: Collins, Brother & Co., 1846.

RT

BENNETT, Emerson. Mike Fink: a legend of the Ohio. Cincinnati: Robinson & Jones, 1848.

LC

Much of this narrative deals with Fink's skill with the rifle.

1853: Mike Fink: a legend of the Ohio. Revised edition. Cincinnati, J. A. & U. P. James.

LC

BENNETT, Gilson M. The great art of taming and training wild horses . . . *See:* RAREY, John Solomon.

BENTWRIGHT, Jeremiah. American horse tamer and farrier . . . Cincinnati, 1857.

Noted in: *Midland Notes*, no. 60. Mansfield, Ohio, 1955. 86 pp. cloth. Otherwise not described.

1858: American horse tamer and farrier. Showing how to cure the wildest and most vicious horse in the world of kicking, balking, and other bad habits: also Directions to purchasers, hints on stable economy, and remedies for all diseases to which horses are liable; such as spavin, distemper, ringbone, etc. By Jeremiah Bentwright, the celebrated American horse-tamer. Cincinnati: H. M. Rulison, Queen City Publishing House, 141 Main St. Philadelphia: D. Rulison, Quaker City Publishing House, 32 South Third Street, 1858. RT

Brown paper wrappers. Diagrams on both sides of frontispiece, and verso title-page. The section: *The American art of subduing wild and vicious horses*, is a piracy of John Solomon Rarey's *Modern art of taming wild horses*.

1858: The American horse tamer, showing how to cure the wildest & most vicious horse in the world of kicking, balking, and other bad habits; also, Directions to purchasers, hints on stable economy, and remedies for all diseases to which horses are liable such as spavin, distemper, ringbone, &c. &c. By Jeremiah Bentwright, the celebrated American horse-tamer. New York: A. O. Moore, Agricultural Book Publisher, (Late C. M. Saxton & Co.) No. 140 Fulton Street, 1858. RT

Diagrams on both sides frontispiece, and verso title-page.

[185–?] The American horse tamer, showing how to cure the wildest & most vicious horse in the world of kicking, balking, and other bad habits; Directions to purchasers, hints on stable economy, and remedies for all diseases to which horses are liable such as spavin, distemper, ringbone, &c. &c. By Jeremiah Bentwright, the celebrated American horse-tamer. New York: George Holbrook. Y

Title from paper wrapper. Inside cover: *The American horse tamer. New York, Hoyt & Co.*

1859: The American horse tamer and farrier. Showing how to cure the wildest and most vicious horse in the world of kicking, balking, and other bad habits . . . Cincinnati.

Paper covers, 86 pp. Noted in Robert G. Hayden. Catalogue 21, no. 181., 1966.

BERIOT, C. de. *See:* BALL, William. Hunter boy.

BERRIMAN, M[atthew] W. The militiaman's manual and sword-play without a master. Rapier and broad sword exercises copiously explained and illustrated. Small-arm light infantry drill of the United States Army; infantry manual of percussion musket; company drill of the United States Cavalry; The most perfect manual ever placed in a soldier's hand. A book to be carried in every soldier's knapsack. Enlarged, revised, corrected, and edited by Capt. M. W. Berriman, engaged for the last thirty years in the practical instruction of military students. New York: Published by the author, 1859.   RT

A pasted correction slip over, and deleting, "Published by the author" reads: *James Miller. 12 numbered plates of rapier exercises.*

BETHUNE, George W[ashington]. A plea for study. An oration before the Literary Societies of Yale College, August 19, 1845 . . . Printed for the Societies. Philadelphia: John C. Clark . . . 1845.   N

Paper covers. *Angling,* pp. 40–43.

1850: *In His:* Orations and occasional discourses. New York, George P. Putnam . . .   N

BETHUNE, George Washington, editor. *See:* WALTON, Isaac. The complete angler.

BEVERL[E]Y, Robert. The history of the present state of Virginia, in four parts. I. The history of the first settlement of Virginia, and the government thereof to the year 1706. II. The natural productions and conveniences of the country, suited to trade and improvement. III. The native Indians, their religions, laws and customs in war and peace. IV. The present state of the country, as to the polity of the government and the improvements of the land, the 10th of June 1720. By Robert Beverly, a native and inhabitant of the place. Reprinted from the author's second revised edition, London, 1722. With an introduction by Charles Campbell. Richmond, Va.: J. W. Randolph, 121 Main Street, 1855.   N

First published Paris, 1707.
Chapter 5. *Fish.*
Chapter 6. *Wild fowl and hunted game.*
Chapter 10. *Sports and pastimes of the Indians.*

56

BEVERLEY, Robert. *Continued:*

Chapter 21. *Recreations and pastimes in Virginia.*

BILSON, Benjamin. The hunters of Kentucky. *See:* PATTIE, James Ohio. The personal narrative of James O. Pattie, of Kentucky.

[BINDLEY, Charles.] Stable talk and table talk; or, Spectacles for young sportsmen. By Harry Hieover [*Pseud.*]. Philadelphia: Lea and Blanchard, 1845. RT

One illustration. First published London, 1845. This edition covers only Vol. 1 of the English edition.

[BINGHAM, Caleb.] The hunters, or the sufferings of Hugh and Francis, in the wilderness. A true story. Boston: Printed by Samuel T. Armstrong, for Caleb Bingham, no. 44, Cornhill . . . 1814. RT

Paper wrappers. Frontispiece pasted against front wrapper. Hugh Holmes and Francis, "an Indian youth," were freshmen at Dartmouth, who after an accident while hunting moose, survived six weeks of winter "in the wilderness." Only known copy. In 1954 a facsimile edition was published by Dartmouth Publications, edited by Richard W. Morin.

BINGLEY, Thomas. Stories about dogs: illustrative of their instinct, sagacity and fidelity . . . New York, 1843. H

Illustrated.

[1850:] Boston: G. W. Cottrell, publisher, 36 Cornhill. RT

Frontispiece and 6 plates.

BISHOP, Sir Henry R[owley]. Foresters sound the cheerful horn. Glee for four voices composed by Henry R. Bishop. Boston: Published by C. Bradlee, 107 Washington Street [ca. 1835]. RT

Words and music. Deer hunting. RT copy lacks covers.

BISHOP, Sir Henry Rowley. Wind thy horn my hunter boy. *See:* MOORE, Thomas.

BISHOP, Joseph. *See:* GRAY, John W. The life of Joseph Bishop.

BLACKWATER chronicle. *See:* KENNEDY, J. Pendleton.

BLACKWELL, Edward. A compleat system on fencing: or, The art of defence, in the use of the small-sword. Wherein the most necessary parts thereof are plainly laid down; chiefly for gentlemen, promoters and lovers of that science in North America . . . Williamsburg: Printed by William Parks, 1734.   BM

Based on Henry Blackwell's *The English Fencing Master,* first published in London, 1702, and republished in 1705. Only 2 copies known, the other in The John Carter Brown Library, Providence, R.I. Not in Evans. *See: Gee.*

BLAKEY, Robert. Angling; or, How to angle, and where to go. A new edition, with illustrations. London: Routledge . . . New York . . . 1859.   N

On cover: *Books for the Country.* First published London, 1854.

BLAKEY, Robert. Shooting: a manual of practical information on this branch of British field sports . . . New Edition. London: G. Routledge & Sons . . . New York . . . [1859.]   LC

On cover: *Books for the Country. First* published London, 1854.

BLANCHOR, F. Schuylkill boat song. *See:* ENGLISH, Thomas Dunn.

BLEWITT, J[onathan]. The hoppulent man. A comic song. Composed by J. Blewitt. New York: Published by E. Riley & Co. [ca. 1835].   RT

Words and music. Lithograph of a "sport," race course in background. Lithograph of Endicott.

BOGART, W[illiam] H[enry]. Daniel Boone, and the Hunters of Kentucky . . . Auburn and Buffalo: Miller, Orton & Mulligan, 1854.   N

Frontispiece, and 3 plates. Small cuts throughout text.

1854: Fifth thousand. Auburn and Buffalo, Miller, Orton & Mulligan . . .   RT

Frontispiece and 4 plates. Small woodcuts throughout text.

1856: Seventh thousand. New York and Auburn, Miller, Orton & Mulligan . . .   N

To this edition is added: *The Hunters of Kentucky,* filling pp. 391–464, and giving sketches of Simon Kenton, Jo Daviess and others. There are

BOGART, W[illiam] H[enry]. *Continued:*

also additional woodcuts, not in former editions, and a new portrait frontispiece of Boone. The 4 pl. remain the same.

1857: New York, Miller, Orton & Co. . . . **RT**

Frontispiece, 4 plates and small cuts throughout text.

1858: New York, C. M. Saxton . . . **N**

Frontispiece and 4 plates. Small cuts throughout text.

1859: New York, C. M. Saxton . . . **RT**

Frontispiece and 4 plates. Small cuts throughout text.

BOLMER, Paul. *See:* BALLMER, Daniel.

BOND, Alonzo. Ashuelot quick step. As performed by the Winchester and Lowell brass bands. Composed and respectfully dedicated to his friend Samuel Graves Jr. Esq. by Alonzo Bond. Boston: Published by Oliver Ditson, 115 Washington St. Lowell, I. N. Metcalf, [cop. 1846]. **RT**

Music only. Lithograph on cover by E. W. Bouve, Boston, "View from Graves & Co's Musical Instrument Manufactory, Winchester, N.H." S. Graves Jr. Del. Fishing and rowing on river. RT copy has cover only.

BOOK of the atmosphere. Boston: Lilly Wait and Company, Portland: Colman, Holden & Co., 1833. **CU**

Vignette of boys' games, including cricket.

The BOOK of games; or, A history of the juvenile sports practised at the Kingston Academy . . . *See:* KINGSTON Academy.

The BOOK of sports. *See:* CLARKE, William.

The BOOK of a thousand songs. The greatest & best collection ever embodied in one work. New York and Philadelphia: Turner & Fisher. James Fisher, Boston, J. Keller, Baltimore. 1843. **RT**

Portrait frontispiece, vignette title page and small cuts throughout. Contains two stories from the Crockett Almanac: *A bundling match* and *Col. Crockett and the elk*. And the following sporting songs: *The hunters of Kentucky, The Irish Duel, The Irish Angler, Hunter of Tyrol, The hunter's horn is sounding, The death of Crockett, The rackoon hunt.*

BOOK of trades, or Library of the useful arts. Illustrated with twenty-four copper-plates. First American edition. White-Hall [Pa.]: Published by Jacob Johnson . . . 1807. 3 vols.   LC

Includes plates: *The Coach-Maker, Wheel-Wright,* etc.

BOOTH, Dr. G. The horseman's friend. Anamosa, Iowa: Crockwell, Parrott & Booth, printers, 1858.

Blank wrappers. 13 pp. 5¼ by 3⅞ inches. Influence of Rarey appears on p. 10, "How to tame a wild horse." Noted in: Midland Notes. Catalogue 96, No. 609, 1966.

BOONE, Daniel. *See:* FILSON, John.

BOSTON Agricultural Association. Grand exhibition for the improvement of horses, by the Association, in Boston, Oct. 21–25, 1856. Boston, 1856.   B

BOSTON, Massachusetts. The by-laws and town orders of the town of Boston, made and passed at several meetings in 1785 and 1786 and duly approved by the Court of Sessions. Boston: Printed by Edmund Freeman . . . 1786.   N

Football, not to be played at, or kicked through any part of the town, p. 43. Also laws regulating galloping horses, dogs, guns and pistols, swimming and skating on the Lord's Day, and snowballing.

BOSTON, Massachusetts. Several rules, orders, and by-laws made and agreed upon by the freeholders and inhabitants of Boston of the Massachusetts, at their Meeting May 12 and September 22, 1701, and approved by His Majestie's Justices for the County of Suffolk, at their general Quarter Sessions held at Boston, Aug. 5th and October 27th next following Annoque Regni Regis Gulielmi Tertij Angliæ, &c. Decimo Tertio. Boston: Printed by Bartholomew Green, and John Allen, for Benjamin Eliot, 1702.   LC

Sabin: 1040. On p. 11, the law passed September, 1701: *For preventing danger by Foot Balls, Squibs and Snow-balls.*

BOSWORTH, N. A treatise on the rifle, musket, pistol, and fowling piece . . . New York: J. S. Redfield . . . 1846.   LC

Paper covers. Diagram (frontispiece).

BOSWORTH, Newton. The accidents of human life; with hints for their prevention, and the removal of the consequences . . . From a London copy, revised, amended, and enriched with a variety of interesting matter . . . New-York: Printed and sold by Samuel Wood, No. 357, Pearl-Street, 1814.　　　RT

Frontispiece and 7 plates. Boards, with same text as title-page on front cover. Chapter VI, *Accidents from water,* contains Franklin's *Advice to swimmers.* Chapter IX, *Accidents at play.—"Dangerous sports,"* First published London, 1813, but contains only part of Franklin's *"Advice to swimmers".*

BOWMAN, Anne. The kangaroo hunters; or, Adventures in the Bush . . . Philadelphia: Porter & Coates [1858].　　　RT

Frontispiece.

The BOY'S book of sports; or, Exercises and pastimes of youth. Embellished with neat and appropriate engravings. New Haven: S. Babcock, 1835.　　　N

Paper covers. Frontispiece, and cuts on covers and throughout text. The selection of games is taken from William Clarke's *Boy's own book,* London, 1829, and Boston, 1829. "Base ball." on pp. 11–12, with illustration "A game at base ball." The illustration was first used in Robin Carver's *Book of sports,* Boston, 1834, under the caption "Playing Ball." It then appeared in an advertisement in T. G. Fessenden's *Complete farmer and rural economist,* Boston, 1834, entitled "Scene on Boston Common." In *The first lie . . .* New Haven, 1835, it again appeared under the caption "The playground of Mr. Watt's School."

1838: The boy's book of sports; or, Exercises and pastimes of youth. Embellished with neat and appropriate engravings. New Haven: S. Babcock—Church Street.　　　RT

1839: The boy's book of sports; a description of the exercises and sports of youth. Embellished with neat and appropriate engravings. New Haven: S. Babcock—Church Street.　　　RT

BOY'S and girl's book of sports. Embellished with cuts. Providence: Published by Cory and Daniels, 1835.　　　B

Paper covers, frontispiece, and woodcuts throughout text. Based on William Clarke's *The Boy's own Book.* London, 1829, and Boston, 1829. Contains "Base, or Goal Ball", which is identical with the game of rounders in the Clarke edition, except for the change in name, and a few minor typographical errors.

1836: Boy's and girl's book of sports. Embellished with cuts. Providence: Published by Geo. P. Daniels.   N

Paper covers, frontispiece, and cuts throughout text, as in 1835 edition, except for typographical changes.

1843: Boy's and girl's book of sports. Embellished with cuts. Providence: Published by Geo. P. Daniels.

1845: Boy's and girl's book of sports. Embellished with cuts. Providence: Published by Geo. P. Daniels.   RT

Text identical with 1843 edition, but paper cover has different vignette on front, and different list of "Children's books" on back.

BOY'S own book. *See:* CLARKE, William.

The BOY'S book of sports and games. *See:* NOYCE, Elisha.

BOY'S own book of amusement and instruction. Embellished with cuts. Providence: Published by J. S. Hammond, 1841.   RT

Frontispiece, vignette on title-page, and cuts throughout text. Frontispiece has two cuts: *Leap frog* and *Playing ball.* A book of moral instruction. Yellow paper covers, with borders. Vignette on cover differs from that on title-page.

BOY'S own book of fun. With two hundred engravings, by Old Comic Elton. N[ew] Y[ork]: T. W. Strong, 98 Nassau-Street [1847].   RT

Bound in paper covered boards. Mentions: Boxing, cycling, hunting, bowling, etc.

BOY'S own book of sports, birds, and animals. *See:* NOYCE, Elisha.

The BOY'S treasury of sports, pastimes, and recreations. With nearly four hundred engravings, designed by Williams, and engraved by Gilbert. First American edition. Philadelphia: Lea and Blanchard, 1847.   RT

Includes archery, golf, hockey, fly-fishing, stoolball.

1848: Third American edition. Boston, J. P. Hill.   LC

1850: Fourth American edition. New York, Published by Clark, Austin & Co. . . .   RT

1851: Fourth American edition. New York: Clark, Austin & Smith. RT

ca. 1852: Fourth American edition. New York: Clark, Austin & Smith. RT

ca. 1855: Fourth American edition. New York: Clark, Austin & Smith. RT

BRACKEN, Henry. Farriery improved; or, A complete treatise on the art of farriery . . . Exemplified by ten elegant cuts, each the full figure of a horse, describing all the various parts of that noble animal. Likewise Rules for breeding and training of colts . . . To which is prefixed, Ten minutes advice to the purchasers of horses. A new edition. Baltimore: Published by Fisher & Coale . . . 1794.

First published London, 1738. Evans: 26696.

1796: Philadelphia, Printed for Mathew Carey . . . AAS

The 10 cuts are on 8 plates. Also pl. 9: *The Age of a Horse by the Teeth*, and frontispiece, *Blacksmith Murdering a Poor Horse*. Evans: 30118.

1798: Second American edition. Philadelphia: Printed for Mathew Carey . . . N

Evans: 33449.

1815: Taplin improved; or a complete treatise on the art of farriery, wherein are fully explained the nature and structure of that useful creature, a horse; with the diseases and accidents he is liable to; and the methods of cure. Exemplified by ten elegant cuts, each with the full figure of a horse, describing all the various parts of that noble animal. Likewise Rules for breeding and training of colts . . . To which is prefixed Ten minutes advice to the purchasers of horses. By Henry Bracken, M.D. Troy: Printed and sold by Francis Adancourt . . . 1815. RT

RT copy has frontispiece and 8 plates, not numbered. Frontispiece has legend: *Fronticepiece* [sic] *to Adancourt's edition of Taplin's Farriery* . . .

1816: A complete treatise on the art of farriery, wherein are fully explained the nature and structure of that useful creature, a horse; with the diseases and accidents he is liable to; and the

BRACKEN, Henry. *Continued:*

methods of cure. Likewise, Rules for breeding and training of colts . . . To which is prefixed Ten minutes advice to the purchasers of horses. New-Haven, Published by Nathan Whiting. Seth Richards, printer. . . . Middletown.   RT

Sub-title on p. [5]: *Taplin improved* . . . Text same as 1815 edition, but contains no plates, nor index.

1826: The American farrier, or New-York horse doctor; being a further improvement upon Adancourt's "Taplin improved," with terms and names of disorders adapted to the nomenclature of farmers, teamsters, and ostlers in the Northern and Middle States. By an experienced American farrier. Troy: Published by F. Adancourt.   RT

Frontispiece as in 1815 edition, but different legend, plates 1–8, and two unnumbered plates.

BRACKEN, Henry. *See also:* TAPLIN, William.

BRACKEN, Henry. The gentleman's pocket farrier.
                    See: BURDON, William.

BRACKEN, Henry. Taplin improved. *See his:* Farriery improved.

[BRADLEY, Abram.] The art of taming horses . . .
                    See: RAREY, John Solomon.

BRAHAM, [John]. Hunter let thy bugle blow, the celebrated hunters duet. Sung by Madame Feron & Mr. Braham, composed by Mr. Braham. New York: Published by Hewitt, 137 Broadway [ca. 1825].   RT

Words and music. Wolf-hunting song. RT copy lacks cover.

BRAHAM, [John.] William Tell the Swiss Patriot. Sung with great applause by Mr. Keene. Composed by Mr. Braham. New York: J., A., and W. Geib, 23 Maiden Lane. [ca. 1819].

Words and music. Archery.

BRANDON, A. C. The horse farrier and breaker: being a familiar treatise on the most prevalent diseases of the horse; containing instructions for the easiest mode of horse-breaking. B. Scibird, General Agent. Eaton, O.: Tizzard & Albright . . . 1856. RT

Paper covers. At head of cover: *Price,—$3.00.*

BRECK, Charles. The fox chase. A comedy. In five acts. As performed at the theatres, Philadelphia and Baltimore. New York: Published by D. Longworth . . . 1808. RT

Paper covers.

BRENHAM, R. L., editor. *See:* The SOUTHERN sportsman . . .

BRISTED, Charles Astor. Five years in an English university . . . Vol.I [–II]. New York: G. P. Putnam, 155 Broadway, 1852. 2 vols. N

Contains: *The boat race,* Vol. 1, pp. 59-66. Originally published in *The Yale literary magazine.* New Haven, Vol. XII, no. 1, November 1841. The author, an American, describes Cambridge University, and contrasts English and American college students.

1852: Second edition. New York, G. P. Putnam & Co., 10 Park Place. N

This edition is in one volume.

BRISTED, C[harles] Astor. The upper ten thousand: sketches of American society. New-York: Stringer & Townsend, 222 Broadway. 1852. RT

Ch. 1: *The Third Avenue in sleighing time.* Ch. 9: *A trot on Long Island.* Vignette t.-p. and three plates by J. W. Orr.

BROCKWAY, W[illiam] H. Dreams of my childhood. Song & chorus composed by W. H. Brockway. Boston: Published by Oliver Ditson & Co., 277 Washington St. 1858. RT

Words and music. Lithograph of childhood games on cover: sleighing, ball playing, kites, fishing.

BRODERICK, David C. The late Hon. David C. Broderick, United States Senator from California. On Friday, Sept. 16th, '59, at half-past 9 a.m., Hon. David C. Broderick died from the effects of a wound received in a duel, fought on Tuesday morning last, with David S. Terry . . . [San Francisco, 1859.]

Broadside. Title noted in Catalogue 158, Edward Eberstadt & Sons.

BROWN, and Miller. The Arabian art of taming and training wild and vicious horses. *See:* RAREY, John Solomon.

BROWN, Barth[olomew]. The archers' song, as sung at the Anniversary of the Robin-Hood Archers October 1st, 1836. Written, composed and respectfully dedicated to the Association by Bart. Brown Esq. Boston: Published by Parker & Ditson, 107 Washn. St. [cop. 1836].   RT

Words and music. Lithograph of meeting of the Robin-Hood Archers, showing encampment and American flag flying, on cover.

BROWN, Francis H., composer. The snow-flake polka. Composed by Francis H. Brown. Boston: Published by G. P. Reed & Co., 17 Tremont Row. 1851.   RT

Music only. Engraving on cover of horse-drawn sleigh. Weller & Greene, Sc.

BROWN, Francis H., composer. *See:* MORRIS, George P. A life in the woods.

BROWN, John. Rab and his friends. By John Brown, M.D. Boston: Ticknor and Fields, 1859.   RT

Paper covers. First appearance in print in his: *Horæ subsecivæ*. Edinburgh, 1858.

[BROWN, John J.] The American angler's guide. Being a compilation from the works of popular English authors, from Walton to the present time; together with the opinions and practices of the best American anglers: containing every variety of mode adopted in ocean, river, lake and pond fishing; the necessary tackle and baits required; manner of making artificial flies, &c. &c. &c.; with engravings on wood. By an American angler. New York: Burgess, Stringer & Co., and for sale by John J. Brown & Co. At the Angler's Depot, 122 Fulton-street, 1845.   RT

BROWN, John J. *Continued:*

Frontispiece: *Trout fishing in Sullivan County, N.Y.,* poem on back of frontispiece, and 2 plates of hooks. One part only, Chapters I–XXII, pp. [v]–viii, [9]–224, 3 leaves of advertisements. No cuts in text. Fisherman in gilt tooling on cover. The Rev. Dr. George Washington Bethune is suggested as the real author of *The American angler's guide* by "Senectutus', in his: "Early American Fly Fishing Literature," *The Angler's Club Bulletin,* 34, no. 1:22-27. New York, 1955.

1846: Second edition. RT

Identical with first edition, including leaves of advertisements, except for "Second edition" and date 1846 on title page. Front cover has same fisherman in gilt, but blind tooling varies, and has gilt fish on back cover.

1849: Third edition. The American angler's guide; a complete fisher's manual, for the United States: containing the opinions and practices of experienced anglers of both hemispheres; with the various modes adopted in ocean, river, lake and pond fishing; the usual tackle and baits required; instructions in the art of making artificial flies; methods of making fish ponds, transportation of fish, etc. etc. etc. Third edition, revised, corrected, and greatly improved with the addition of a Second Part, containing over one hundred pages of useful and instructive information. Handsomely illustrated with twenty engravings of the principal angle fish of America, and embellished with numerous engravings on steel, stone and wood, by the best artists. New York: H. Long & Brother, 43 Ann Street, and John J. Brown & Co., Angler's Depôt, 103 Fulton Street. N

1 leaf of advertisements; p. 1. with poem, v.b.; engraved frontispiece, *Trouting,* by Wier, pl. 1-2 of hooks and 18 other plates. Part 2 has engraved title page, 4 plates (additional to 18 in Part 1). Small engravings throughout text. Part 1: Chapters I–XXII. Part 2: pp. [225]-332; 3 leaves of advertisements.

1849: Fourth edition. The American angler's guide, containing the opinions and practices of the best English and American anglers, with the modes usually adopted in all descriptions of fishing, method of making artificial flies, etc. Fourth edition, revised, corrected and improved. New-York: H. Long & Brother, 43 Ann-Street, John J. Brown & Co., Angler's Depot, 103 Fulton-Street. N

BROWN, John J. *Continued:*

Frontispiece, 2 plates of hooks and text as in first edition. Chapters I-XXII. Contains first part only, but not called Part I. Poem before title-page on separate leaf. Lacks *The* and small cut of fish as in 1845 edition. Pp. [1-8] *Opinions of the press.* 3 leaves of advertisements at end, as in 1845 edition, except for change in date to 1849.

1850: The American angler's guide; or, Complete fisher's manual, for the United States: containing the opinions and practices of experienced anglers of both hemispheres; with the various modes adopted in ocean, river, lake, and pond fishing; the usual tackle and baits required; instructions in the art of making artificial flies; methods of making fish ponds, transportation of fish, etc., etc., etc. Fourth edition, revised, corrected, and greatly improved, with the addition of a Second part, containing over one hundred pages of useful and instructive information, handsomely illustrated with twenty engravings of the principal angle fish of America, and embellished with numerous engravings on steel, stone, and wood, by the best artists. New York: H. Long & Brother, 43 Ann Street, and John J. Brown & Co., Angler's Depôt, 103 Fulton Street.   RT

Advertisements pp. [1]-[viii].; 1 l. with poem, v.b.; engraved frontispiece: *Trouting* by Wier, text and illustrations as in 3.ed., 1849, 3 pp. of advertisements at end. Pamphlet laid in: Brown, John J. *Stealing or steeling,* accusing H. W. Herbert of plagiarism, in Van Winkle copy.

1857: The American angler's guide; or, Complete fisher's manual, for the United States: containing the opinions and practices of experienced anglers of both hemispheres; with the various modes adopted in ocean, river, lake, and pond fishing; the usual tackle and baits required; instructions in the art of making artificial flies; methods of making fish ponds, transportation of fish, etc., etc., etc. Fourth edition, revised, corrected, and greatly improved, with the addition of a Second part, containing over one hundred pages of useful and instructive information, handsomely illustrated with twenty engravings of the principal angle fish of America, and embellished with numerous engravings on steel, stone, and wood, by the best artists. New York: D. Appleton and Company, 346 & 348 Broadway.   RT

68

BROWN, John J. *Continued:*

Text and plates same as 3.ed. of 1849. No advertisements.

[Brown, John J.] The angler's almanac, for 1848 . . . Anecdotes of angling, &c. &c. New York: Published by John J. Brown & Co. . . . 1848.   RT

Engraved paper cover with title: *Brown's Angler's Almanac for 1848.*

1849: New York.   Y

Similar title and cover.

1851: The fisher's vade mecum: or, Angler's almanac for 1851 . . . Beautifully illustrated . . . New York.   Y

Cover title: *Brown's Angler's Almanac for 1851.*

BROWN, William Linn. *See:* WATMOUGH, Edward Coxe.

BROWNING, Meshach. Forty-four years of the life of a hunter; being reminiscences of Meshach Browning, a Maryland hunter, roughly written down by himself. Revised and illustrated by E. Stabler. Philadelphia: J. B. Lippincott Company [1859].   RT

This is first edition, in spite of "revised" in title. Fourteen plates, including frontispiece, (two, p. 28 and p. 42 not in *List of illustrations*) and 13 engravings in text.

BRYAN, Daniel. The mountain muse. Comprising The adventures of Daniel Boone . . . Harrisonburg [Va.]: Printed for the author, by Davidson & Bourne, 1813.   RT

BUCHAN, William. Every man his own doctor . . . With an Appendix containing A complete treatise on the art of farriery. New Haven, 1816.

The Farriery is probably based on: BURDON, William. The gentleman's pocket farrier. Copy in University of Vermont Medical Library.

BULLOCK, William. A concise and easy method of preserving objects of natural history, intended for the use of sportsmen, travellers, and others . . . From the third London edition, with additions by a Naturalist in America. New York: Printed for the Publisher, 1829.   RT

First published London, 1817. Paper covers.

69

BUNBURY, [Henry William]. An academy for grown horse-men; containing the completest instructions for walking, trotting, cantering, galloping, stumbling, and tumbling. By Geoffrey Gambado, Esq. [*Pseud.*] . . . Illustrated with twelve caricatures, from designs by Bunbury . . . Philadelphia: Published by M. Carey . . . 1813. RT

First published London, 1787.

[1828:] Gambado's horsemanship. New York: S. King.

Advertised in *Twin sisters*. New York: S. King, 1828. With colored engravings. Copy in Vassar College Library.

BUNG, *pseud.* The sports and joys of fishing. A humorous song as sung by Ossian's Bards. Written and composed for the piano, and respectfully inscribed to Oliver Optic, Esq., by Bung. Boston: Published by C. H. Keith. . . , 1854.

Words and music. No cover illustration.

BURDON, William. The gentleman's pocket farrier, shewing how to use your horse on a journey, and what remedies are proper for common misfortunes that may befal him on the road. By Capt. William Burdon. London printed: Reprinted by Lewis Timothy in Charleston, South Carolina, 1734.

First published London, 1730. No copy known. Advertised in *The South-Carolina Gazette* of October 19, 1734, as "Just published and sold by the Printer . . . (Price neatly bound 15s.)" In the advertisement the name of the printer is misspelled "Thimothy." First Bracken edition London, 1748. Published in America under several authors, and anonymously, in numerous editions, with various titles. Not in Evans.

1735: London printed: Reprinted by B. Franklin, Philadelphia.

Published anonymously. Evans: 3882.

1775: Ten minutes advice to every gentleman going to purchase a horse out of a dealer, jockey, or groom's stables. In which are laid down established rules for discovering the perfections and blemishes of that noble animal. Philadelphia: Printed by Joseph Crukshank, for W. Aikman, Bookseller in Annapolis, 1775. [*Second title on E2.*]:
The gentleman's pocket farrier; shewing how to use your horse on a journey; and what remedies are proper for common accidents

70

that may befal him on the road . . . Philadelphia: Printed by Joseph Crukshank, for W. Aikman, Bookseller in Annapolis, 1775. RT

1778: Boston: N.E., Printed and sold by N. Coverly. AAS

Published anonymously. Not in Evans.

1787: Philadelphia, Printed and sold by Joseph Crukshank. *Bound with:* Ten minutes' advice to every gentleman . . . Philadelphia, 1787. AAS

Published anonymously. Not in Evans.

1790: . . . With a copperplate, shewing the age of a horse by his teeth . . . London. Printed: Middletown: Re-printed and sold by Moses H. Woodward. RT

Evans: 22327, under: Bartlet, J. Published anonymously.

1791: . . . With a copperplate . . . Philadelphia, Printed by William Spotswood. AAS

Evans: 23157, under: Bartlet, J.

1793: . . . With a copperplate . . . Springfield, Massachusetts, Printed by James R. Hutchins. AAS

Evans: 25238, under: Burdon, William.

1795: The complete farrier; wherein is contained almost every disorder to which American horses are incident to, with proper directions how to perfect the care of them. Lexington, Printed by James H. Stewart.

Published anonymously. Evans: 28460.

1796: Bracken's Farriery abridged; or, The gentleman's pocket farrier . . . Baltimore, Printed for George Keatinge.

Evans: 30117, under: Bracken, Henry.

1797: The gentleman's pocket farrier; shewing how to use your horse on a journey; and what remedies are proper for common accidents, that may befal him on the road. Philadelphia: Printed by Francis Bailey, at Yorick's Head.

BURDON, William. *Continued:*

Plate: *The age of a horse by its teeth.*

1797: The gentleman's pocket farrier . . . WHSHINGTON (sic.): Printed by John Colerick.   RT

[ca. 1800:] The complete pocket farrier, wherein is contained almost every disorder to which American horses are incident to . . . Frederick-Town [Md.], Printed by Matthias Bartgis.   RT

Published anonymously.

1816: . . . To which is added, Ten minutes' advice to every purchaser of a horse . . . Carlisle, Printed by Archibald Loudon.   AAS

Published anonymously.

1816: Buchan, William. Every man his own doctor . . . With an Appendix containing A complete treatise on the art of farriery [probably based on: Burdon, William. The gentleman's pocket farrier]. New Haven, [Conn.].

Copy in University of Vermont Medical Library.

1828: The gentleman's pocket-farrier. Showing how to use a horse on a journey. And what remedies are proper for common accidents that may befal him on the road. A new edition, improved and carefully revised by a veterinary surgeon. With additions by Mr. Blyth, Riding Master at the Circus, Philadelphia, and lately from Astley's Theatre, London. Philadelphia: Published by Thomas Desilver, 253 Market St.   RT

1832: The pocket farrier, showing how to use a horse on a journey, and what remedies . . . With additions by Mr. Blyth, Riding Master at the Circus, Philadelphia . . . Wheeling, Va. Printed and Published by A. & E. Picket . . .   AAS

Published anonymously.

1832: The gentleman's pocket farrier . . . By F. Tuffnell, Veterinary Surgeon. Boston, Carter & Hendee.   RT

1836: The gentleman's pocket farrier . . . By F. Tuffnell, Veterinary Surgeon. Baltimore, Published by John Plaskitt. . . .
                                                                    JLO

BURDON, William. *Continued:*

1843: Every man his own farrier. Containing Ten minutes advice how to buy a horse. To which Is added Directions how to use your horse at home or on a journey. . . . Philadelphia, J. B. Perry . . . New York, Nafis and Cornish.   RT

Published anonymously. Wood engravings.   RT

1845: Every man his own farrier. Containing ten minutes advice how to buy a horse. To which is added Directions how to use your horse at home or on a journey . . . Philadelphia, J. B. Perry . . . New York, Nafis & Cornish . . .   RT

Identical with 1843 edition, except for copyright date, plate added at p. 98: *The age of a horse by his teeth,* and at end: Books, published and for sale . . . by John B. Perry, pp. [1]–8.

BURKE, B. W. A compendium of the anatomy, physiology, and pathology, of the horse . . . Together with a concise examination of the economy and structure of the foot, and observations on shoeing. Philadelphia: Printed and sold by James Humphreys . . . 1806.   RT

Two engraved anatomical plates. First published London, 1806.

BURNHAM, Calvin. The thorough bred horse *Obscurity,* will stand at the stable of Calvin Burnham, near the Court House in Lenox, where he will cover mares at   dollars the season . . . Good pasture provided for mares by CALVIN BURNHAM. April 1807.   RT

Horse breeding broadside, cut of horse at head, 10½" by 8¾".

BURNHAM, George P. Western trappers camp song. As sung by Francis H. Brown's Concert Troupe. Also by Miss C. Hiffert. Written by George P. Burnham, Esq. Composed by Francis H. Brown. New York: Published by Firth, Pond & Co., 547 Broadway [1856].   RT

Words and music. Stag hunting and angling lithograph by Sarony, Major & Knapp on cover. At head of cover: *To George P. Morris, Esq.*

BURRIS, William, The farmer's farrier book . . . Wilmington, O.: Rice Gaddis, Printer, 1819.

No copy known. Title from Copyright Book for the District of Ohio, 1806–1828.

BURTON, William E., editor. *See:* The GENTLEMAN'S magazine.

BUTLER, Francis. Breeding, training, management, diseases, &c. of dogs . . . Illustrated by T. C. Carpendale. New York, 1857.
BM

BUTLER, Francis. Dogo-graphy. The life and adventures of the celebrated dog Tiger, comprising a variety of amusing and instructive examples, illustrative of the happy effects of the appropriate training and education of dogs . . . Stereotype edition. New York: Published by Francis Butler . . . 1856.   RT

Paper covers.

The CABINET of natural history and American rural sports with illustrations. Philadelphia: J. & T. Doughty, 1830–1834.
AAS

Issued in monthly parts, dated 1830 to 1834, and bound in three volumes dated respectively 1830, 1832 and 1833. Ceased publication with vol. 3, pt. 4. Vol. 3 is rare. Of great importance because it contains the first colored sporting prints made in America. The wild turkey plate in vol. 3, pt. 1 is almost as rare as the famous Audubon folio wild turkey plate. Sets in the original wrappers are of the utmost rarity. Two sets in parts, AAS and Arents copies, and two bound sets, N and RT, have been compared. The conclusion is drawn that as the plates were printed, they became worn and were then strengthened by a border line. In some cases (See below) they were replaced by plates drawn by different artists.

The following description of the AAS set was made by Mr. R. W. G. Vail and variations are noted in the set of Mr. George Arents (in parts) and the RT copy (bound).

Volume I.

The cabinet of natural history, and American rural sports, with illustrations. Vol. 1. [vignette of hunter and two dogs] Philadelphia Published by J. & T.

Doughty. 1830 [Engraved title signed: *T. M. Raser Scr. C. G. Childs Sculp.* Vignette signed: *T. Doughty Del. W. E. Tucker Sc.*].

Cover title:
No. 1. The cabinet of natural history and American rural sports. [filet] *With illustrations.* [rule] *A monthly publication.* [filet] *Vol. I.* [thin-thick rule] *Philadelphia: Published by J. & T. Doughty, No. 80 Walnut Street. Russell & Martien, Printers.* [dotted rule] *1830.* Index on verso of front wrapper. Back wrapper (recto and verso) contains adv. of the work, announcing that it would contain 24 p. of text and 2 colored plates per

CABINET of natural history. *Continued:*

part, issued monthly at $8.00 per year. With No. 5 the publisher's address becomes: *S. E. Corner Walnut & Fourth Streets.* With no. 12 their address becomes: *Library Street, above Fourth.* With Vol. 2, No. 1 the address reads: *No. 5, Library Street, above Fourth. William Stavely, Printer.* With No. 3 the publisher becomes: *John Doughty.* The advertisements on back wrapper vary.

Note: This set has been bound up as issued, not with the extra plates and introductory pages placed according to the directions to the binder. It is therefore exactly as issued and is so described. When the wrappers contain exact dates, they are given.

No. 1. 1830. Engraved title as above, pp. [1]-24 and two colored plates: *Pl. 1. Common deer. Doughty pinxt. Sartain sc. Pl. 2. Ruffed grouse, or pheasant. From nature by T. Doughty. On stone C. G. Childs Direx.*

No. II. 1831. pp. 25-48 and 2 colored plates: *Pl. 3. Red fox. From nature and on stone by T. Doughty. Childs Lith. Pl. 4. Quails, or partridges. From nature & on stone by T. Doughty. Childs & Inman Lithr Philada.*

No. III. 1831. pp. 49-72 and 2 colored plates: *Pl. 5. Newfoundland dog. From nature and on stone by T. Doughty. from Childs & Inman's Press. Pl. 6. Pelican. From nature and on stone by T. Doughty. from Childs & Inman's Press.*

No. IV. 1831. pp. 73-96 and two colored plates: *Pl. 7. Prairie wolves. From nature and on stone by T. Doughty from Childs & Inman's Press. Pl. 8. Meadow lark. Snow bird. From nature and on stone by T. Doughty. from Childs & Inman's Press.*

No. V. 1831. pp. 97-120 and two colored plates: *Pl. 9. Woodcock shooting. On stone by T. Doughty. from Childs & Inman's Press. Pl. 10. Goosander. Golden eye. From nature and on stone by T. Doughty. from Childs & Inman's Press.*

No. VI. 1831. pp. 121-144 and 2 colored plates: *Pl. 11. Grizzly bears. On stone by T. Doughty from a drawing by T. R. Peale. From Childs & Inman's Press. Pl. 12. Blue bird. Robin. From nature and on stone by T. Doughty. From Childs & Inman's Press.*

No. VII. 1831. pp. 145-168 and 2 colored plates: *Pl. 13. 1. Trout of Silver Lake, drawn from one 24½ inches long. 2. Male brook trout drawn from one 9 inches long in Septemr. T. Doughty on stone from a drawing by a Lady. From Childs & Inman's Press Phil. Pl. 14. Woodcock. From nature & on stone by T. Doughty. From Childs & Inman's Press.*

No. VIII. 1831. pp. 169-192 and 2 colored plates: *Pl. 15. Ground squirrel. From nature and on stone by T. Doughty. from Childs & Inman's Press. Pl. 16. Swans. From nature and on stone by T. Doughty. from Childs & Inman's Press.*

75

CABINET of natural history. *Continued:*

No. IX. 1831. pp. 193–216 and 2 colored plates: *Pl. 17. Argali. On stone by T. Doughty. from Childs & Inman's Press. Pl. 18. Rail. From nature & on stone by T. Doughty. from Childs & Inman's Pr.*

No. X. 1831. pp. 217–240 and 2 colored plates: *Pl. 19. Varying hare. From nature and on stone by T. Doughty. from Childs & Inman's Press. Pl. 20. Red tailed hawk. American sparrow hawk. From nature and on stone by T. Doughty. From Childs & Inman's Press.*

No. XI. 1831. pp. 241–264 and 2 colored plates: *Pl. 21. American porcupine. From nature and on stone by T. Doughty. From Childs & Inman's Press. Pl. 22. Summer duck. From nature and on stone by T. Doughty. From Childs & Inman's Press*

No. XII. 1831. pp. 265-288 and 2 colored plates: *Pl. 23. Great tailed squirrel. From nature and on stone by T. Doughty. From Childs & Inman's Press. Pl. 24. Raven. From nature & on stone by T. Doughty. From Childs & Inman's Press.*

Extra. 1831. [Port. of Peale was supposed to be inserted facing the engraved title page of the volume]. *Biographical sketch of Charles Willson Peale,* p. [i]–vii; *Embellishments to Volume I.,* verso of p. vii; [main text continued, pp. 289-298: *End of the first volume.;* Index to Volume I., [2] p. Facing the Biog. sketch: stipple port. of *C W Peale Engraved by J. B. Longacre from an original painting by Rembrandt Peale.*

Volume II

The cabinet of natural history and American rural sports with illustrations. Volume II. [vignette of man fishing] 1832. Philadelphia Published by J. & T. Doughty. [Vignette signed: T. Doughty del. W. E. Tucker sc.]

No. I. 1832. Engraved title as above, pp. [1]-24 and 2 colored plates: *Pl. 1 Vol. 2. Wild horses. MED Brown Delt his Lith. No. 5 Library St. Phila. Pl. 2 Vol. 2. Great horned owl. From nature & on stone by MED Brown. his Lith. No. 5 Library St. Phila.*

No. II. 1832. pp. 25-48 and 2 colored plates: *Pl. 3 V. 2. Cougar—Panther. From life & on stone by MED Brown; his Lith. No. 5 Library St. Pha. Pl. 4 Vl. 2. Canvas-Back duck. Red-headed duck. From nature & on stone by MED Brown his Lith. N 5 Library St. Phila.*

No. III. 1832. [On recto of back wrapper:] "The copartnership heretofore existing between the Subscribers, was dissolved by mutual consent on the 16th inst. The Work will be continued by John Doughty, who is duly authorized to settle all accounts of the late firm./Jno. Doughty,/Thomas Doughty./Philadelphia, May 17, 1832." "With much pleasure we refer our readers to the elegant Engraving, of 'Breaking Cover,' which accompanies the present number. It is the second effort of a young and talented artist, who has just commenced business."

CABINET of natural history. *Continued:*

pp. 49-72 and one copperplate engraving and one colored plate: *Breaking cover. Engraved for the Cabinet of Natural History and American Rural Sports. Painted by Philip Reinagle A. R. Engraved by F. Humphrey. Pl. 6 Vol. 2. Ruby-crowned wren. Blue jay. From nature & on stone by MED Brown his Lith. No. 5 Library St. Phila.*

No. IV. 1832. pp. 73-96 and 2 colored plates: *Vol. 2 Pl. 7. Raccoon. Drawn from life & on stone by MED Brown his Lith. No. 5 Library St. Phila. Vol. 2 Pl. 8. Maryland yellowthroat. American redstart. From nature & on stone by MED Brown. his Lith. No. 5 Library St. Phila.*

No. V. 1832. pp. 97-120 and 2 colored plates: *Pl. 9 Vol. 2. Esquimaux dog. Drawn & printed by Childs & Inman. Pl. 10. Vol. 2. Humming birds. From life & on stone by MED Brown. his Lith. No. 5 Library St. Phila.*

No. VI. 1832. [Announces discontinuance at end of the volume unless receives better support]. pp. 121-144 and 2 colored plates: Vol. 2 Pl. 11 misnumbered *Vol. 2 Pl. 12. Birds eggs.* [25 eggs numbered and identified] *From nature and on stone by J. G. Clonney. E. S. Mesier's Lith. N.Y. Plate XII. Scarlet tanager. Blue eyed yellow warbler. Drawn on stone from nature by M. E. D. Brown, No. 5 Library St. Printed by Childs & Inman.*

No. VII. 1832. pp. 145-168 and 2 colored plates: Vol. 2 [Pl. 13] misnumbered *Vol. 2 Pl. 14. Grey fox. On stone by J. G. Clonney from a drawing by E. Landseer. E. S. Mesier's Lith. N.-York. Plate 14. Vol. 2. Blue crane. Hudsonian godwit. From nature & on stone Childs & Inman's Lith.*

No. VIII. 1832. pp. 169-192 and 2 colored plates: *Pl. 15 Vol. 2. American buffaloe. Drawn on stone by M. E. D. Brown from a sketch by R. M. E. D. Brown's Lith No. 5 Library St. Phila. Pl. 16. Vol. 2. Flicker, or golden-winged woodpecker. Printed by Mesier, N.Y. Drawn on stone from nature by J. C. Clonney.*

No. IX. 1832. pp. 193-216 and 2 colored plates: *Pl. 17. Vol. 2. Skunk. On stone by J. G. Clonney from a drawing by R. E. S. Mesier's Lith. N.-York. Pl. 18. Vol. 2. Gannet. (Young.). Gannet. (Adult.) From nature and on stone by J. G. Clonney. Mesier's Lith.*

No. X. 1832. pp. 217-240 and 2 colored plates: *Vol. 2. Pl. 19. Polar bear. Childs & Inman Lithrs. Vol. 2. Pl. XX. Snipe. From nature and on stone by J. G. Clonney. Mesier's Lith. N.York.*

No. XI. 1833. pp. 241-264 and 2 colored plates: *Vol. 2. Pl. XXI. Grey squirrel. From nature and on stone by J. G. Clonney. Mesier's Lith. New-York. Vol. 2. Pl. XXII. Pine finch. Purple finch. from nature on stone by J. G. Clonney. Mesier's Lith. N.York.*

No. XII. 1833. pp. 265-288 and 2 colored plates: *Vol. 2. Pl. XXIII. Black wolf. From Childs & Inman's Press. Vol. II. Pl. XXIV. Belted king fisher. Buffel headed duck. From nature by M. E. D. Brown.*

CABINET of natural history. *Continued:*

Extra. 1833. [Portrait of Bartram to face engraved title page]. *Biographical sketch of William Bartram,* p. [i]–vii; *Embellishments to Volume II,* verso of p. vii; *Index to Volume II,* [2] p. Facing the biog. sketch is a stipple engraved portrait of: *Will. Bartram Engraved by T. B. Welch from an original painting by C. W. Peale.* Notice to subscribers on back wrapper explains delay in publication on account of a five months trip to the southern states where the editor secured new materials for the work and enough new subscribers to warrant its continuance for another volume.

Volume III.

The cabinet of natural history and American rural sports with illustrations Vol. III. [vignette of duck hunter] Philadelphia Published by John Doughty. 1833. [Vignette signed:] *W. E. Tucker Sc. T. Doughty Del.* [Engraved title]

No. 1. 1833. Engraved title, pp. [1]–24 and 2 colored plates: *Vol. III. Pl. I. Beaver. From nature by M.E.D. Brown From Childs & Inman's Press.* Vol. III pl. II misnumbered *Vol. III. Pl. I. Wild turkey. From nature by M. E. D. Brown From Childs & Inman's Press.*

No. II..1834. pp. 25–48 and 2 colored plates: *Vol. III. Pl. III. Golden winged warbler. Indigo bird. From Childs & Inman's Press. From nature by MED Brown. Vol. III. Pl. IV. Red flamingo. From nature on stone by G. Lehman. Childs & Inman Lithrs.*

No. III. 1834. pp. 49–72 and 2 colored plates: *Pl. V. Vol. III. Prong-horned antilope. Drawn on stone by. A. Rider. Printed by Childs & Lehman. Plate VI. Vol. III. Chesnut sided warbler. Baltimore oriole. From nature by M. E. D. Brown Printed by Pendleton, Boston.* [Inserted in AAS copy of the work is an extra uncolored print from this stone printed on a coarser paper than that used with the published work].

No. IV. 1834. pp. 73–96, 1 engraved and 1 colored lithographed plate: [Copperplate engraving, uncolored:] *Death of the fox. Engraved for the Cabinet of Natural History and American Rural Sports. Painted by Sawry Gilpin R. A. Engraved by Francis Humphreys. Plate VIII. Vol. III. Spotted grouse. From nature by M. E. D. Brown. Printed by Pendleton, Boston.*

Note: Though there is no notice to subscribers on the wrappers of Vol. III that the work would not be continued, part IV, ending with p. 96 and plate VIII, seems to have been the last published.

Variations, Mr. George Arents copy:
Vol. 1, nos. 1–4. Address on cover *No. 80 Walnut Street* does not appear. Instead imprint reads: *Published by J. & T. Doughty, S. E. Corner Walnut & Fourth Streets.*

CABINET of natural history. *Continued:*

Vol. 1, no. 1, pl. 2. Names of artist and engraver not legible.

Variations, Racquet and Tennis Club copy:
Vol. 1, pl. 7. Prairie wolves: *On stone A. Newsam from Childs & Inmans Press.*

Vol. 1, pl. 10. Goosander, Golden eye: *On stone by J. G. Clonney from a drawing by T. Doughty. P. A. Mesier's Lith. N.York.*

Vol. 1, pl. 11. Grizzly bears: *Grisly bears. Lith. by J. F. & C. A. Watson. Philada.*

Vol. 1, pl. 15. Ground squirrel: *Lith. by J. F. & C. A. Watson.*

Vol. 1, pl. 17. Argali. *Lith. by J. F. & C. A. Watson.*

Vol. 1, pl. 21 American porcupine. Misnumbered *PL. 12: E. S. Mesier's Lith. J. G. Clonney del.*

Vol. 2, pl. 10. Humming birds. Not numbered.

CADWALADER, M. D. New manuel [sic.] of veterinary medicine, or the treatment of the diseases of the horse. By M. D. Cadwalader, veterinary surgeon. [Ohio?], 1854.   RT

Bound in flexible cloth. Entered according to Act of Congress, in the year 1854 . . . in . . . the District Court of the United States for the District of Ohio.

CALDWELL, Charles. A discourse on the vice of gambling, delivered by appointment, to the Anti-Gambling Society of Transylvania University, November 2nd and 3rd, 1835 . . . Lexington, Ky.: J. Clarke & Co., 1835.   HCL

Paper covers.

CALDWELL, Charles. Thoughts on physical education: being a discourse delivered to a convention of teachers in Lexington, Ky., on the 6th & 7th of Nov., 1833. Boston: Marsh, Capen & Lyon, 1834.   N

CALIFORNIA spirit of the times. San Francisco: Published by Jno. Phenix 1854–1860.

Not in Library of Congress nor Union List of Periodicals.

CALTHROP, S. R. Lecture on physical development, and its relations to mental and spiritual development, delivered before The American Institute of Instruction, at their twenty-sixth Annual Meeting in Norwich, Conn., August, 1858, by S. R. Calthrop, of Bridgeport, Conn., formerly of Trinity College, Cambridge, England. Boston: Ticknor and Fields, 1859.

Green paper covers, lettering as on title-page. 36 pp. Copy owned by Warder H. Cadbury, Albany, N.Y.

CAMPBELL, Walter. The old forest ranger; or, Wild sports of India on the Neilgherry Hills, in the jungles, and on the plains. Edited by Frank Forester. [*Pseud.* of Henry William Herbert.] . . . New York: Stringer & Townsend . . . 1853.　　　Y

Frontispiece, engraved title-page, and 4 plates from sketches by Major Campbell. First published London, 1842.

1855: New York, Stringer & Townsend.

1856: New York, Stringer & Townsend.

1859: New York, Stringer & Townsend.　　　Y

The CANINE race. A brief natural history of the dog. Interspersed with interesting characteristic anecdotes, and embellished with sixteen beautiful wood engravings. New Haven [Conn.]: Printed and published by S. Babcock [ca. 1840]. Babcock's moral, instructive, and amusing toy books.　　　RT

Paper wrappers with sporting designs. Vignette title-page, and illustrations throughout text.

1841: Identical with above, except for date on title-page.　　　RT

[CANNING, Josiah Dean] The shad fishers. By the "Peasant Bard." Greenfield: Published by R. C. Graves, 1854.　　　N

A 24p. poem.

[CAREY, David.] Life in Paris; or, The rambles and sprees of Dick Wildfire, Squire Jenkins and Captain O'Shuffleton; with the whimsical adventures of the Halibut family, and other eccentric characters in the French metropolis. In two volumes. New Orleans: For sale by W. M'Kean; James Rice Jr., Louisville;

Flash, Ryder and Co. Cincinnati . . . 1837. 2 vols.　　　RT

[CAREY, David.] *Continued:*

First published, with illustrations by Cruikshank, London, 1820. Not illustrated. Boards, labels.

CAREY, Mathew. Proposals for publishing the beauties of the Sporting Magazine. Philadelphia, 1817.

A prospectus for a periodical or book which evidently was never published. Contains 4 plates and several sample articles. Copy owned by Mr. Lindley Eberstadt.

CARSON, Kit. *See:* PETERS, DeWitt Clinton.

CARUSI, Nath[anie]l The chace. A favorite discriptive [sic] piece. Composed & arranged for the pianoforte and dedicated to Miss H. Berry by Nathanl. Carusi. Baltimore: Published by Saml. Carusi [1845].   RT

Sheet music. Lithograph of fox-hunting scene on cover, by Ed. Weber & Co., Baltimore.

CARVER, James. A treatise on the age of the horse, being a true delineation, with instructions how to tell his age, from a foal to the period of sixteen years . . . Philadelphia: Published for the author by Littell & Henry . . . 1818.   N

Two engraved plates.

CARVER, James. Veterinary science important to . . . the gentlemen of Philadelphia . . . Also, Comparative shoeing explained . . . [Philadelphia:] T. S. Manning, Printer, 1817.   LC

CARVER, James. *See also:* The FARRIER'S magazine.

CARVER, Robin. The book of sports. By Robin Carver. Boston: Lilly, Wait, Colman, and Holden, 1834.   RT

Vignette title-page, illustrations throughout text. "Base, or Goal Ball," with illustration of game, is first appearance in America of rules of baseball, and earliest *American* illustration of game. The rules are taken from the game of rounders in William Clarke's *The boy's own book,* London, 1829. The illustration appeared in an advertisement in T. G. Fessenden's *Complete farmer and rural economist,* Boston, 1834, entitled "Scene on Boston Common." It was also repeated in: *The first lie* . . . New Haven, 1835, as "The playground of Mr. Watt's School," and in *The boy's book of sports,* New Haven, 1839. *See:* Clarke, William. *The boy's own book.* Boston, 1829. *See* p. xxi.

81

CARVER, William. The practical horse farrier; or, The traveller's pocket companion. Shewing the best method to preserve the
horse in health; and, likewise, the cure of the most prominent
diseases to which this noble animal is subject in the United States
of America . . . Philadelphia: Printed and Published by M'Carty
& Davis . . . 1818.   RT

1820: Second edition, much enlarged, and embellished with three
engravings. Philadelphia, M'Carty & Davis.   AAS

1826: Second edition.   RT

Identical with 1820 edition.

The CASKET. Flowers of literature, wit and sentiment. No. 2.
Philadelphia, February, 1830.   RT

The Gloucester Fox Hunting Club, by Lang Syne. An article based on
the manuscript of *Memoirs of the Gloucester Fox Hunting Club,* by
William Milnor, Jr., pp. 49-51. Full page engraving of two hounds killing
a fox.

CASPAR, the hunter, a story for young people. Boston: Brown,
Bazin & Co., 1854.   RT

Vignette title-page, frontispiece, and 31 full-page illustrations, tailpieces.
Hunting general. Dark brown cloth. Another copy in red cloth, otherwise
identical.   RT

CAVEAT Emptor, *pseud. See:* STEPHEN, Sir George.

CHALLENGE, The. New York, 1854.

Merged with *The New York Clipper.*

CHANNEL, Solomon. The Arabian art of taming and training
wild & vicious horses. *See:* RAREY, John Solomon.

CHAPMAN, John Ratcliffe. Instructions to young marksmen,
in all that relates to the general construction, practical manipula-
tion, causes and liability to error in making accurate performances, and the theoretic principles upon which such accurate performances are founded, as exhibited in the improved American
rifle. By John Ratcliffe Chapman . . . New-York: D. Appleton
& Company, 200 Broadway. Philadelphia: Geo. S. Appleton, 148
Chesnut-St. 1848.   RT

7 plates, including frontispiece, and small woodcuts in text.

CHEEK, Henry. Cheek's farriery: a complete treatise on the causes and symptoms of the diseases of the horse, and their remedies. Being an improvement upon the methods of treating diseases . . . Memphis: 1845.   RT

Folded frontispiece, 1 plate and 1 full-page cut.

CHEYNE, George. An essay on health and long life . . . New York: Printed and published by Edward Gillespy . . . 1813.
                                                                            AAS

CHILD, L. Maria. The girls' own book, by Mrs. L. Maria Child. New York: Clark Austin & Co., 3 Park Row & 3 Ann-St. [Copyright, 1833].   RT

Frontispiece and engraved title page, small engravings throughout text. A collection of girls' games.

1837: The little girl's own book. By Mrs. Child, author of "The frugal housewife," "Mother's book," &c. Boston: American Stationers Company. John B. Russell.   RT

Colored frontispiece and small engravings throughout text. Cover title: *Girl's own book*. Identical with 1833 edition, except for frontispiece, title-page and cut on p. [ix].

CHILDREN at play. Cincinnati: William T. Truman [ca. 1830].
                                                                            RT

Cover: *Truman's entertaining toy books*. Paper covers. Small woodcuts throughout. Children's games, including "ball", with illustration.

CHILDREN'S amusements. When school is over for the day, The sprightly boys run off to play. New-York: Published by Samuel Wood & Sons, No. 261 Pearl-street; and Samuel S. Wood & Co. No. 212, Market-street, Baltimore. 1820.   AAS

Paper covers. Vignette title-page, and woodcuts illustrative of games throughout text. Includes: archery, playing ball, sailing, skating, fives. The illustration *Playing ball* was used in: *New York primer*. New York, 1823.

The CHILD'S pictorial mentor . . . Worcester: Howland, 1845.

Contains plates showing children skating, fishing and partridge shooting. Second edition.

CHILD's pictorial music book. Hartford, Conn. and Berea, Ohio: E. B. and E. C. Kellog, 1842.

Copy in Connecticut Historical Society. Illustrations of badminton, kite flying, etc.

CHINKS, *pseud. See:* STEDMAN, Charles Ellery.

CHIOSSO, [James]. The gymnastic polymachinon. Instructions for performing a systematic series of exercises on the gymnastic & calisthenic polymachinon, by Captain Chiosso . . . London: Walton & Maberly . . . Paris and New York:—H. Balliére . . . 1855. RT

Frontispiece, illustrations throughout text.

The CHOICE medley; or, "Here a little and there a little." By a Mother. Written for the American Sunday-School Union, and revised by the Committee of publication. Philadelphia: American Sunday-School Union, No. 146 Chestnut Street [1843]. RT

5 plates, including frontispiece. *The game at ball,* pp. [7]-19 is a description of the Indian game.

CHOULES, *Rev.* John Overton. The Cruise of the steam yacht *North Star;* a narrative of the excursion of Mr. Vanderbilt's Party to England, Russia, Denmark, France, Spain, Italy, Malta, Madeira, etc. . . . Boston: Gould and Lincoln. New York: Evans and Dickerson, 1854. RT

Vignette on title-page, 2 ports., 9 plates, 5 illustrations in text. Dark green cover, with two emblems on spine, and cut of yacht on front cover, gilt. Title in red and black.

1854: Boston, Gould and Lincoln . . . RT

Same as above, but with variant binding: Light green binding, with only one of the emblems on the spine. Same cut of yacht on front cover, gilt. Publisher and place in cursive lettering.

CHRISTMAS blossoms, and New Year's wreath for MDCCCLI. By Uncle Thomas. Philadelphia: Published by E. H. Butler & Co. 1851. RT

Extra engraved title-page and 5 engravings. *The sport of fishing,* pp. 74-113.

CILLEY, Hon. Jonathan. The funeral oration delivered at the Capitol in Washington . . . with full account of the late duel, comprising many facts never before published. Embellished with an elegant likeness of Mr. Cilley . . . New York: Wiley & Putnam, 1838.

Paper boards. 44 pp. Jonathan Cilley at the time of the duel was Senator from Maine. Noted in Catalogue no. 2, 1964, Edward C. Fales, Salisbury, N.H.

CINCINNATI Angling Club. Proceedings of the Cincinnati Angling Club. (From the Cincinnati Chronicle, October 23, 1830.) Cincinnati: Printed at the Chronicle Office, 1831.   RT

Title from cover. Harvard has 2 copies. In one there is a mss. list of members of the Club, on p. [2]. Device: 2 fish, crossed, on cover. This Club was organized on 25th August, 1830. See: *The American turf register and sporting magazine.* Baltimore, 1832. Vol. 3, p. 355.

CLARK, F. H. & Co. Clark's illustrated treatise on the rifle, shotgun and pistol . . . Together with F. H. Clark & Co.'s Catalogue of Guns, Watches . . . Memphis, Tenn.: F. H. Clark & Co., 1850.   Y

Paper covers.

CLARK, James. A treatise on the prevention of diseases incidental to horses . . . From the second Edinburgh edition. Corrected and enlarged. Philadelphia: Printed by William Spotswood, 1791.   RT

First published Edinburgh, 1788. Evans: 23262.

[CLARKE, William.] The boy's own book; a complete encyclopedia of all the diversions, athletic, scientific, and recreative, of boyhood and youth. First American edition. Boston: Munroe and Francis, 128 Washington-Street; and Charles S. Francis, New York, 1829.   Y

A collection of boys' games, with many woodcuts throughout text. First published London, 1828. Second London edition, 1828 or 1829 probably has earliest account of the game of rounders. It is included in the 3d. London edition of 1829. The Boston 1829 edition makes the first mention of "rounders" in the United States, with a "diamond" typographically indicated. Clarke's name does not appear on any edition. Small engravings throughout text.

CLARKE, William. *Continued:*

1830: The boy's own book; a complete encyclopedia of all the diversions, athletic, scientific, and recreative, of boyhood and youth. Second American edition. Boston: Munroe and Francis, 128 Washington-Street; and Charles S. Francis, New-York. RT

Small engravings throughout text. Rounders, p.. 20.

1831: The boy's own book . . . Boston: Munroe and Francis. New York: Charles S. Francis. The second American edition.

In: Heyl, Edgar. A contribution to conjuring bibliography . . .

1832: The boy's own book . . . Second American edition. Boston: Munroe and Francis. RT

1834: The boy's own book . . . Second American edition. Boston: Munroe and Francis. LC

1834: The boy's own book . . . Boston: Munroe and Francis. The sixth American edition.

In Heyl, Edgar. A contribution to conjuring bibliography . . .

1834: *See:* Carver, Robin. The book of sports. Boston.

1835: *See:* Boy's and girl's book of sports . . . Providence.

1836: *See:* Boy's and girl's book of sports . . . Providence.

1838: *See:* Boy's book of sports. New Haven.

1838: The boy's own book . . . Sixth American edition. Boston: Munroe and Francis. RT

1839: *See:* Boy's book of sports. New Haven.

1844: The boy's own book; a complete encyclopedia of all the diversions athletic, scientific, and recreative, of boyhood and youth . . . Sixth American edition. Boston: Munroe and Francis; Joseph H. Francis. New-York: Charles S. Francis. RT

Small engravings throughout text.

1847: The book of sports. Philadelphia: Edward W. Miller, No. 11 George St. RT

Lacks frontispiece.

CLARKE, William. *Continued:*

1847: The boy's own book . . . Boston: Munroe and Francis. The sixth American edition.

In Heyl, Edgar. A contribution to conjuring bibliography . . .

1849: The boy's own book; a complete encyclopedia . . . Boston: Munroe and Francis. RT

Text identical with 1844 edition, but with two leaves of advertisements at end. Binding on 1844 edition boards. 1849 edition brown cloth.

1851: Boy's own book, extended, illustrated. Boston: Munroe & Francis. N

1854: Boy's own book, illustrated. Louisville, Morton & Griswold.

1857: Boy's own book, extended . . . New York, C. S. Francis and Co. N

[ca. 1858]: The book of sports. Philadelphia: H. C. Peck & Theo. Bliss. RT

Appears to be from same plates as Philadelphia 1847 edition, except for added text, p. [192]: *Miniature juveniles* . . .

1859: Boy's own book, extended . . . New York and Boston, C. S. Francis and company. RT

Bound with this is: *Paul Preston's book of gymnastics; or, Sports for youth* . . . No imprint, separate pagination. Small cuts throughout text.

CLASSICAL and Scientific Seminary. Prospectus of the Classical and Scientific Academy, at Ballston, N.Y. [By Jonathan R. Paddock]. N.p. [ca. 1825]. RT

Designed "to develop and confirm the physical powers, by a regular and systematic course of gymnastic exercises."

CLATER, Francis. Every man his own farrier: containing the causes, symptoms, and most approved methods of cure, of the diseases of horses. By Francis Clater . . . and his son, John Clater. First American from the Twenty-eighth London edition. With notes and additions, by J. S. Skinner. Philadelphia: Lea and Blanchard, 1845. RT

First published Newark, England, 1783.

CLAY, Henry. *See:* The GREAT duellist.

CLIFTON, William. Our boat sets lightly on the wave. A duet and trio written, composed and arranged, and respectfully dedicated to the New York Boat Clubs, by William Clifton. Boston: Published by Oliver Ditson, 115 Washington St. 1838.   RT

Words and music. Illustration on cover.

CLINTON, De Witt. An introductory discourse, delivered before The Literary and Philosophical Society of New-York, on the fourth of May, 1814, by De Witt Clinton, LL.D. . . . New York: Published by David Longworth, At the Shakespeare-Gallery. N. Van Riper, Print. 1815.   RT

Contains many references to game and game birds in America.

CLIPPER. *See:* NEW YORK Clipper.

[COBBIN, Ingram]. The faithful dog; an interesting story: with instructive remarks for the use of young people. By the author of "Memoirs of my dog," etc. etc. . . . New-York: M. W. Dodd, Brick Church Chapel, opposite the City Hall, 1842.
RT

Paper covers. Cover title: *The faithful dog: by the Rev. Ingram Cobbin, M. A.* [Cut of dog rescuing a boy.] From the London edition. . . . Small cuts on title-page and throughout text.

COBB'S toys. Second series, No. 11. Pretty stories for pretty children. Newark, N.J., Benjamin Olds, 1835.   RT

COBB'S toys. Third series, no. 6. Stories about the salmon, turbit, pike, mackerel, roach, cod, carp, gar-fish, and bream, in words of one, two and three syllables. Newark, N.J.: Benjamin Olds [1835].

Printed wrappers. 16pp. 4½ by 2¾ inches. Copyright and preface dated 1835. Noted in: Midland Notes. Catalogue 96, no. 299. 1966.

COFFIN, John G. Discourses on cold and warm bathing; with remarks on the effects of drinking cold water in warm weather. Boston: Printed by John Eliot, 1818.   RT

Includes outdoor swimming.

1826: Second edition. Boston, Cummings, Hilliard, and Company.   RT

COLE, Lamb. Poor Old Bob. Words by Lamb Cole. Music by Phil Coachee. New York: Published by Horace Waters, 333 Broadway, 1856. RT

Words and music. At head of cover: Old Dog Tray has passed away, and now we'll sing of . . . Cut of horse's head on cover.

COLE, S. W. The American veterinarian, or diseases of domestic animals, showing the causes, symptoms, and remedies, and rules for restoring and preserving health, by good management; with directions for training and breeding . . . Boston: John P. Jewett & Co., No. 23 Cornhill, 1847. RT

At head of title: *A book for every farmer.* Frontispiece and illustrations.

1848: The American veterinarian, or diseases of domestic animals, showing the causes, symptoms, and remedies, and rules for restoring and preserving health, by good management; with directions for training and breeding . . . Twentieth thousand. Rochester, David Hoyt, 6 State Street, 2d Floor. RT

At head of title: *A book for every farmer.* Frontispiece and illustrations. Probably from same plates as 1847 edition.

[COLEMAN, William.] A collection of the facts and documents relative to the death of Major-General Alexander Hamilton; with comments: together with the various orations, sermons, and eulogies, that have been published or written on his life and character. By the Editor of The Evening Post. New-York: Printed by Hopkins and Seymour, for I. Riley and Co. Booksellers, No. 1 City-Hotel, Broadway, 1804.

COLMAN, Benjamin. Death and the grave without any order. A sermon preached July 7, 1728. Being the Lord's Day after a tragical duel, and most lamented death . . . Boston in New-England: Printed for John Phillips & Thomas Hancock, near the Town Dock, 1728. RT

Probably issued in paper wrappers.

COLTON, Walter. Remarks on duelling . . . Published by Jonathan Leavitt, New York: Crocker & Brewster, Boston: 1828. N

Paper covers.

The COLUMBIAN magazine. [New York] January, 1844.   RT

Contains: *The white-footed deer*, by William Cullen Bryant. *Recollections of the Western Wilds*, by G. Wilkins Kendall. Deer hunting.

The COMPLETE art of boxing; teaching the practical and elementary principles, attitudes, and movements of the science in the present day. Also, the art of attack, as practised by the most celebrated pugilists . . . With Broughton's Rules, as was observed at his Amphitheatre in Tottenham-Court Road. Philadelphia: Sold wholesale and retail, No. 118 North Fourth Street. William Sharpless, Printer, 1829.   RT

Paper wrapper continues title: *To which is added, biographical sketches of the most celebrated pugilists.* Frontispiece folding plate. Based on, but considerably re-written and enlarged: *A treatise on boxing, including a complete set of lessons on the art of self defence* . . . London, 1802. The 7 plates in the London edition are condensed on the folding plate in the Philadelphia edition, on which there are 9 small cuts. One is taken from Sir Thomas Parkyns' *Inn Play.*

The COMPLETE farrier, or Gentleman's travelling companion, comprising a general description of the perfections and imperfections of that noble animal the horse . . . Compiled . . . a gentleman of known experience in the United States. Philadelphia: Bradford and Inskeep . . . 1809.   RT

3 folding plates.

1810: Second edition. Philadelphia, Published by Bradford and Inskeep.   JLO

The COMPLETE farrier, or horse doctor . . . *See:* SLOAN, W. B.

COMSTOCK, J[ohn] L[ee]. Outlines of physiology, both comparative and human; in which are described the mechanical, animal, vital, and sensorial organs, and functions; including those of respiration, circulation, digestion, audition and vision, as they exist in the different orders of animals, from the sponge to man. Also, The application of those principles to muscular exercise, and female fashions, and deformities. Illustrated by numerous engravings. Intended for the use of schools and heads of families. Second edition. By J. L. Comstock, M.D. . . . New York: Robinson, Pratt & Co. 63 Wall Street, 1837.   N

Contains: Calisthenics, field sports, riding, archery, etc. Entered according to Act of Congress, in the year 1836.

1839: Second edition. New York: Robinson, Pratt & Co., 63 Wall Street.   RT

A CONCISE system of farriery. Newbern [N.C.]: J. C. Osborn & Co., 1798.   AAS

CONNECTICUT. Statutes. Acts and laws, made and passed by the General Assembly of the State of Connecticut, in America, holden at New-Haven, on the second Thursday of October, Anno Domini 1786. [New-London: Printed by T. Green, 1786.]
                                                            RT

Pages 347–359 of the *Acts and Laws.* Contains: An act in addition to a law of this State, entitled, *"An act against gaming,"* which prohibits playing at billiards and the keeping of billiard tables.

CONN[ECTICUT] River Railroad. Notice! New England Horse Show at Brattleboro! . . . Ladies' Horsemanship at 11 a.m. and the trial Run for the Sweepstakes, to come off on Friday Oct. 20 . . . J. I. Briggs, M. T. October 19, 1854.

Broadside, 16″ x 11″. Cut of locomotive and carriage. Noted in: Old Print Shop Portfolio. New York, vol. 13, no. 9, May 1954.

CONVERSATIONS of a father with his children. Concluded . . . New York: Published by B. Waugh and T. Mason, for the Sunday School Union of the Methodist Episcopal Church . . . J. Collard, printer, 1834.   CU

At head of title: *Offering for October 1834.* Illustrations throughout text. *Tiger hunting,* p. 55 ff.

[COOK, Eliza.] The fisher boy. Music by G. F. H. Jaurence. Boston: Published by Gei. P. Reed & Co., 17 Tremont Row [ca. 1850–52.]   RT

Lithograph of boy with fishing net, signed J. H. Bufford's Lith. Boston. At head of cover: To his friend Horatio Robinson, Jr. Words and music.

COOK, Eliza. The Indian hunter. A song written by Eliza Cook, the music composed & dedicated to Henry John Sharpe, Esq. by his friend Henry Russell. New York: Published by Jas. L. Hewitt & Co., 239 Broadway. [ca. 1840.]   RT

Words and music. Lithograph of Indian hunter on cover.

1844: Indian hunter quick step, arranged from Henry Russell's popular song of the Indian Hunter by Allen Dodworth, and respectfully dedicated to Henry John Sharpe, Esq. by the publishers. New York: Published by Firth, Hall & Pond, 239 Broadway, cor. of Park Place . . . [cop. 1844].   RT

Music only. Lithograph of Indian hunter on cover, by Thayer & Co., Boston.

COOK, T. The wolf is out. *See:* ARNOLD, J. The wolf is out.

COOKE, P[hilip] St. G[eorge]. Scenes and adventures in the Army; or, Romance of military life . . . Philadelphia: Lindsay & Blakiston, 1850.   LC

Covers period 1827–1845 in Western America. Many incidents of hunting buffalo, bear, beaver, elk and other game.

1857: Philadelphia, Lindsay & Blakiston.   N

1859: Philadelphia, Lindsay & Blakiston.   N

COOPER, J. W. A treatise on cocking, giving a history of the various breeds of imported and American game fowls; the manner of feeding and training them for the pit, a scientific mode of gafting for battle . . . Media, Delaware County, Pa.: Cooper & Vernon, 1859.   RT

Colored frontispiece and folding plate of cockpit. The folding plate is so scarce that there has been doubt as to its existence. However, copy owned by Ernest J. Wessen has both frontispiece and folding plate. See Midland Notes, no. 60. Mansfield, Ohio, 1955.

[COOPER, Susan Fenimore.] Rural hours. By a Lady. [Verse.] New York: George P. Putnam, 155 Broadway, London: Putnam's American Agency, 1850.   RT

Contains many references to hunting and fishing.

The CORSAIR. A gazette of literature, art, dramatic criticism, fashion and novelty. Edited by N. P. Willis and T. O. Porter. Vol. 1 no. 1–52. New York, March 16, 1839–March 7, 1840.   RT

Complete in 52 parts. Contains a series of six articles by Frank Forester [Henry William Herbert], *A week in the Woodlands,* which form the first six chapters of *The Warwick Woodlands,* with additions to *Second day* in the book. They were reprinted in *The American turf register and sporting magazine,* May to November, 1839. Also Frank Forester's *The last bear,* which was reprinted in *The American turf register and sporting magazine,* March 1840, and again in *The sporting sketch book,* London, 1843. *See: Van Winkle.*

The COUNCIL of dogs. Illustrated with suitable engravings. Philadelphia: Published by Johnson & Warner . . . 1809.   RT

1821: Philadelphia, Published by Benjamin Warner.   RT

Reissue of 1809 edition, the imprint on title-page identical. The 1821 date and imprint are at the foot of the frontispiece. Original wrappers, with title on front cover, advertisement on the back. First leaf pasted down on front cover. Copies also issued in plain salmon wrappers.

A COURSE of calisthenics for young ladies, in schools and families. With some remarks on physical education. With sixty-two engraved illustrations. Hartford: H. and F. J. Huntington . . . 1831.   RT

Illustrations in text show dainty, doll-like mannequins going through prescribed exercises.

COWPER, [William]. John Gilpin. The words by Cowper. Music by W. A. Nield. Philadelphia: Published by George Willig, 171, Chesnut St. J. F. & C. A. Watson Lithrs. [ca. 1828.]   N

Four riding cuts on cover.

[COX, William]. Crayon sketches. By an amateur. Edited by Theodore S. Fay. In two volumes. Vol. I [–II]. New-York: Conner and Cooke, Franklin Buildings. Press of G. P. Scott & Co. Nassau Street, 1833.

Essay: *Morality, Horse-racing,* Vol. 1, pp. 214–220.

COYNER, David H. The lost trappers; a collection of interesting scenes and events in the Rocky Mountains; together with a short description of California: also, Some account of the fur trade . . . Cincinnati: J. A. & U. P. James . . . 1847.   RT

Dark brown cloth binding, blind tooled. Purports to be based on the lost *Journal* of Ezekiel Williams, and other sources.

1850: Cincinnati: E. D. Truman.   RT

Dark blue cloth binding, blind tooled.

1850: Cincinnati: E. D. Truman.   RT

Green patterned cloth binding, blind tooled.

1858: Cincinnati: Anderson, Gates & Wright.   LC

1859: Cincinnati: Anderson, Gates & Wright.   N

COZZENS, Frederic S[wartwout]. Acadia; or, A month with the Blue Noses . . . New York: Derby & Jackson . . . 1859.
Two lithographic portraits.   RT

COZZENS, Frederic S[wartwout]. The Sparrowgrass papers: or, Living in the country . . . New York: Derby & Jackson, 119 Nassau St. Cincinnati: H. W. Derby, 1856.   N

A novel of country life, with special interest in horsemanship.

1857: New York, Derby & Jackson, 119 Nassau St. Cincinnati: H. W. Derby.   N

CRAIG, Robert H. Rules and regulations for the sword exercise of the cavalry. To which is added, The rules for drill, and the evolutions of the light cavalry. Baltimore: Published by Robert H. Craig. B. Edes, printer, 1812.   RT

Plates 1-26, some folded. Error in numbering: 22 omitted, and 23 *bis*. First published as: Great Britain. Adjutant General's Office. *Rules and regulations for the sword exercise.* London, 1796. Editions of this book also published by Robert Hewes. First Hewes edition was in 1802. Preface signed: Robert H. Craig. Teacher of military tacticks. *Drill and evolutions for light cavalry* not in Hewes, and the Craig plates differ from the Hewes' plates. A folded plate: *Post of Officers,* between pp. 172 and 173.

94

CRAIGE, Thomas. A conversation between a lady and her horse. By Thomas Craige, of the Philadelphia Riding School. Philadelphia: Published by Thomas Craige, and for sale at the N. W. corner of Fifth and Arch streets, 1851.   RT

Frontispiece.

CRIB, Tom. *See:* MOORE, Thomas.

The CRICKET field; or, The history and science of cricket. *See:* PYCRAFT, James.

The CRICKET player's pocket companion. *See:* A MANUAL of cricket and baseball.

The CRICKETER'S hand-book: containing the origin of the game, remarks on recent alterations, directions for bowling, striking, and placing the players; and the laws as altered by the Marylebone Cricket Club. With a view of Lord's Cricket Ground. First American, from a new English edition . . . Boston: Published by Saxton, Pierce & Co. . . . New York: Saxton & Miles, 1844.

Lithographed frontispiece.   RT

CROCKETT, [David]. An account of Col. Crockett's tour to the North and Down East . . . Written by himself. Philadelphia: E. L. Carey and Hart . . . 1835.   RT

Engraved portrait frontispiece.

1837: Tenth edition. Philadelphia, E. L. Carey and A. Hart. N

1845: New York, Published by Nafis & Cornish . . .   RT

1848: New York, W. H. Graham.   N

CROCKETT, [David]. Col. Crockett's exploits and adventures in Texas . . . Written by himself . . . Philadelphia: T. K. & P. G. Collins, 1836.   N

Engraved portrait frontispiece. Mostly fiction. Part based on life of Parson Weems, especially the imaginary fight of *Georgia Scenes.*

1837: Sixth edition. Philadelphia, T. K. & P. G. Collins.   N

1839: Cincinnati, U. P. James.

1845: New-York, Published by Nafis & Cornish . . . Philadelphia, John B. Perry.   RT

1848: New York, W. H. Graham.   LC

CROCKETT, [David]. Crockett's yaller flower almanac for '36 . . . Snagsville, Salt River: Published by Boon Crockett and Squire Downing, Skunk's Misery, Down East . . . New York: Sold by Elton . . . [1836].   AAS

Similar to, but independent of, the regular Crockett series of almanacs.

CROCKETT, David. Davy Crockett's Almanack of wild sports of the West, and life in the backwoods. Calculated for all the States in the Union. 1835. Nashville, Tenn.: Published for the author.

At head of cover: "*Go Ahead!*" Probably the first edition.

1835: Nashville, Tenn., Snag & Sawyer.   RT

1836: Vol. 1, no. 2. Nashville, Tenn., Published for the author.

The 1835 and 1836 editions were published during Crockett's life. They continued to be published by various publishers up to 1855. A complete list will be found in: Constance Rourke's *Davy Crockett.* New York: Harcourt, Brace and Company, [1934]. The 1835 edition has 2 woodcuts taken from Lloyd's *Field sports of the north of Europe,* London, 1830. Page 29 shows a charging bear, with caption: "Desperate attempt to tree a bear," taken from vol. 2, p. 345 of the second edition of Lloyd, where the caption is: "The author in personal conflict with a bear." The caption appears in the edition "Published by the author," but not in the Snag & Sawyer edition. The outside rear cover of both 1835 editions of the *Almanac* show "Col. Crockett's desperate fight with the great bear." This is from Lloyd, vol. 2, p. 382, second edition. These illustrations show a Norwegian elk hound, the first to be pictured in America.

CROCKETT, David. The life and adventures of Colonel David Crockett, of Tennessee . . . Cincinnati: Published for the proprietor, 1833.

CROCKETT, David. Life of Col. David Crockett. Written by himself . . . Philadelphia: Published by G. G. Evans, 1859.   RT

Illustrations.

CROCKETT, David. A narrative of the life of David Crockett

CROCKETT, David. *Continued:*

. . . of the State of Tennessee. Written by himself. Philadelphia: E. L. Carey and A. Hart . . . 1834.   RT

Paper label on spine. Six editions published in 1834.

1835: Twelfth edition. Philadelphia.

1837: New York.

1845: New York.   LC

1848: New York, Wm. H. Graham.

CROCKETT, David. Pictorial life and adventures of Davy Crockett. An autobiography—Written by himself. Embellished with life-like illustrations. Engraved in the finest style of the art, from original designs drawn by Henry L. Stephens . . . Philadelphia: T. B. Peterson & Brothers . . . [1852].   N

Paper covers.

CROCKETT, David. Sketches and eccentricities of Col. David Crockett of West Tennessee . . . New York: J. & J. Harper, 1833.   LC

1833: New edition. New-York, Printed and published by J. & J. Harper . . .   RT

1837: Tenth edition. New York, Published by Harper & Brothers . . .   RT

1847: Tenth edition. New York: Harper & Brothers, Publishers . . .   RT

Text identical with 1837 edition, but imprint varies, as does pages of advertisements at end of volumes.

CROSBY, L. V. H. Kitty Clyde, written and composed by L. V. H. Crosby. [Verse.] Syracuse: Published by T. Hough . . . [cop. 1854].   RT

At head of cover: *To his Friend T. Hough.* Words and music. Lithograph on cover of young girl fishing, by Sarony & Co., New York City.

1854: Boston, G. P. Reed & Co. [cop. 1854].   N

Plate Peale no. 2423.

97

CUMMING, Roualeyn Gordon. *See:* GORDON-CUMMING, Roualeyn.

CUZENT, Paul. Pick-pocket. Quadrille des exercices de Mme. Lejars, pour le piano, composé et dedié à Son Altesse Madame La Princesse Liechtenstein, née Comtesse de Wrbna, Dame du Palais de S. M. l'Imperatrice. Par Paul Cuzent. Philadelphia: Lee & Walker, No. 120 Walnut Str. . . . [ca. 1845]. ᴿᵀ

Music only. Lithograph of woman circus rider on cover.

CYPRESS, J., Jr., *pseud. See:* HAWES, William Post.

D. D. The Echo horn, a favourite hunting air. Composed for the pianoforte by D. D. Philadelphia: Pub. & sold by G. Willig, 171 Chestnut St. & to be had at E. Johns & Co., New Orleans [1832]. ᴿᵀ

Words and music. Deer hunting.

DADD, George H. The advocate of veterinary reform and outlines of anatomy and physiology of the Horse . . . Also, A veterinary dictionary, selected from the Works of R. White . . . Boston: Published by the author, 1850.

Two folding plates, illustrations. On cover: *Dadd's Reformed Veterinary and Dictionary.*

DADD, George H. The Anatomy and physiology of the horse . . . To which is added, glossary of veterinary technicalities . . . Boston: J. P. Jewett & Co., 1857. ɴ

Twenty plates, each followed by leaf of descriptive letterpress.

DADD, G[eorge] H. The horseowner's guide: being a synopsis of the causes, treatment, and cure of the most common diseases of live stock, selected from "Dadd's Chart of veterinary practice," with additions and improvements . . . Boston: Press of Geo. C. Rand & Avery, 1855. ᴬᴬˢ

1856: Boston, Press of Bazin and Chandler. ᴿᵀ

DADD, George H. The modern horse doctor: containing practical observations on the causes, nature, and treatment of disease and lameness in horses. Embracing the most recent and approved methods . . . With illustrations . . . Third thousand. Boston: Published by John P. Jewett and Company. Cleveland, Ohio:

DADD, George H. *Continued:*

Jewett, Proctor, and Worthington, 1854. AAS

Frontispiece, woodcuts in text.

1856: Eleventh thousand. Boston, John P. Jewett and Company. RT

[ca. 1857:] Twelfth thousand. New York, A. O. Moore . . . RT

DADD, George H., editor. *See also:* The AMERICAN veterinary journal.

DAGLEY, R[ichard]. Death's doings: consisting of numerous original compositions in verse and prose . . . Principally intended as illustrations of thirty copperplates, designed and etched by R. Dagley . . . From the second London edition, with considerable additions. Boston: Charles Ewer . . . 1828. 2 vols. RT

Contains angling, cricket, boxing, gambling, and other sporting subjects. First published London, 1826, with 24 plates. Second London edition published 1827.

DARDIN, Amey. *See:* UNITED STATES. House of Representatives. Report of the Committee of Claims.

DARROW, Pierce. The artillerist; comprising the drill without arms, and exercises and movements of the light and horse artillery, together with a sword exercise for the light artillery . . . Second edition, improved and enlarged. Hartford: Oliver D. Cooke, 1821. RT

The *Sword exercise* is substantially taken from Taylor's *Art of Defence on Foot.* 7 plates.

DARROW, Pierce. Cavalry tactics; comprising the modern mode of discipline and sword exercise, for the cavalry generally. Adapted to the rules and regulations of infantry, as prepared by Gen. Scott, and established by a resolve of Congress. To which is added. The review exercise. In five parts. Illustrated by eight copper-plate engravings. By Pierce Darrow, Lt. Colonel, Military Instructor . . . Hartford: Oliver D. Cooke, 1822. RT

8 plates of military diagrams.

DAVIE, Allen J., editor. *See:* AMERICAN turf register and sporting magazine.

DAVIE, William Richard. Instructions to be observed for the formations and movements of the cavalry. Published agreeably to a resolution of the Legislature of North-Carolina. By William Richardson Davie, Esquire. Governor, Captain-General and Commander in Chief of the Militia of the State of North-Carolina. Halifax [N.C.]: Printed by Abraham Dodge, 1799.

RT

Three folding plates. Sabin: 18748.

DAVIS, B. F. *See:* NASH, Ephraim.

[DAVIS, J.] Essays on various subjects. Written for the amusement of everybody, by one who is considered nobody . . . New York: Printed by J. W. Bell, 17 Ann-Street, near Broadway, 1835.

Y

Contains: *Hints to Young Sportsmen,* and other sporting subjects. Van Winkle copy, sold at Parke-Bernet Galleries, May 16, 1949 is inscribed ". . . with the complts. of J. Davis Author." *See: GEE.*

1835: New York.

Second issue, with the letter s in the word *Sportsman* in the second line of text, p. [1] dropped. *See: MACLAY.*

1835: New York.

Another variation, Third issue. The letter s, p. [1] second line from different font.

RT

[DAVY, Sir Humphrey.] Salmonia; or Days of fly fishing. In a series of conversations. With some account of the habits of fishes belonging to the Genus Salmo. By An Angler . . . First American, from the second London edition. Philadelphia: Carey and Lea . . . 1832.

RT

First published London, 1828. Three engraved plates of flies. Does not contain the 6 additional engraved plates of the 2d. London edition.

DAVY, [John]. The morn unbars the gates of light. A favorite hunting song. Composed by Davy. Sung by Mrs. Burke. Philadelphia: Published and sold at G. Willig's Music Store. [ca. 1810.]

RT

Words and music. Deer hunting.

1814: The morn unbars the gates of light. A favorite hunting song; sung with great applause by Mrs. Burke. Philadelphia: Published by A. Bacon & Co., and Vallotte & Co. New York [ca. 1814–1819.]

RT

DAVY, [John]. *Continued:*

RT copy lacks covers. Title from head of music, which omits name of composer.

1815: The morn unbars the gates of light. A favorite hunting song; sung with great applause by Mrs. Burke. Composed by John Davy. Philadelphia: Published by G. E. Blake. No. 13 South 5th Street [ca. 1815].   RT

RT copy lacks covers.

1816: The Morn unbars the gates of light. A favorite hunting song. Composed by Davy. Sung by Mrs. Burke. New York: Engraved, printed and sold by E. Riley, 23 Chatham Street [ca. 1816].   N

Advertised in *New York Post* April 1st, 1816.

DECATUR, Stephen. Correspondence, between the late Commodore Stephen Decatur and Commodore James Barron, which led to the unfortunate meeting of the twenty-second of March. Washington: Printed by Gales & Seaton, 1820.   RT

An eight page pamphlet.

DEIGENDESCH, Johann. Nachrichters: oder Nützliches und aufrichtiges Ross-Artzney-Büchlein. Germantown: Gedruckt bey Christoph Saur, 1770.   AAS

Evans: 11627. First published in Germany, Freiburg, 1716.

1771: Second edition. Germantown: Zum zweyten mal gedruckt bey Christoph Saur, 1771.   RT

Evans: 12026.

1791: Third edition. Germantown: Zum dritten mal gedruckt und zu finden bey Peter Liebert.   RT

Not in Evans.

1822: Nachrichters nutliches und aufrichtiges Pferd-Arzneybuch. Harrisburg.

Copy in Pennsylvania State University Library. The 1822 edition apparently was copied from a different German original than the earlier American editions. *See:* COWEN, David L. Deigendesch's *Nachrichters Rossartzneybüchlein.* In: American Veterinary Medical Association Journal 139, no. 3, August 1, 1961:359-66.

DENNEY, J. W. A new and certain way of taming horses. *See:*

RAREY, John Solomon. The modern art of taming wild horses.

DENNIE, Joseph. *See:* PORT folio.

D'EON, Frederick. System of fencing as arranged and systematically taught by Frederick D'Eon, Fencing Master. In thirty-one sections, for the first quarter's tuition. Boston: Published for the Author, 1823. HCL

Paper covers.

DE PINNA, Josh[ua]. Huntsman rouse thee, hark the horn. A hunting cavatina, as sung by Mr. Salmon. Composed by Josh. De Pinna. New York: Thomas Birch, Music Engraver, Printer and Publisher, Wholesale and Retail, 95 Canal St. RT

Words and music. Lithograph of fox hunt on cover by Endicott & Swift.

DEPPING, J. B. Evening entertainments; or, Delineations of the manners and customs of various nations, interspersed with geographical notices, historical and biographical anecdotes, and descriptions in natural history. Designed for the instruction and amusement of youth. Philadelphia: Published and sold by Towar & Hogan . . . 1827. N

Frontispiece. Includes skating, horse-racing and hunting stories.

1827: Philadelphia. RT

Fourth Edition. A reprint of first edition, with the addition of: [*Fourth edition*] in imprint on title-page.

DEVEREAUX, L. The Bohemian hunter's return. Written and arranged by L. Devereaux. Philadelphia: A. Fiot . . . no. 196 Chestnut St. [ca. 1840].

Words and music. Lithograph on cover of hunters returning, by G. Lehman. Lehman and Duval, Lithrs. First line: *When the sunbeam gilds the fountain.*

[ca. 1850:] The Bohemien [sic] hunter's return. Written and arranged by L. Devereaux. Philadelphia: Fiot, Meignen & Co. . . . 217 Chestnut Street. RT

Lithograph on cover by G. Lehman, Lehman & Duval, Lithrs.

DEVEREAUX, L. The Maltese boatman's song. For one, two or

three voices, by L. Devereaux. Boston: Published by C. Bradlee Washington Street [ca. 1835].   RT

Words and music. A fishing song.

DEVEREAUX, L. The mountaineer's return. The evening song of the Alpine peasants. Composed & arranged by L. Devereaux . . . New York: Published by James L. Hewitt & Co., 137 Broadway [ca. 1830–1835].   RT

Lithograph on cover of hunter with chamois over shoulder, returning home, by Pendleton. Words and music.

DEVEREAUX, L. The Swiss hunters welcome home. Arranged by L. Devereaux. Boston: Published by James L. Hewitt & Co. . . . [1829].

Words and music. Hunting scene, lithograph signed G. L. B., 1829. Senefelder Lith. Co. First line: When the hunter o'er the mountain. Chamois hunting.

1829: The Swiss hunters welcome home. Arranged by L. Devereaux. New York: Published by Geib & Walter, no. 23 Maiden Lane [ca. 1829–1832].   RT

Words and music. Lithograph of hunter returning home by P. Desobry's Lithy. on cover.

DIELITZ, Theo[dore]. The hunters of the world: or, Wild sports and adventures in encounters with wild animals in every part of the world . . . Translated from the German, by a Lady. With illustrations on stone. Philadelphia: Willis P. Hazard . . . 1854.   Y

1856: Philadelphia, Willis P. Hazard.   BM

1857: Philadelphia, Willis P. Hazard.   Y

DIELITZ, Theodore. Travellers' adventures in all countries. Abridged from the best writers for young persons. Philadelphia: Willis P. Hazard . . . 1854.   RT

Colored plates, and colored vignette on title-page.

"DINKS", *pseud. See:* PEEL, Jonathan.

DIXON, Edmund Saul. A treatise on the history and management of ornamental and domestic poultry . . . With large additions by J. J. Kerr, M.D. Illustrated with sixty-five original portraits engraved expressly for this work. Second edition. Philadelphia: E. H. Butler & Co., 1851.   LC

Copyrighted 1851. First published separately London, 1848, a reprint, with additions, from *Gardener's Chronicle and Agricultural Gazette.* Chapter XIII: *The Game Fowl. The Mexican Hen-cock Game Fowl.*

1855: Fourth edition, revised. Philadelphia, Published by E. H. Butler & Co.   RT

1859: Fourth edition, revised. New York, A. O. Moore & Co. N

DODWORTH, Allen. Mahopac Lake waltz. Club boat Gazelle. Composed and respectfully dedicated to The Amateur Cornet Club, by Allen Dodworth. New York: Published by Firth Hall & Pond, no. 239 Broadway, and Firth & Hall, no. 1 Franklin Square. 1846.   RT

Lithograph on cover of six-oared boat, with coxswain, and view of lake. C. Parsons del. G. & W. Endicott, Lith. Music only.

The DOG as an example of fidelity. New York, 1848.   W & M

First published London. Illustrated.

1850: The DOG, as an example of fidelity. . . . From the London edition. New York: General Protestant Episcopal S. S. Union. Depository 20 John Street.   RT

Four plates.

The DOMESTIC animal's friend; or, The complete Virginia and Maryland farrier, being a copious selection from the best treatises on farriery now extant in the United States . . . Winchester, Va.; Printed and published by J. Foster, 1818.   RT

Illustrated with cuts.

[DOWLING, Frank Lewis.] Fights for the championship of England; or, Accounts of all the prize battles for the championship, from the days of Figg and Broughton to the present time; including also the recent contests between Tom Sayers, Benjamin and Brettle. To which is added the New rules of the ring . . . Compiled from "Bell's Life in London," "Boxiana," and

DOWLING, Frank Lewis. *Continued:*

other original sources, by the editor of Bell's Life in London. New York: Robert M. De Witt, Publisher . . . [1859].   RT

Paper covers, with woodcut of Tom Sayers. First published London, 1855.

DRAYSON, Alfred W[ilks]. Sporting scenes amongst the kaffirs of South Africa. Illustrated by Harrison Weir, from designs by the author. London: G. Routledge & Co. New York . . . 1858.   N

Colored plates.

DRAYTON, Frank. My old thatched cot. By Frank Drayton. Philadelphia: Lee & Walker, 722 Chestnut St. [cop. 1858].

Words and music. Lithograph on cover, signed O.K., of hunter returning home, with gun and birds. At head of title: *To Miss Mary Stretch.*

DROWN, William. Compendium of agriculture, or The farmer's guide, in the most essential parts of husbandry and gardening; compiled from the best American and European publications, and the unwritten opinions of experienced cultivators . . . By William Drown, with the aid and inspection of Solomon Drown, M.D. Providence: Printed by Field & Maxcy, 1824.   RT

Section on horses, pp. 158-159.

DUELLING incompatible with true honor. *See:* JEWETT, Stephen.

DUFFERIN [and Ava, Frederick Temple Hamilton—Temple—Blackwood,] Lord. A yacht voyage. Letters from high latitudes; some account of a voyage in the schooner yacht "Foam," 85 O.M. to Iceland, Jan Mayen, and Spitzbergen, in 1856. By Lord Dufferin. Boston: Ticknor and Fields, 1859.

Vignette on title-page.

[DUNCAN, James.]Political running, or An account of a celebrated race over the Pennsylvania course, in the year 1823, for the Governor's Purse. Dedicated, without permission, to all true admirers of the turf, political and sporting, by their humble servant, Jehu, the younger. "Castigat ridendo mores." [Philadelphia:] Printed and published for the use of the buyer, 1823. RT

[DUNCAN, James.] *Continued:*

Vignette of horse race on title page. No cover on RT copy. A political pamphlet relating to the contest for the Governorship of Pennsylvania, 1823. Written by the Auditor General, i.e. James Duncan. *See:* PURDY, Jr.

DUNLAP, William. *See:* SOUTHEY, Robert.

DURIVAGE, Francis A[lexander]. The three brides, Love in a cottage, and other tales. Boston: Sanborn, Carter & Bazin [1856].

Contains story: *He wasn't a horse jockey.*

DWIGHT, Timothy. The folly, guilt, and mischiefs Of duelling: a sermon preached in the College Chapel at New Haven, on the Sabbath preceding the Annual Commencement, September 1804. By Timothy Dwight, D.D. President of Yale-College. Hartford: Printed by Hudson and Goodwin, 1805.   RT

The sermon was inspired by the duel between Dwight's cousin, Aaron Burr and Alexander Hamilton.

1805: A sermon on duelling, preached in the Chapel of Yale College, New Haven, September 9th, 1804, and in the Old Presbyterian Church, New York, January 21st, 1805 . . . New York: Printed by Collins, Perkins and Co. No. 189 Pearl-Street.
                                                                RT

EAGLE Ball Club. Revised constitution, by-laws and rules of the Eagle Ball Club, adopted in 1857. Organized in 1840. New York, 1858.

Frontispiece: *Plan of the Eagle Ball Club bases.*

EASTMAN, Mary H[enderson]. Chicóra and other regions of the conquerors and the conquered. By Mrs. Mary H. Eastman. Philadelphia: Lippincott, Grambo, and Co., 1854.   RT

21 engraved plates, numbered I-XXI in *List of Illustrations,* but variously numbered on plates. A collection of engravings from drawings by Capt. Seth Eastman, accompanied by descriptive text illustrative of the history and customs of various tribes of North American Indians.

ECKLEY, David. *See:* SMITH, Jerome Van Crowinshield.

EDGAR, Patrick Nisbett. The American race-turf register, sportsman's herald and general stud book. Containing the pedigrees of the most celebrated horses, mares and geldings, that have distinguished themselves as racers on the American turf . . . By Patrick Nisbett Edgar. In two volumes. Vol. I. New York: Press of Henry Mason . . . 1833.   N

Only first volume issued.

[EGAN, Pierce.] The American fistiana: containing a history of prize fighting in the United States, with all the principle battles for the last forty years, and a full and precise account of all the particulars of the great $10,000 match between Sullivan and Hyer, with their method of training for the fight, as described by Patrick Timony, Esq. [*pseud.*] New York: H. Johnson, 108 Nassau Street [cop. 1849].   RT

Yellow wrappers. Wording, but not lettering same as on title-page except for added border, date on cover, and at head of cover: *Price Twelve and a Half Cents.* Cut of Tom Hyer on cover, cut of unnamed boxer on title-page.

EGAN, Pierce. Life in London: or, The day and night scenes of Jerry Hawthorn, Esq. and Corinthian Tom, accompanied by Bob Logic, the Oxonian, in their rambles and sprees through the Metropolis. In two volumes. For sale by W. M'Kean, New Orleans; James Rice, Jr. . . . Louisville . . . 1837.   RT

Not illustrated. First published, with illustrations by Cruikshank, London, 1821.

EGAN, Pierce. Sporting anecdotes, original and selected . . . the whole forming a complete delineation of the sporting world. Philadelphia: H. C. Carey and I. Lea . . . 1822.   N

Illustrated with English plates. First published London, 1820.

1823: New York, Johnstone & Van Norden . . . 2 vols.   Y

Frontispiece in each volume an American wood engraving. Boards, with paper labels. RT copy: 2 vols. in 1.

EGGHARD, Jules. Les chasseurs. The hunters. Ancien choeur de chasse. Par Jules Egghard. Op. 194. Philadelphia: Louis Meyer, 1413 Chestnut St. [1854].   RT

Music only. Lithograph of deer hunting scene in forest, by Holmes. Thos. Bovell Lith.

The ELEMENTS of gymnastics; containing The origin of gymnastics . . . with a variety of other useful and entertaining matter on the subject of gymnastics. New-York: Published by William Fuller, 1830. RT

Folded frontispiece. First published in London. William Fuller ran a gymnasium on lower Broadway, New York City.

ELLIOTT, William. Carolina sports by land and water; including incidents of devil-fishing &c., Charleston: Burges and James . . . 1846. N

Paper covers. Also in cloth.

1850: New York, Trehern & Williamson. N

1859: . . . Wild-cat, deer and bear hunting, with six illustrations. New York: Derby & Jackson. RT

ELWORTH, Thomas. Sketches of incidents and adventures in the life of Thomas Elworth, the American pedestrian. Written by himself . . . Boston: Printed for the author, 1844. RT

EMPEROR. The thorough bred bay horse, *Emperor*, will cover this season, at the stable of the subscriber in the Town of , at dollars the season . . . [Hartford, Conn.? ca. 1810.] RT

Horse breeding broadside, cut of horse at head, 10½″ by 8¾″.

ENGELBRECHT, J. C. "All aboard." A brilliant polka composed by J. C. Engelbrecht. Boston: Published by Oliver Ditson & Co., 277 Washington St. . . . [cop. 1855]. RT

At head of cover: *To Miss E. J. Caperton.* Music only. Lithograph on cover of sled drawn by two horses, by J. H. Bufford's Lith. Boston.

ENGLISH, Thomas Dunn. Schuylkill boat song. Poetry by Thomas Dunn English, M.D. Music composed and dedicated to the Atalanta Barge Club by F. Blanchor. Philadelphia: Osbourn's Music Saloon, 30 South Fourth Street [ca. 1835–1842].

Words and music. Lithograph on cover showing two eight-oared boats racing, signed Sinclair Lithr., Phila.

EPICURE. Salad for the solitary. *See:* SAUNDERS, Frederick.

ERRA PATER, [*pseud.*] The book of knowledge: treating of the wisdom of the ancients. In four parts . . . IV. The farmer's calendar . . . 3. The complete and experienced farrier and cowleech &c. . . . Written by Erra Pater, a Jew Doctor in astronomy and physic . . . Made English by W. Lilly . . . Boston: Sold by John W. Folsom . . . [1787].   N

Frontispiece. Not in Evans.

[1790:] Boston, Sold by J. White and C. Cambridge.   AAS

Evans: 22489.

1793: Philadelphia; Printed in the year 1793.   RT

1793: Exeter, Henry Raulett.

Not in Evans.

1794: Albany, For sale by T. Spencer, and A. Ellison.

Evans: 26948.

1794: Canaan [New York], Printed by Elihu Phinney.   BM

Evans: 26949.

1795: Haverhill, Printed by Peter Edes.   AAS

Evans: 28633, 22488.

1795: Portsmouth, N. H., Printed and sold by Charles Peirce.
                                                                                      N

Evans: 28364.

1799: Suffield, Printed by Edward Gray.   N

Evans: 35451.

ERRA PATER, [*pseud.*] The fortune teller, and experienced farrier. In two parts. By Ezra [*sic.*] Pater, a Jew Doctor in astronomy and physic . . . Exeter: Printed [by William Stearns and Samuel Winslow] . . . 1794.   AAS

Evans: 26950.

ESSAYS on various subjects . . . *See:* DAVIS, J.

ESTELLE. Estelle's stories about dogs. For good boys and girls. With six plates with illuminated borders. Boston: Phillips, Sampson, and Company, Publishers [1854]. RT

The six plates include an extra title-page.

EVERY boy's book: a complete encyclopaedia of sports and amusements . . . London, New York: G. Routledge & Co., 1858. Y

EVERY man his own farrier: containing the mode of treatment and cure of the various diseases incident to that noble animal the horse. By an old farrier. Re-printed from an English edition. Ann Arbor: Published by Edw. & Wm. Wallington. Davis & Cole, printers, 1857.

Engraved frontispiece: *The name & situation of the external parts of a horse.* First published Halifax, England, 1852. Should not be confused with William Burdon nor Francis Clater.

The FAMILY magazine; or, Monthly abstract of general knowledge. Illustrated with several hundred engravings. Vol. 1. 1836. Cincinnati: Published by Eli Taylor, 1836. RT

Contains several articles on natural history, including sporting birds and animals. *The American rail; Black-tailed deer of North America* (cut); Large cut of Col. Daniel Boon[e], of Kentucky, in the costume of a Western hunter, and *Adventures of Captain Daniel Boon[e], written by himself;* Arabian horses (cut); Racehorse (cut); *Life in the East* [Tiger-hunting] (Cut), and others.

The FAMILY receipt book, containing eight hundred valuable receipts in various branches of domestic economy; selected from the works of the most approved writers, ancient and modern; and from the attested communications of scientific friends. Second American edition. Pittsburgh: Published by Randolph Barnes, Third Street, 1819.

Chapter II: *Angling-fishing.* Chapter XXI: *Farriery.* Chapter XXIII: *Fire-arms.*

FANCHER, O. H. P. The Arabian farrier and horse-breaker. Lowell, Mass., 1852.

Copy formerly in LC.

1855: Second edition. Norfolk, Va., J. B. Taylor, printer.

Green paper covers. At head of title-page: *Price Twenty-Five Dollars.* Double-line border. Copyright notice on verso of title-page, 1852, filed in the clerk's office of the District Court of Massachusetts.

FANCHER, O. H. P. *Continued:*

1858: Sixth edition. [Leesburg?] Va., J. B. Taylor.   RT

At head of paper cover: *Price Fifty Dollars.*

[1858:] Sixth edition . . . By George Harris, n.p.   N

At head of paper cover: *Price $50.* No copyright note.

[1859:] Seventh edition . . . By George Harris, n.p.   RT

At head of paper cover: *Price Fifty Dollars.* No copyright note.

1860: Seventh edition. [Leesburg? Va.] J. B. Taylor.

Copy in Virginia State Library.

1860: The Persian and Arabian farrier, and horse breaker. By J. S. Watkins. Third edition, n.p.   RT

At head of paper cover, and at head of title: *Price, Fifty dollars.*

The FARMERS' Association of Christiana Hundred, for the Recovery of Stolen Horses, and Detection of Thieves. Wilmington [Del.]: Printed by Geo. W. Vernon, 1859.   RT

Paper covers. Names of members on p. [12].

The FARMER'S and farrier's almanac for 1846 . . . Philadelphia: John B. Perry . . . New York: Nafis & Cornish, 1846.

Published from 1846 to 1849. Illustrated with woodcuts.   AAS

The FARMER'S guide and western agriculturist . . .
          See: The WESTERN agriculturist . . .

The FARMER'S and horsemen's true guide, pointing out the perfections and imperfections of the horse, with cures for his diseases, and for neat cattle and sheep. Together with useful recipes in gardening, horticulture and domestic economy. From practical experience. Well tried and approved by farmers, farriers, &c. Owego [N.Y.]: Published and sold by A. P. Searing. Printed at the Gazette office, 1834.   RT

Small cuts of teeth on p. 6.

1841: [Title as above.] Rochester: Published by G. W. Fisher & Co., for Johm [*sic*] M. Clark, 1841.   RT

Small cuts of teeth on p. 7. Cut of horse on verso title-page.

111

The FARMER'S, mechanic's, manufacturer's and sportsman's magazine. By George Houston, member of the New York and Paris Linnæn Societies: editor and proprietor. New York: Printed by Vanderpool & Cole . . . 1827. Y

Twelve monthly numbers, beginning March, 1826. First two numbers have title: *The Farmer's Mechanic's and Manufacturer's Magazine.* Three full page engravings, and some woodcuts. *See: Gee.*

The FARMER'S own book. *See:* KOOGLE, J. D.

The FARMER'S practical horse farriery. *See:* NASH, Ephraim.

The FARMER'S receipt book; and pocket farrier. Being a choice selection of the most approved and valuable receipts, designed for the benefit of farmers, and heads of families generally. Stereotyped at the Concord Foundry. Boston: Published by Charles Gaylord, 1831. RT

Frontispiece, repeated on the back cover. Front cover same as title-page. Copyright granted to David D. Fisk and Daniel Chase.

1836: The pocket farrier, or Farmers' receipt book; a selection of receipts for the cure of disease in horses, cattle, sheep and swine. With directions to farmers for choosing good stock . . . Boston, Charles Gaylord. RT

Frontispiece differs from 1831 edition, and is: *Pl. 9. The Age of a Horse by its Teeth.* Drawn and engraved by E. Martin from the Bones. Woodcut vignette on title-page. Front cover same as title-page. Woodcut on back cover of cattle. Copyright granted to David D. Fisk and Daniel Chase.

1840: The pocket farrier . . .

Title, frontispiece, copyright, and front cover as in 1836 edition. Back cover has *The Age of a Horse by his teeth.* RT

FARREN, P. The horn of chace. Words by P. Farren, Esq. Dublin, the music by Chas. Gilfert, Esq. Sung by Mr. Keene, in the romantic opera of Der Freischutz at the Park Theatre. New York: Engraved, printed & sold by E. Riley, 29 Chatham Street, 1823. RT

Words and music. First line: *To join the chase, at break of day.*

The FARRIER'S magazine, or The archives of veterinary science; containing the anatomy, physiology and pathology of the horse . . . By James Carver. Philadelphia: Printed for the author, 1818.   LC

Published quarterly. 2 issues only. Plates.
[pt. 1.] "containing the anatomy, physiology and pathology of the horse . . ."
[pt. 2.] "containing—the pathology of the horse's eye . . ."

The FATHER'S gift; containing an interesting description of one hundred and eight objects. With plates. Philadelphia: Published by Jacob Johnson . . . J. Rakestraw, printer, 1804.   N

Woodcuts: *Battledoor, A Shuttlecock, A Postillion, A Fisherman,* etc. Companion to: *The Mother's Gift.*

FAULKS. Mr. Faulks, the noted performer in horsemanship . . . [Advertising his performances. Dated,] Philadelphia, Sept. 23, 1771.

Broadside. Evans: 12041.

FEMALE Robinson Crusoe, a tale of the American wilderness. [Verse.] New-York: Printed by Jared W. Bell, No. 17 Ann-Street, 1837.   N

Game of ball, closely resembling baseball, pp. 176–178.

FIEHRER, Joseph. A short general adviser in the most common diseases of horses . . . Harrisburg [Pa.], 1840.   H

FIELD, Joseph M. *See:* THORPE, Thomas Bangs. Colonel Thorpe's scenes in Arkansaw.

FIELDS, J. T. O swift we go, a sleighing song. The poetry by J. T. Fields, Esq. The music composed and dedicated to S. Parkman Tuckerman, Esq. by Joseph Philip Knight. Boston: Published by W. H. Oakes, 8½ Tremont Row, 1840.   RT

Words and music. Lithograph on cover of sleigh drawn by four horses, B. Champney, del.

FILSON, John. The discovery, settlement, and present state of Kentucke: and an essay towards the topography, and natural history of that important country: to which is added, an Appendix, containing, I. The adventures of Col. Daniel Boon[e], one of the

FILSON, John. *Continued:*

first settlers . . . Wilmington: Printed by James Adams, **1784**.
LC

Folded map. The first appearance of the story of Daniel Boone, as dictated
to Filson. Evans: 18467.

1786: The adventures of Colonel Daniel Boon[e], one of the
first settlers of Kentucke: containing the wars with the Indians
of the Ohio, from **1769** to **1783**, and the first establishment and
progress of the settlement on that river. Written by the Colonel himself. To which are added, A narrative of the captivity,
and extraordinary escape of Mrs. Francis Scott . . . Norwich:
Printed by John Trumbull.

Title from: *One hundred and Fifty Years of Printing in English America*,
The Free Library of Philadelphia, 1940. Only known copy owned by the
late Dr. A. S. W. Rosenbach. Not in Evans.

1787: *In:* The American museum, or Repository . . . Vol. **2.**
Philadelphia, Printed by Mathew Carey.
LC

Evans: 20193.

1793: *In:* Imlay, Gilbert. A topographical description of the
Western Territory of North American. New York, Printed by
Samuel Campbell.
N

Evans: 25648.

[1794]: Adventures of Col. Daniel Boon[e], one of the original
settlers at Kentucky . . . *In:* Beers's almanac and ephemeris of
the motion of the sun and moon . . . for . . . **1795.** Hartford:
Printed by Hudson and Goodwin.
N

1821: *In:* Metcalf[e], Samuel L[ytler]. A collection of some of
the most interesting narratives of Indian warfare in the West
. . . Lexington, Ky., Printed by William G. Hunt.
N

1823: Life and adventures of Colonel Daniel Boon[e], the first
white settler in the State of Kentucky . . . Written by himself
. . . Annexed, is an eulogy on Col. Boon[e], and choice of life,
by Lord Byron. Brooklyn, for C. Wilder.
N

Portrait frontispiece.

1824: Life and adventures . . . Brooklyn, Printed for C. Wilder.

FILSON, John. *Continued:*

Portrait frontispiece. **N**

1824: Life and adventures . . . Providence, Printed by H. Trumbull. **Y**

The 1823 and two 1824 editions are printed from the same type. *See:* Jillson, Willard Rouse. *The Boone narrative.* Louisville, Ky., The Standard Printing Co., 1932.

FISHER, James. A spring day; or, Contemplations on several occurrences which naturally strike the eye in that delightful season . . . New York: George Lindsay, 1813.

Contemplation X. *On Fishing.*

FITCH, Elijah. The beauties of religion. A poem. Addressed to youth. In five books . . . Providence: Printed by John Carter, **1789.** **RT**

Protests the killing of fish and game for sport.

FITZSIMONS, E. F. The hunter's horn, a new sporting cavatina. Sung by Mr. Philipps with the most unbounded applause at the vocal concerts, Dublin at the Theatre Royal Crow St. and at the New York Theatre. Composed by T. Philipps. New York: Published for the composer by Geib & Co., 23 Maiden Lane [ca. 1820]. Copyright secured. **RT**

At head of music: The words by E. F. Fitzsimons, Esqr.

1820: The hunter's horn. A new sporting cavatina. Composed and written by Mr. Philipps. New York: Engraved, printed & sold, by E. Riley, 29 Chatham Street [ca. 1820]. **RT**

1820: The hunter's horn. A new sporting cavatina. Composed and sung by Mr. Philipps. Philadelphia: Published and sold at G. Willig's Musical Magazine [ca. 1820]. **RT**

FLAGG, John W. [Copy book.] Made and sold by John W. Flagg. Bennington, N.H. [1846.] **RT**

Cut of bear hunt on cover.

FLAGG, Wilson. Studies in the field and forest . . . Boston: Little, Brown and Company, 1857. **N**

Chapter XXVI: *Angling.*

FLEMING, Joseph H. Six essays on taxing dogs, published originally in the Freeman's journal, in 1805, '6 and '7. Dedicated to the Legislature of Pennsylvania. With certificates of recommendation from the Hon. John D. Coxe . . . Philadelphia: Printed for the author, 1807. Stiles, Printer.   RT

An anti-dog tract.

FLINT, Micah P. The hunter and other poems. Boston: Cummings, Hilliard, and Company, 1826.   RT

Paper covers and contemporary boards.

FLINT, Timothy. Biographical memoir of Daniel Boone, the first settler of Kentucky . . . Cincinnati: N. & G. Guilford & Co., 1833.   LC

Woodcut portrait frontispiece and full page woodcuts in text. Also published under the title: *The First White Man of the West.*

1834: Cincinnati, George Conclin.

1836: Cincinnati, George Conclin.

1837: Cincinnati, George Conclin.   RT

1839: Cincinnati, George Conclin.   AAS

1840: Cincinnati, George Conclin.   N

1841: Cincinnati, George Conclin.

1842: Cincinnati, George Conclin.

1845: Cincinnati, George Conclin.   N

1846: Cincinnati, George Conclin.

1847: Cincinnati, George Conclin.   Y

1849: Cincinnati, George Conclin.

1850: Cincinnati, George Conclin.   N

1851: Cincinnati. H. S. & J. Applegate & Co.

1854: Cincinnati, Applegate & Co.   RT

1855: Cincinnati, Applegate & Co.

1856: Cincinnati, Philadelphia, H. M. Rulison.   LC

1858: Cincinnati, Anderson, Gates & Wright.

FLUVIATULIS Piscator, *pseud. See:* SECCOMBE, Joseph.

The FOOT ball controversy between the classes of '55 and '56.
See: YALE University.

FORESTER, Frank, *pseud. See:* HERBERT, Henry William.

FOSTER, Stephen Collins. Old dog Tray . . . Written and
composed by Stephen C. Foster. New York: Firth, Pond & Co.
cop: 1853. W & M

Music. Publication plate no. 2384. At head of title: *Foster's Melodies.*
No. 21.

FRANKLIN, Augustus. The American farrier: adapted for the
convenience of the farmer . . . gentleman . . . and smith; being
a sure guide to prevent and cure all maladies and distempers that
are incident to horses . . . Strasburg: Printed & sold by Brown
& Bowman . . . 1803. RT

FRANKLIN, Benjamin. The art of swimming. *See:*

The ART of swimming . . . Baltimore [1821]. RT

BOSWORTH, Newton. The accidents of human life . . .
New York, 1814. RT

FROST, J. The art of swimming . . . New York, 1818.
RT

FREITAG, Eberhard. Der Deutsche Pferd-Arzt. Herausgegeben
von Doctor Eberhard Freitag in Bethlehem. Copy right secured
according to law. Easton, Pennsylvanien, Gedruckt bey Christ.
Jac. Hütter, 1809. RT

FRIENDS, [Society Of]. The book of discipline, agreed on by
the Yearly Meeting of Friends for New-England. Containing
extracts of Minutes, Conclusions and Advices, of that Meeting;
and of the Yearly-Meetings of London, Pennsylvania and New-
Jersey, and New-York; from the first institution. Alphabetically
digested. Providence: Printed by John Carter, M,DCC,LXXXV.
RT

Sports and games, p. 135, advises against racing on foot or horse. Youth,
p. 155, advises against "foolish and wicked pastimes . . . particularly
balls, gaming-places, horse-races, and play-houses."

117

FROST, J. The art of swimming; a series of practical instructions, on an original and progressive plan, by which the art of swimming may be readily attained, with every advantage of power in the water: accompanied with twelve copper-plate engravings, comprising twenty-six appropriate figures . . . To which is added, Dr. Franklin's Treatise, also some anecdotes respecting swimming. New York: Published by P. W. Gallaudet, 49 Fulton Street. Birch and Kelley, printers, 1818.   RT

12 folding plates. RT copy lacks plates, as does others examined. Not to be confused with: *The Art of swimming* . . . Baltimore, W. Turner [1821].

[FROST, John.] Heroes and hunters of the West: comprising sketches and adventures of Boone, Kenton, Brady, Logan, Whetzel . . . Philadelphia: H. C. Peck & T. Bliss [1853].   LC

Frontispiece, plates, illustrations.

1854: Philadelphia, H. C. Peck & Theo. Bliss.   RT

Frontispiece, plates, illustrations.

1858: Philadelphia, H. C. Peck & T. Bliss.   N

Some of the sketches taken from John A. McClung's *Sketches of Western Adventure.*

[FROST, John.] Robert Ramble's Scenes in the country. Boston: W. H. Hill, Jr., [1850].   N

Frontispiece, plates. Illustrated section: *Angling.*

[ca. 1855:] Robert Ramble's Scenes in the country. Boston: Joseph H. Francis, 128 Washington Street, New York: C. S. Francis & Co., 252 Broadway.   RT

Frontispiece and plates as in 1850 edition. With this is bound his: *City scenes.* By Robert Ramble, with separate title-page. Imprint same as first title. Illustrated sections: *The horse auction* and *A rowing match.*

FROST, J[ohn]. Wild scenes in a hunter's life. Including Cumming's Adventures among the lions . . . Compiled by J. Frost. Auburn: Derby & Miller, 1851.   VW

Illustrations. Added illustrated title-page.

1851: Third thousand. Cincinnati, H. W. Derby & Company.   RT

1852: Sixth thousand. Auburn, Derby & Miller.   N

FROST, John. *Continued:*

1853: Twelfth thousand. Wild scenes in a hunter's life. Including Cumming's Adventures among the lions . . . Compiled by John Frost, LL.D. Auburn: Derby and Miller. Buffalo: Derby, Orton and Mulligan, 1853. N

Added colored title-page with imprint: New York & Auburn: Miller, Orton & Mulligan, 1855.

1854: Sixteenth thousand. Wild scenes in a hunter's life. Including Cumming's Adventures among the lions, and other wild animals of Africa, etc. With three hundred illustrations. Compiled by John Frost, LL.D. Auburn and Buffalo: Miller, Orton & Mulligan. RT

Colored frontispiece and added colored title-page, same imprint and date as title-page. Illustrations throughout text.

1855: Eighteenth thousand. Wild scenes of the hunter's life; or, The hunting and hunters of all nations . . . With three hundred illustrations. New York and Auburn, Miller, Orton & Mulligan. LC

1856: Twenty-sixth thousand. New York and Auburn, Miller, Orton & Mulligan . . .

Same title as 1855 edition.

1857: Thirty-first thousand. New York and Auburn, Miller, Orton & Co. RT

Same title as 1855 edition.

FRY, W[illiam] H[enry]. A complete treatise on artificial fish-breeding: including the reports on the subject made to the French Academy and the French Government; and particulars of the discovery as pursued in England. Translated and edited by W. H. Fry. Illustrated with engravings. New York: Appleton and Company . . . 1854. N

FULLER, R. M. A reminiscence. *In:* The Nassau literary magazine. Princeton, February 1857. Vol. 17, no. 5. pp. 201–207. RT

Article signed: B * * *An account of a deer hunting expedition on Eddings Island, South Carolina.*

FULLER, William. Elements of gymnastics. *See:* ELEMENTS of gymnastics.

GAMBADO, Geoffrey, *pseud. See:* BUNBURY, Henry William.

GAMES and sports for young boys: comprising athletic games, country games, games with balls, marbles, buttons, tops, hoops, kites. Miscellaneous toys. Rhymes and calls. Romps. Athletic feats. Table games. Games with toys. Forfeits. Penances. With ninety illustrations. London: Routledge, Warne, and Routledge . . . New York: 56, Walker Street, 1859.   RT

Frontispiece, and illustrations throughout text.

GANO, Daniel. Blooded horses in the west. *See:*

The WESTERN agriculturist, Cincinnati, 1830.

BARNUM, H. L. Farmer's farrier, Cincinnati, 1831.

FARMER'S guide and western agriculturist, Cincinnati, 1832.

GARLICK, Theodatus. A treatise on the artificial propagation of certain kinds of fish . . . Also Directions for the most successful modes of angling for such kinds as are herein described. Cleveland: Tho. Brown . . . 1857.   RT

Plates and illustrations in text.

1858: New York, A. O. Moore . . .   RT

GEAR, Joseph. A favorite old song on mortality and smoke tobacco. Made agreeable & pleasing to all classes . . . Set to music for a single voice and may be repeated as a chorus. With an accompaniment for the pianoforte by Joseph Gear . . . Boston: Pubd. by John Ashton & Co. . . . 1836.   N

Words and music. Smoking lithograph on cover designed by Joseph Gear.

The GENERAL advertiser. Philadelphia, June 1st, 1799.

Contains a long advertisement: *Celebrated running horse* PUNCH. This horse is described in: *American turf register and sporting magazine.* Baltimore, 1829. Vol. 1 pp. 14-16.

The GENERAL character of the dog . . . *See:* TAYLOR, Joseph.

The GENERAL stud book. Containing pedigrees of English race horses, &c., &c., from the earliest accounts to the year 1831, inclusive. With an Appendix, giving extended pedigrees of stallions imported into the United States, and their most noted progeny. Three volumes in two. First American from the second London edition. Baltimore: Published by J. S. Skinner . . . 1834. RT

Usually bound in one volume with binder's title: *British American Stud Book*. A reprint of the English book, but the *Appendix* was added by J. S. Skinner. *See: Gee; Harrison.*

The GENTLEMAN'S magazine. Edited by William E. Burton. Philadelphia: Published by Charles Alexander . . . 1837–1840. 7 vols. N

From July 1837 to December 1840. Vol. 5–7; *Burton's Gentleman's Magazine*. Edgar Allan Poe was associate editor of volumes 5 to 6. In January 1841 it united with the *Casket*, to form *Graham's American Monthly Magazine of Literature, Art and Fashion*. Occasional sporting articles throughout, especially in vol. 5 (1839), a series of chapters on *Field Sports and Manly Pastimes. By An Experienced Practitioner.*

The GENTLEMAN'S pocket farrier. *See:* BURDON, William.

The GENTLEMAN'S vade mecum: or, The sporting and dramatic companion. Published by Smith and Alexander, Athenian Buildings, Philadelphia, 1835–1836.

"Published every Saturday on fine imperial paper of the largest class." Second volume of smaller size. Includes *Dramatic Literature, the Turf and the Fashions*. Illustrated with woodcuts of horses, dogs, etc. The following numbers are the only known copies:

Vol. 1: No. 18. May 2, 1835.	No. 41. Oct. 10.	
No. 19. May 9, 1835.	No. 42. Oct. 17.	
No. 20. May 16.	No. 44. Oct. 31.	
No. 22. May 30.	No. 45. Nov. 7.	
No. 23. June 6.	No. 46. Nov. 14.	
No. 24. June 13.	No. 47. Nov. 21.	
No. 26. June 27.	No. 48. Nov. 28.	
No. 27. July 4.	No. 49. Dec. 5.	
No. 28. July 11.	No. 50. Dec. 12.	
No. 29. July 18.	No. 51. Dec. 19.	
No. 30. July 25.	No. 52. Dec. 26.	
No. 31. Aug. 1.	Vol. 2: No. 69. April 23, 1836.	
No. 32. Aug. 8.	No. 70. April 30.	
No. 33. Aug. 15.	No. 71. May 7.	
No. 34. Aug. 22.	No. 72. May 14.	
No. 35. Aug. 29.	No. 73. May 21.	
No. 36. Sept. 5.	No. 74. May 28.	
No. 38. Sept. 19.	No. 75. June 4.	
No. 39. Sept. 26.	No. 78. June 25.	

GERARD [Cecile Jules Basile]. The adventures of Gerard, the lion killer, comprising a history of his ten years' campaign among the wild animals of northern africa. Translated from the French by Charles E. Whitehead. New York: Derby & Jackson . . . 1856.   RT

Portrait frontispiece, and plates. First published Paris, 1850, in: Houdetot, C.F.A.d', *Chasses Exceptionelles*.

1857: New York, Derby & Jackson.   N

GERSTAECKER, F[riedrich] W[ilhelm] C[hristian]. Wild sports in the Far West . . . With tinted illustrations by Harrison Weir. London and New York: G. Routledge & Co., 1854.
                                                                    LC

1855: Third thousand. London and New York, Geo. Routledge & Co.   RT

1859: Boston, Crosby Nichols & Co.   AAS

GIBSON, William. The farrier's dispensatory, in three parts. Containing I. A description of the medicinal simples . . . made use of in the diseases of horses . . . Philadelphia: Printed by Samuel Keimer, 1724.

First published London, 1721. Evans: 2535.

[GILMAN, Chandler Robbins.] Life on the lakes: being tales and sketches collected during a trip to the pictured rocks of Lake Superior. By the author of "Legends of a Log Cabin." In two volumes. New York: George Dearborn . . . 1836.   N

Each volume has a lithographed frontispiece. Attributed by Halkett & Laing to Thomas Bangs Thorpe; by Cushing to Margaret Fuller Ossoli, by Boston Athenaeum to Charles Lanman.

GIRARDEY, G. The North American compiler containing a large number of selected receipts; for the use of the artist, mechanic, agriculturist, farrier, house-keeper and the community in general. By G. Girardey, M.D. . . . Rossville, O.: Published by the Author, 1844.   RT

Chapter IV: *Veterinary in general.*

The GIRL'S book of healthful amusements and exercises. 4th series, no. 6. New York: J. S. Redfield [ca. 1840].

[ca. 1855:] The young girl's book of healthful amusements and exercises. New York: Kiggins & Kellog, publishers, Nos. 113 & 125 William Street, between John and Fulton.   RT

Engraved title on wrapper: *Fourth series.—No. 6.* List of Redfields Toy Books on back. Illustrations throughout text. Includes: *Riding on horse-back.*

GLOUCESTER Fox Hunting Club. *See:*

The CASKET.

The GREAT Western almanac.

MILNOR, William, Jr.

GOOD Intent Horse Company, of Sellersville and its Vicinity. Routes of the Good Intent Horse Company, of Sellersville and its Vicinity, for detecting horse thieves and other villains. [Philadelphia? ca. 1855.]   RT

Broadside.

[GOODRICH, Samuel Griswold.] Enterprise, industry and art of man, as displayed in fishing, hunting, commerce, navigation, mining, agriculture and manufactures. By the author of Peter Parley's Tales . . . Boston: Bradbury, Soden & Co., 1845.   RT

Woodcuts throughout text. Chapters on *Cattle hunting, Buffalo hunting.* and *Bear hunting.*

[1845:] Boston, Thompson, Brown & Company.   N

1845: New York, John Allen, 139 Nassau St.   RT

1848: Boston, C. H. Peirce and G. C. Rand, No. 3 Cornhill.   RT

Frontispiece, extra engraved title page, and small engravings throughout text.

1852: Boston, Published by Geo. C. Rand, Cornhill. Wm. J. Reynolds and Company.   RT

[GOODRICH, Samuel Griswold.] The every day book, for youth. By Peter Parley [*Pseud.* of Samuel Griswold Goodrich]. Illustrated by numerous engravings. Boston: Carter, Hendee and Co. 1834.   RT

GOODRICH, Samuel Griswold. *Continued:*

Contains the fable: *The Angler and the little fish,* with wood engraving of angler, *Council of horses,* with wood engraving. *Boat song,* etc.

GOODRICH, Samuel Griswold. Peter Parley's story of the soldier and his dog. Boston, 1830.   W & M

[GOODRICH, Samuel Griswold.] A tale of adventure: or, The Siberian sable hunter . . . New York: Wiley & Putnam, 1843.

Frontispiece, and illustrations in text.

GOODWIN, Joseph. A new system of shoeing horses, abridged from the work of Joseph Goodwin . . . To which are added, observations on bleeding and the pulse . . . By John B. Brown. Boston: Printed by Wells and Lilly, 1821.   RT

Five plates. First published London, 1820.

GORDON-CUMMING, Roualeyn [George]. Five years of a hunter's life in the far interior of South Africa . . . In two volumes. New York: Harper & Brothers . . . 1850.   RT

Added illustrated title-page reads: *A Hunter's Life in South Africa.* First published London, 1850.

1851: New York: Harper & Brothers.   N

1856: A hunter's life among lions, elephants, and other wild animals of South Africa. With an Introduction by Bayard Taylor. Complete. Two volumes in one. New York, Derby & Jackson.

Colored frontispiece and vignette on title-page. Illustrations.   CU

1857: New York, Derby & Jackson.   LC

Same title as 1856. Not colored.

1858: New York, Derby & Jackson.   Y

Same title as 1856. Not colored.

1859: New York, Harper & Brothers.

Same title as 1850. *See also:* FROST, John.

GRANDFATHER Merryman, *pseud.* Home recreation: a collection of tales of peril and adventure, voyages and travels, biography, manners and customs, poetry, and other entertaining sketches. A new gift-book for young readers. By Grandfather Merryman. With colored illustrations. New-York: D. Appleton

& Company, 200 Broadway. Philadelphia: Geo. S. Appleton, 164 Chesnut-St., 1850.   RT

Contains five *Sporting and hunting sketches,* reprints from other works, with and without acknowledgment.

GRAHAM, Archibald H. History of Young America Cricket Club. [1854–1889.] Title 128 pp. typescript.   RT

Number of copies made unknown. Accounts of matches with various teams in the Philadelphia area, New York, Boston, Baltimore, and other cities, including matches with English professional teams. On some occasions the Club also played baseball, but played cricket against a team of professional baseball players from the Philadelphia (Athletics) and Boston teams, among them George Wright and Harry Wright.

GRAU, Charles William. Medical parlor gymnastics, or Systematic explanations and prescriptions of movements and exercises practicable under all circumstances for the cure and prevention of diseases . . . With 59 woodcuts. Springfield: Samuel Bowles & Co., 1859.   DCL

GRAY, John W. The life of Joseph Bishop, the celebrated old pioneer in the first settlements of Middle Tennessee, embracing his . . . remarkable hunting excursions . . . Nashville, Tenn.: Published by the author, 1858.   LC

Autobiography of Bishop, related by him to Gray, who added three chapters.

[GRAYDON, Alexander.] Memoirs of a life, chiefly passed in Pennsylvania within the last sixty years; with occasional remarks upon the general occurrences, character and spirit of that eventful period. Harrisburg: Printed by John Wyeth, 1811.   N

On p. 59 a reference to Sir William Draper who "frequently amused himself with the game of rackets," and a mechanic, "the hero of the tennis court" who played with him [1770]. Also mentions foot races, sailing, swimming, skating, fencing.

1846: Memoirs of his own time. With reminiscences of the men and events of the Revolution. Edited by John Stockton Littell . . . Philadelphia, Lindsay & Blakiston.   N

The GREAT duellist. A sketch of the duelling practices of the Hon. Henry Clay. Boston, [ca. 1845].

Leaflet, 8 pp. Noted in *Catalogue* of E. Morrill, Boston, 1974.

The GREAT Western almanac for 1849. Philadelphia: Published and sold by Jos. McDowell . . . 1849. AAS

Illustrated with wood engravings. Article on The Gloucester Fox Hunting Club.

GREEN, J[onathan] H. An exposition of games and tricks with cards. By J. H. Green, the reformed gambler. New York: Published by G. & S. Bunce, 37 Chatham Street, 1850. RT

Paper covers. Cover reads: *Price 25 cents. Gamblers' tricks with cards exposed and explained. By J. H. Green, the reformed gambler.* Same imprint. Border device of cards.

GREEN, J[onathan] H. An exposure of the arts and miseries of gambling; designed especially as a warning to the youthful and inexperienced, against the evils of that odious vice. By J. H. Green. Revised by a literary friend. Cincinnati: Published by U. P. James, 1843. RT

Includes chapters on horse racing and cock-fighting.

1847: An exposure of the arts and miseries of gambling; designed especially as a warning to the youthful and inexperienced against the evils of that odious and destructive vice. By J. H. Green. Revised by a literary friend. Fifth edition improved. Philadelphia: Published by G. B. Zieber & Co. Ledger Building. RT

GREEN, J[onathan] H. The gambler's mirror: By J. H. Green, The reformed gambler, author of "Green on gambling:" designed to expose the wiles practised by the gambling and sporting gentry, and intended to warn the community against the evil tendency of their desperate habits. Illustrated by appropriate engravings. Vol. 1. Boston: Published by Redding & Co., No. 8, State Street, 1845. RT

Paper covers. Cover title: *The gambler's mirror,* Vol. 1, no. 1. No more published. Engraved title-page and cuts throughout text.

GREEN, Jonathan H. Gamblers' tricks with cards, exposed and explained. New York, [1850?].

Wrappers, 114 pp. Noted in: *Midland notes,* no. 60. Mansfield, Ohio, 1955.

GREEN, J[onathan] H. Gambling in its infancy and progress; or a dissuasive to the young against games of chance. New York: Published by Lewis Colby, 122 Nassau Street, 1849. RT

Frontispiece and 3 plates. "Entered according to act of Congress. in the year 1848."

126

GREEN, Jonathan H. The reformed gambler; or The history of the later years of the life of Jonathan H. Green (the "Reformed Gambler"), to which is added a complete and full exposition of the game of thimbles; diamond cut diamond . . . Written by himself . . . Philadelphia: T. B. Peterson and Brothers, 306 Chestnut Street [1858]. RT

Frontispiece.

GREEN, J[onathan] H. A report on gambling in New York: made by J. H. Green, General Executive Agent of the New York Association for the Suppression of Gambling. New York: J. H. Green, 37 Chatham Street, 1851. RT

Paper covers. Cover title: *Green's report, No. 1, on gambling and gambling houses in New York. New York: J. H. Green, 37 Chatham Street. And sold by all booksellers, 1851.*

GREEN, J[onathan] H. The secret band of brothers; or, The American outlaws . . . Compiled from original papers, by J. H. Green, the reformed gambler. Third edition. Philadelphia: Published by the author, 1848. RT

Frontispiece and 4 plates.

GREENE, Nathaniel. Tales and sketches. Translated from the Italian, French and German by Nathaniel Green. Boston: Charles C. Little & Brown, 1843. RT

The artist's excursion, pp. 5-27, is on game bird shooting.

GREENWOOD, Grace. *See:* LIPPINCOTT, Sara Jane (Clarke).

GRISWOLD, E. D. Fox hunter. Orwell, Vt., 1858. RT

A two page circular advertising a Black Hawk stallion, *Fox Hunter,* at stud, dated Orwell, Vt., April 1858. Engraving of horse at head.

GUENTHER, F[riedrich] A[ugust]. New manual of homœopathic veterinary medicine; or, The homœopathic treatment of the horse, the ox, the sheep, the dog, and other domestic animals. By F. A. Gunther. Translated from the third German edition, with considerable additions. Second American edition. Boston: Otis Clapp, 3 Beacon Street. New York: William Radde. Philadelphia: Rademacher & Sheek, 1856. RT

Translator's notice dated London, 1846.

H., W. The Tally ho! Galop. Composed by W. H. New York: Firth, Pond & Co. Montreal: H. Prince. [1854.] RT

Sheet music. Colored lithograph of fox-hunting scene Lithographed by Sarony & Co., N.Y.C. At head of cover: *J. H. Daley, Esq. and the members of the Montreal "Fox Hounds."*

HAMILTON, R. P. Prof. R. P. Hamilton's Great original secrets & discoveries in taming and subduing the horse. n.p. [ca. 1859].

Purple paper covers. RT

HAMILTONIAD: or, The effects of discord. *See:* HOPKINS, Joseph R.

HARK the Goddess Dianna. *See:* SPOFFORTH, Reginald.

[HAMMETT, Samuel Adams.] A stray Yankee in Texas. By Philip Paxton. [*Pseud.* of Samuel Adams Hammett.] New York: Redfield . . . 1853.

Frontispiece and engraved title-page. A novel, with descriptions of hunting, wild fowling, etc.

[HAMMETT, Samuel Adams] The wonderful adventures of Captain Priest. A tale of but few incidents, and no plot in particular. With other legends. New York: H. Long & Brother, 121 Nassau-Street [cop. 1855]. RT

Frontispiece and extra illustrated title-page. 3 pp. of advertisements at end. Humorous incidents in the life of the skipper of a "sloop-rigged vessel," of fishing interest, with some mention of horse racing on Long Island.

HAMMOND, S[amuel] H. and Mansfield L[ewis] W[illiam]. Country margins, and rambles of a journalist. New York: J. C. Derby . . . Boston: Phillips, Sampson & Co. Cincinnati, H. W. Derby, 1855. N

Contemplative essays descriptive of life and travel in New York State, appreciative of nature and out-of-doors. First published in *Albany State Register.*

HAMMOND, S[amuel] H. Hills, lakes, and forest streams: or, A tramp in the Chateaugay Woods. By S. H. Hammond . . . New York: J. C. Derby . . . Boston: Phillips, Sampson & Co. Cincinnati: H. W. Derby, 1854. RT

Engraved half-title, frontispiece and 2 plates.

HAMMOND, Samuel H. *Continued:*

1855: Hunting adventures in the Northern Wilds: or, A tramp in the Chateaugay Woods, over hills, lakes, and forest streams. By S. H. Hammond. New York, J. C. Derby.

1856: Hunting adventures in the Northern Wilds . . . New York, Derby & Jackson: Cincinnati: H. W. Derby.   LC

Frontispiece and plates.

1856: Hunting adventures in the Northern Wilds . . . New York; J. C. Derby . . . Boston, Phillips, Sampson & Co.: Cincinnati, H. W. Derby.   RT

Engraved half-title, frontispiece and 2 plates.

1859: Hunting adventures in the Northern Wilds . . . New York, Derby & Jackson . . .   Y

HAMMOND, S[amuel] H. Wild northern scenes; or, Sporting adventures with the rifle and the rod. New York: Derby and Jackson . . . 1857.   N

Illustrations.

1858: New York, Derby and Jackson.   H

1859: New York, Derby and Jackson.   Y

HARE. Hare's complete farrier: containing full and complete directions for choosing, breeding, rearing, and general management of the horse: together with accurate descriptions, causes, peculiar symptoms, and the most approved method of curing all diseases to which the horse is subject. Newcomerstown, Ohio: [Printed at the "Preacher" Office, Washington, O.] 1853.   RT

Cloth spine, boards with lettering: *Hare's complete horse farrier. Price twenty-five cents. A very valuable work for every farmer.*

The HARE; or, Hunting incompatible with humanity: written as a stimulus to youth towards a proper treatment of animals. [Verse] Philadelphia: Printed for Benjamin Johnson, No. 31 High Street, and Jacob Johnson, No. 147 High-Street, 1802.   RT

Engraved frontispiece. Half title reads: *The hare. In two books. Book I.* Half-title of Book II on p. [61] reads: *The hare. Book the second. Poor is the triumph o'er the timid hare. Thomson.* p. 63 numbered 64 in error.

HARRINGTON. How sweet in the woodlands. A favorite duett. Composed by Harrington. New York: Published by W. Dubois . . . no. 126 Broadway [ca. 1818–1821].

Words and music. Deer hunting. RT

HARRIS, George Harris. *See:* FANCHER, O. H. P.

HART, Joseph. The Tyrolese peasants' song. Arranged by Joseph Hart. New York: Published by J. L. Hewitt, no. 137 Broadway [ca. 1830]. RT

Second edition. Music and words. Lithograph of peasants in hunting costume on cover.

HARTLEY, Cecil B. Hunting sports in the West, comprising adventures of the most celebrated hunters and trappers. Philadelphia: Published by G. G. Evans, no. 439 Chestnut Street, 1859 RT

Extra illustrated title-page. Frontispiece and 14 plates. This is the first edition, the following undated copy is a reprint of the same year..

[1859]: Philadelphia: J. E. Potter & Co. Y

HARTLEY, Cecil B. Life and times of Colonel Daniel Boone . . . To which is added Colonel Boone's Autobiography complete, as published in 1784 . . . Illustrated with engravings . . . Philadelphia: Published by G. G. Evans . . . 1859. N

Engraved title-page.

[HARVARD UNIVERSITY]. Regattas on Lake Winnipissiogee! *See:* BAKER, N. B.

HASLAM, John. A few brief observations on the foot of the horse, and on shoeing. Baltimore: Samuel Harker, 1832. vw

[HAWES, William Post], possible author. Nixon's Creek, or, A fisherman's tale. N.p., ca. 1840.

26 pp. Title from *The Thomas Winthrop Streeter Collection of Americana.* New York: Parke-Bernet Galleries, 1969.

[HAWES, William Post.] A shark story. *See:* PORTER, William Trotter. A quarter race in Kentucky.

[HAWES, William Post.] Sporting scenes and sundry sketches; being the miscellaneous writings of J. Cypress, Jr. [*Pseud.* of William Post Hawes.] Edited by Frank Forester. [*Pseud.* of Henry William Herbert.] In two volumes . . . New York: Published by Gould, Banks & Co. . . . 1842.   RT

See: Van Winkle.

HAWKER, P[eter]. Instructions to young sportsmen, in all that relates to guns and shooting. First American, from the ninth London edition . . . To which is added, The hunting and shooting of North America . . . Collated from authentic sources, by Wm. T. Porter, Esq. . . . With illustrations. Philadelphia: Lea and Blanchard, 1846.   RT

Contributions by H. W. Herbert. First published London, 1814. Illustrated with the "Wild Turkey" frontispiece, by J. J. and J. W. Audubon, and other illustrations.

1853: Second American edition. Philadelphia, Blanchard & Lea.

See: Van Winkle.

[HAWKS, Francis Lister.] The adventures of Daniel Boone, the Kentucky rifleman. By the author of "Uncle Philip's conversations" . . . New York: D. Appleton & Co., 200 Broadway. Philadelphia: George S. Appleton, 148 Chesnut St., 1844.   RT

Frontispiece. Volume V of *A library for my young countrymen.*

1846: New York: D. Appleton & Co. . . .   RT

Frontispiece.

1850: New York: D. Appleton & Co. . . .   RT

Frontispiece.

1854: New York: D. Appleton & Company.   RT

Frontispiece.

1856: Life of Daniel Boone. Dayton, O., Ells, Marquis & Company.   N

Frontispiece and illustrations throughout text. Vignette title-page. Includes: *The hunters of Kentucky.*

HAWTHORNE, Alice, [*pseud.*]. *See:* WINNER, Septimus.

HAZEN, Edward. The panorama of professions and trades; or, Everyman's book. Embellished with eighty-two engravings. Philadelphia: Published by Uriah Hunt. Sold by the booksellers generally, 1836.   N

Frontispiece and vignette title-page, with engravings for each subject throughout text. Includes: *The saddler and harness maker, The hunter, The fisherman, The gunsmith.*

1837: The panorama of professions and trades; or, Every man's book. Embellished with eighty-two engravings. Philadelphia: Published by Uriah Hunt. . . .   RT

Includes: *The saddler and harness-maker, The fisherman, The hunter, The gunsmith.* Bound in boards, with cover title same as title-page, except for date 1841.

1841: Popular technology; or, Professions and trades . . . Embel-with eighty-one engravings. In two volumes. Vol. I [–II]. New-York, Harper and Brothers, 82 Cliff-St.   RT

Vignette title-pages, with engravings for each subject throughout text. Includes: *The saddler and harness-maker, The hunter, The fisherman, The gunsmith.*

1845: The panorama of professions and trades . . . Philadelphia.

HEADLEY, J[oel] T[yler]. The Adirondack; or, Life in the woods. New York: Baker and Scribner . . . 1849.   RT

Frontispiece, plates. Includes parts of his: *Letters from the Backwoods.*

1853: New York, Baker & Scribner.   RT

Frontispiece, plates.

HEADLEY, J[oel] T[yler]. Letters from the backwoods and the Adirondack. New York: John S. Taylor . . . 1850.   N

Portrait frontispiece.

HENRY, T[homas] Charlton. An inquiry into the consistency of popular amusements with a profession of Christianity. By T. Charlton Henry, D.D. . . . Charleston, S.C.: Printed and published by Wm. Riley, Church-Street, 1825.   RT

Discusses theater, dancing, and recreation in general. Boards. Cover title identical with title-page, with additional border.

HERBERT, Henry William. American game in its seasons . . . Illustrated from nature, and on wood, by the author. New York: Charles Scribner . . . 1853.

The works of Henry William Herbert are of major importance to collectors of American sporting books. The many editions with their variations are exhaustively covered in: *Henry William Herbert [Frank Forester]: a bibliography of his writings 1832–1858,* compiled by William Mitchell Van Winkle, with the bibliographical assistance of David A. Randall, published in Portland, Maine, by The Southworth-Anthoensen Press, 1936. Only brief entries to each title are made here. For full details see the Van Winkle-Randall bibliography. Also *see:* White, Luke, Jr., *Henry William Herbert. The American publishing scene 1831–1858.* Newark, N.J., The Carteret Book Club, 1943.

[HERBERT, Henry William.] The complete manual for young sportsmen: with directions for handling the gun, the rifle, and the rod; the art of shooting on the wing; the breaking, management, and hunting of the dog; the varieties and habits of game; river, lake, and sea fishing, etc., etc., etc. Prepared for the instruction and use of the youth of America. By Frank Forester . . . New York: Stringer & Townsend . . . 1856.

[HERBERT, Henry William.] The deerstalkers; or, Circumstantial evidence: a tale of the South-Western counties. By Frank Forester . . . Illustrated by the author. Philadelphia: Carey and Hart, 1849.

[HERBERT, Henry William.] Fishing with hook and line; a manual for amateur anglers. Containing also descriptions of popular fishes, and their habits, preparation of baits, &c. &c. By Frank Forester. New York: Published at the Brother Jonathan Office [1858].

[HERBERT, Henry William.] Frank Forester's Field sports of the United States, and British provinces, of North America. By author of "My shooting box" . . . In two volumes. Vol. I [–II]. New York: Stringer & Townsend . . . 1849.

HERBERT, Henry William. Frank Forester's Fish and fishing of the United States and British provinces of North America. Illustrated from nature by the author . . . New York: Stringer & Townsend . . . 1850.

HERBERT, Henry William. Frank Forester's Horse and horse-

HERBERT, Henry William. *Continued:*

manship of the United States and British provinces of North America . . . With steel-engraved original portraits of celebrated horses. In two volumes, Vol. I [–II]. New York: Stringer & Townsend . . . 1857.

HERBERT, Henry William. Frank Forester's Sporting scenes and characters. Containing full remarks on all kinds of English and American shooting, game, and all kinds of sporting. In two volumes.—Volume one. [Volume two.] With numerous illustrations, from original designs by Darley. Philadelphia: T. B. Peterson . . . [1857].

HERBERT, Henry William. Hints to horse-keepers, a complete manual for horsemen . . . With additions, including "Rarey's Method of horse-taming," and "Baucher's System of horsemanship" . . . and A memoir of the author. New York: A. O. Moore & Company . . . 1859.

[HERBERT, Henry William.] My shooting box. By Frank Forester . . . Philadelphia: Carey and Hart, 1846.

HERBERT, Henry William. The Quorndon hounds; or, A Virginian at Melton Mowbray . . . With illustrations by the author. Philadelphia: Getz, Buck & Co., 1852.

HERBERT, Henry William. Supplement to Frank Forester's Fish and fishing of the United States and British provinces of North America. By William Henry [*sic*] Herbert . . . New York: Stringer & Townsend . . . 1850.

[HERBERT, Henry William]. Tricks and traps of New York City . . . [Part I]. Boston: Published by C. H. Brainard . . . 1857.   N

Paper covers. *Brainard's Half-Dime Handbooks.* Chapter V: *Gamblers and Gambling Houses.*

1858: The tricks and traps of horse dealers. By Frank Forester. Part 1. New York: Dinsmore and Company.   RT

Paper covers, lacking from RT copy. White wrappers, lettered: Tricks & traps of Horse dealers . . . Portrait frontispiece and 5 full-page illustrations, and smaller cuts in text. Verso title-page has notice: "Tricks and traps." listing nos. 1-7. *The tricks and traps of horse dealers* is no. 5, [Part 1]. No. 6 is *Tricks and Traps of Horse Dealers* [Part 2] (In preparation). There is no evidence that this second part was ever issued.

HERBERT, Henry William. The Warwick woodlands, or Things as they were there, ten years ago, by Frank Forester . . . Philadelphia: G. B. Zieber & Co., 1845.

HERBERT, Henry William. *See also:*

BROWN, John J. The American angler's guide, 1850.

The CORSAIR.

HAWKER, Peter. Instructions to young sportsmen.

HAWES, William Post. Sporting scenes and sundry sketches.

HOOPER, Johnson Jones. Dog and gun.

PEEL, Jonathan. The sportsman's vade mecum.

SUE, Eugene. The Godolphin Arabian.

SURTEES, Robert Smith. Mr. Sponge's sporting tour.

TRICKS and traps of the city.

WALTON, Isaac. The complete angler.

HERNE, Peregrine, [*pseud.*] Perils and pleasures of a hunter's life; or, The Romance of hunting . . . Boston: L. P. Crown; Philadelphia: J. W. Bradley, 1854.   RT
Colored frontispiece and plates, added colored title-page.

[1855:] Philadelphia, John E. Potter.   LC
Colored frontispiece and plates.

1857: Philadelphia, Evans & Co. . . .   RT
Colored frontispiece and plates.

HEROES and hunters of the West. *See:* FROST, John.

HERSHBERGER, H. R. The horseman. A work on horsemanship; containing plain practical rules for riding, and hints to the reader on the selection of horses. To which is annexed a sabre exercise for mounted and dismounted service. With cuts, illustrating the various kinds of bits . . . And Practices for the accomplished horseman. New York: Henry G. Langley . . . 1844.   RT

1847: New York, Wilson and Company . . .   RT
Paper covers.

HEWES, Robert. An elucidation of regulations for the formations and movements of cavalry. The first American from the third London edition. Revised and corrected by Robert Hewes . . . Salem: Printed by Joshua Cushing, For W. Norman, Boston, 1804.   RT

HEWES, Robert. Rules and regulations for the sword exercise of the cavalry. To which is added, The review exercise. The first American, from the London edition. Revised and corrected by Robert Hewes, teacher of the sword exercise for the cavalry. Boston: Printed for William Norman, book and chart seller [1802].   RT

28 plates, numbered 1–28. First published as: Great Britain. Adjutant General's Office. *Rules and regulations for the sword exercise*. London, 1796.

[1802:] Rules and regulations for the sword exercise of the cavalry. To which is added, The review exercise. The second American, from the London edition. Revised and corrected by Robert Hewes, teacher of the sword exercise of the cavalry. Philadelphia, Published by M. Carey, No. 122 Market-Street. Alexander & Phillips, printers, Carlisle [1802].   N

Plates numbered 1–27, and *Explanatory Plate*.

1808: Rules and regulations for the sword exercise of the cavalry. From the copy printed by His Brittannic Majesty's Command for the War Office, London, 1805. Philadelphia, Printed and sold by James Humphreys on Change Walk.   RT

Frontispiece only: The six cuts. Hewes name does not appear in this edition.

1812: *See:* Craig, Robert H.

1813: Rules and regulations for the sword exercise of the cavalry. To which is added, The review exercise. The second Albany edition. Revised and corrected by Robert Hewes, teacher of the sword exercise for cavalry. Albany, puplished [*sic*] by G. Forbes, Court-Street, J. Buel—printer.   RT

No plates.

HEWITT, John H. The mountain bugle. For one or two voices. Written, composed, & inscribed to Miss Mary Margaret Houck, by John H. Hewitt. Baltimore: Published and sold by Geo. Willig, Jr., 1833.   RT

Words and music. Deer hunting.

HIEOVER, Harry, *pseud. See:* BINDLEY, Charles.

HINDS, John, *pseud. See:* BADCOCK, John.

A HISTORY of my father's dog Towzer. Go, mark his true, his faithful way, And in thy service copy Tray. Providence: Geo. P. Daniels, 1843.   RT

Wrappers. Small woodcuts on wrappers, title-page and throughout text.

The HISTORY, treatment, and diseases of the horse . . .
See: YOUATT, William.

HODSON, G. A. The Lake of Como. Morning . . . The symphonies & accompaniments by G. A. Hodson. Philadelphia: Fiot, Meignen & Co., 217 Chesnut St. . . . [ca. 1837].   RT

Words and music. Arranged for the guitar by L. Meignen. Hunting lithograph by Lehman & Duval on cover.

HOFFMAN, C[harles] F[enno]. Wild scenes in the forest and prairie. With sketches of America life . . . In two volumes. New York: William H. Colyer . . . 1843.   N

First edition London, [1839?]. Chapters include: *A mountaineer of the Hudson, A Bear Story, Camping Out, A Wolf Encounter, The Dog and the Deer Stalker.*

HOHMAN, John George. Der lange verborgene Freund, oder: Getreuer und Christlicher Unterricht für Jedermann, enthaltend: wunderbare und probmässige Mittel und Künste, sowohl für die Menschen als das Vieh. Mit vielen Zeugen bewiesen in diesem Buch, und wovon das Mehrste noch wenig bekannt ist, und zum allerersten Mal in America im Druck erschient. Herausgegeben von Johann Georg Hohman, nahe bey Reading, in Elsass Taunschip, Berks Caunty, Pennsylvanien. Reading: Gedruckt für den Verfasser, 1820.   RT

Boards.

[ca. 1820] Der lange verborgene Freund, oder: Getreuer und Christlicher Unterricht für Jedermann, enthaltend: wunderbare und probmässige Mittel und Künste, sowohl für die Menschen als das Vieh. Mit vielen Zeugen bewiesen in diesem Buch, und wovon das Mehrste noch wenig bekannt ist, und zum allerersten Mal in America im Druck erschient. Herausgegeben von Johann George Hohman, nahe bey Reading in Elsass Taunschip, Berks Caunty, Pennsylvanien. Zweite und verbesserte Auflage.   LC

137

HOHMAN, John George. *Continued:*

1828: Der lange verborgene Freund, oder; Getreuer und Christlicher Unterricht für Jedermann, enthaltend, wunderbare und probmässige Mittel und Künste, sowohl für die Menschen als das Vieh. Ephrata.

Noted in Ernest J. Wessen. Midland Notes, 89, No. 216, 1963.

1829: Der lange verborgene Freund, oder: Getreuer und Christlicher Unterricht für Jedermann, enthaltend: wunderbare und probmässige Mittel und Künste, sowohl für die Menschen als das Vieh . . . Herausgegeben von Johann George Hohman, nahe bey Reading, in Elsass Taunschip, Berks Caunty, Pennsylvanien. Chambersburg: Nachgedruckt in Jahr 1829.   RT

1856: The long lost friend. A collection of mysterious & invaluable arts & remedies, for man as well as animals. With many proofs of their virtue and efficacy in healing diseases, &c., the greater part of which was never published until they appeared in print for the first time in the U.S. in the year 1820. By John George Hohman. Harrisburg, Pa.: T. F. Scheffer, printer, 1856.   RT

Boards.

HOHMAN, John George. Die Land-und Haus-Apotheke, oder getreuer and gründlicher Unterricht für den Bauer und Stadtmann, enthaltend die allerbesten Mittel, sowohl für die Menschen als für das Vieh besonders für die Pferde. Nebst einem grossen Anhang von der Aechten Färberey, um Türkisch-Roth, Blau, Satin-Roth, Patent-Grün und viele andere Farben mehr zu Färben. Erste americanische Auflage. Herausgegeben von Johann George Homan, in Elsass Taunschip, Berks Caunty, Pennsylvanien. Reading: Gedruckt bey Carl A. Bruckman, 1818.   RT

Boards.

HOLCROFT, Thomas. The road to ruin: a comedy. As it is acted at the Theatre Royal, Covent-Garden. London: Printed: New York: Reprinted for Berry and Rogers . . . 1792.   AAS

Game of tennis played off stage. First published Dublin, 1789.

1806: New York, D. Longworth.   N

1819: New York, D. Longworth.   N

HOLCROFT, Thomas. *Continued:*

1822: . . . With prefatory remarks . . . as it is performed at the Theatres Royal. By W. Oxberry, Comedian. Boston, Published by Wells and Lilly . . .   RT

1847: New York, Berford & Co.   N

1848: New York, J. Douglas.   LC

HOMAN, Johann George. *See:* HOHMAN, John George.

HOOK, James. Bright Phoebus. A favorite hunting song, composed by Mr. Hook. Philadelphia: Printed and sold by G. Willig, Mark: Street no. 185 [1798].   RT

Words and music. Fox hunting.

HOOK, James. Diana, a favorite hunting cantata. Composed by James Hook. Boston: Published and sold by G. Graupned, at his music store, no. 6 Franklin Street [ca. 1821–1825].   RT

Words and music. Fox hunting.

HOOPER, Johnson J[ones]. Dog and gun; a few loose chapters on shooting . . . among which will be found some anecdotes and incidents . . . New York: C. M. Saxton & Co. . . . 1856.
                                                    HTP

Paper covers, with woodcut on front. Two articles by H. W. Herbert.

HOOTON, James. Ladies cavalcade quick step. Composed and respectfully dedicated to Miss Susan W. Bartlett, by James Hooton. Boston: Published by Wm. H. Oakes, 8½ Tremont Row, 1840.   RT

Sheet music. "Entered according to act of Congress in the year 1840 . . ." Male and female riders on cover, *E. W. Bouvé's Lith. Boston.*

[HOPKINS, Joseph R.]. Hamiltoniad: or, The effects of discord. An original poem. In two books. With an Appendix; containing a number of papers relative to this late unfortunate duel. By a Young Gentleman of Philadelphia. Philadelphia, 1804.

Wegelin no. 998.

HORN, Charles E., composer. *See:* POWER, Thomas.

The HORNET. "To true republicans I'll sing, Aristocrats shall feel my sting." Fredericktown, Maryland: Printed and published by M. Bartgis, April 11th, 1809.

4 pages, quarto. Woodcut of Merry Andrew, the famous stallion.

The HORSE: its habits, diseases and management, in the stable and on the road: with advice to purchasers . . . New York: Homans & Ellis, 1846.   N

1847: New-York: Published by Wm. H. Graham . . .   RT

Cover title: *The complete horse doctor* . . .

1849: New York: Dewitt & Davenport.

Cover title: *The complete horse doctor.*

HORSE-RACING, and Christian principle and duty, incompatible. Charleston, 1837.   HCL

HOUSTON, George. *See:* The FARMER'S, mechanic's, manufacturer's, and sportsman's magazine.

HOUSTOUN, Mrs. [Matilda Charlotte (Jesse) Fraser.] Texas and the Gulf of Mexico: or, Yachting in the New World. Philadelphia: G. B. Zieber & Co., 1845.   RT

Frontispiece, plates, illustrations. First published London, 1844. Also included in: *Smith's Weekly Volume,* Philadelphia, 1845.

HOWARD, W[illia]m. Narrative of a journey to the summit of Mont Blanc, made in July 1819. By Wm. Howard, M.D. [verse]. Baltimore: Published by Fielding Lucas, Jr. J. Robinson, printer, 1821.   RT

Engraved frontispiece. Boards. First published in *Analectic Magazine,* Philadelphia. May, 1820. First edition. First ascent of Mont Blanc by an American.

HOWITT, William. The boy's country book, of amusements, pleasures, and pursuits. Illustrated with twenty-two original designs. Edited by William Howitt. [From the London edition]. New York: Published by Samuel Colman, 1840.   RT

Mentions angling, swimming, horsemanship, dogs, etc. Extra engraved title-page.

[1843:] New York, Published by Edward Kearney.   AAS

HOYLE [Edmond]. Hoyle's Games improved: being practical treatises on the following fashionable games, viz. whist, quadrille, piquet, back-gammon, chess, billiards, and tennis. With the established rules of the game. By James Beaufort . . . Philadelphia: Printed for and sold by H. P. Rice . . . 1796.   RT

Evans: 30599. The article on tennis is based on: *Annals of gaming*, London, 1790.

1796: Boston, Printed and sold by William Spotswood.   RT

Evans: 30598.

1796: New York, William Pritchard.   AAS

Not in Evans.

1803: The pocket Hoyle. New York, David Longworth.   RT

1805: The new pocket Hoyle, containing the games of whist, reversis, quadrille . . . chess, back-gammon, billiards, pool and hazard. Philadelphia: Printed and published by H. Maxwell, opposite Christ Church.   RT

One plate: backgammon table. Contains no outdoor games.

1814: Boston, Published by Edward Cotton . . .   RT

Includes golf.

1817: Hoyle's games, containing as follows, whist, quadrille, piquet, quintze, vingt-un, lansquenet, pharo, rouge et noir, cribbage, matrimony, cassino, reversis, put, connexions, all fours, speculation. To which is added, The games of brag and chess. With the practice and rules, as established by the most correct players. Philadelphia, Printed and sold by John Bioren, Chesnut-Street.   RT

1819: Hoyle's games improved; containing whist, piquet, quadrille, lansquenet, pharo, rouge-et-noir, cribbage, matrimony, cassino, put, all fours, speculation, draughts, hazard, billiards, brag, cricket, tenis [*sic*] back-gammon, chess . . . New York: Printed and sold by G. R. Waite, No. 54, Maiden-Lane.   RT

1821: New York, George Long.   RT

1823: New York, George Long.   RT

1825: New York, George Long.   AAS

141

HOYLE, Edmond. *Continued:*

1829: New York, George Long.   N

1830: New York, W. C. Borrodaile.   RT

Includes horse racing and cocking.

1836: Philadelphia, John Locken.   N

1838: Philadelphia, Thomas, Cowperthwaite & Co.   RT

1841: Philadelphia, Thomas, Cowperthwaite & Co.   RT

1842: Philadelphia, John Locken.   AAS

1844: Philadelphia, Henry F. Anners.   RT

1845: Philadelphia, Henry F. Anners.   AAS

Includes archery, bowls, golf.

1850: Hoyle's games, or Card player's assistant; Containing the established rules and practice of whist, Loo . . . Philadelphia: Fisher & Brother. . . , ca. 1850.

Frontispiece. Bound with: *The AMATEUR, or Guide to the stage* . . . By a Retired Person. Philadelphia: Fisher & Brother, ca. 1850.

1857: Boston, G. W. Cottrell.

HOYT, E[paphratas]. A treatise on the military art; in four parts. Containing: I. A comprehensive system of discipline, for the cavalry of the United States; adapted to the principles of Baron Steuben's Regulations for the infantry . . . Illustrated with plates . . . Vol. 1. Part I & II . . . Printed at Brattleborough, by Benjamin Smead, for the author. Sold by him . . . Greenfield, 1798.   RT

Binder's title: *Cavalry discipline.* 10 folding plates.

1813: Rules and regulations for drill, sabre exercise, equitation, formation and field movements of cavalry. Illustrated with plates. Being a second edition of Cavalry discipline. Revised, corrected and enlarged by the author. Greenfield (Mass.), Printed by and for Denio and Phelps . . .   RT

14 folded plates.

HOYT, E[paphratas]. *Continued:*

1816: Rules and regulations for the drill, sabre exercise, equitation, formation and field movements of cavalry. Illustrated with plates. Being a third edition of Cavalry discipline. Revised, corrected and enlarged by the author. Greenfield, (Mass.): Printed and published by Ansel Phelps . . .   RT

Fourteen folded plates.

1818: Greenfield, Mass. Printed by and for Denio and Phelps.   N

HUENTEN, Franz. Quatre rondeaux de chasse. No. 1. La chasse au loup. No. 2. La chasse au renard. No. 3. La chasse au cerf. No. 4. La chasse a la bécasse. Par François Hünten. New York: Published by Torp & Viereck, 465 Broadway [ca. 1850].   RT

Music only. RT has only No. 1. La chasse au loup. Four small hunting cuts on cover of wolf, fox, deer, and woodcock hunting.

HUGHS, Willis. An introduction to farrierry [*sic*], being a description of the most common diseases to which the horse is incident, together with the most approved remedies for relieving the same. By Willis Hughs, of Gallatin County, Kentucky. Madison, Ia.: Printed by C. P. J. Arion [1829].

Boards with brown leather strip. Preface dated "Gallatin county, Ky. Dec. 4th, 1828." Verso title-page: notice of application for copyright by William [*sic*] Hughs, dated December 8, 1828. Page [72] contains testimonial dated "21st day of February, 1829." Copy in Indiana Historical Society, Indianapolis, Ind.

1835: An introduction to farriery, being a description of the most common diseases to which the horse is incident, together with the most approved remedies for relieving the same. By Willis Hughs. Crawfordsville, Indiana, 1835.

Boards, with green cloth backstrip. Verso title-page: [copyright secured]. Record Press. Copy in Purdue University Library, Lafayette, Ind.

The HUMOURIST: a collection of entertaining tales. Baltimore, 1829. 2 vols. in 1.

14 colored plates by C. V. Nickerson. Sporting, theatre, etc.

HUNT, [James Henry] Leigh. The indicator: miscellany for the fields and the fireside. In two parts. Part I [–II]. First American edition. New York: Wiley and Putnam, 161 Broadway, 1845. N

Angling, pt. I, ch. XI. First published London, 1820-1822. 2 vols.

The HUNTERS or the sufferings of Hugh and Francis . . . *See:* BINGHAM, Caleb.

The HUNTERS of Kentucky . . . [By Ben Bilson]. *See:* PATTIE, James Ohio. The personal narrative . . .

HUNTING song. *See:* BENHAM, Asahel.

HUNTINGTON, J[edidiah] V[incent]. The forest. By J. V. Huntington, author of "Alban" and "Lady Alice." Redfield: Clinton Hall, New York, 1852. N

Contains fishing and deer hunting in the Adirondacks. The first Adirondack novel.

The HUSBAND-MAN'S guide: in four parts . . . Part Third: The experienc'd farrier, containing many excellent and profitable receipts for the curing of all diseases in horses, sheep, cowes, oxen, & hogs. . . . Boston: Printed by John Allen, for Eleazar Phillips, 1710.

Copy in John Carter Brown Library, Providence, R. I.

1711: Boston. Evans 1500. Printed by B. Green.

1712: The second edition, enlarged. New York: Printed by Will & Andrew Bradford. N

This edition not in Evans.

1712: The second edition, enlarged. Printed for, & sold by Eleaz. Phillips, Book-seller in Boston.

In John Carter Brown Library.

1723: Philadelphia.

Listed in: Guerra, F. *American medical bibliography. Colonial Period and Revolutionary War.* New York, 1961.

1727: New York: Printed by William Bradford.

Evans: 2884.

HYATT, George W. The mellow horn. A very popular song

HYATT, George W. *Continued:*

[by George W. Hyatt]. Composed & sung with rapturous applause, by Mr. Jones. Boston: Published by C. Bradlee, No. 164 Washington Street [ca. 1830].   RT

Lithograph of fox hunting scene, by Pendleton's Lithog. Boston.

[ca. 1831:] The mellow horn. A very popular song. Composed and sung with rapturous applause. By Mr. Jones at the Park Theatre. [The words by G. W. Hyatt Esq. and respectfully dedicated, to J. H. Eastburn, of Boston.] Baltimore, Published by George Willig Junr.   RT

Lithograph of fox-hunting scene within horn, on cover.

[ca. 1834:] The mellow horn, written by G. W. Hyatt, Esqr. Composed and sung by Mr. Jones. Philadelphia, Kretschner & Nunns, No. 70 So. Third & 196 Chesnut St.   RT

No cover on RT copy.

[ca. 1835:] The mellow horn. Composed and sung with rapturous applause by Mr. Jones. Written by G. W. Hyatt, Esqr., and respectfully dedicated to J. H. Eastburn (of Boston), New York, Firth & Hall, 1 Franklin Square.   N

No cover on N copy.

[1842:] The mellow horn, a very popular song, written by George W. Hyatt. Composed, arranged and sung, with rapturous applause, by Mr. Jones. New York, Published at Atwill's Music Saloon, No. 201 Broadway.   N

No cover on N copy.

HYDE, Eli. A sermon; in which the doctrine of the lot, is stated, and applied to lotteries, gambling and card playing, for amusement. By Eli Hyde, A.M. Pastor of a church in Oxford, New-York. Oxford [N.Y.]: Printed by John B. Johnson, 1812.   RT

RT copy lacks wrappers.

The ILLUSTRATED manners book: a manual of good behavior and polite accomplishments. New York: Leland Clay, & Co., 1855.   RT

Engraved title page, by N. Orr, N.Y. At bottom of title page: *Stringer & Townsend, 222 Broadway, N.Y.* Small engravings throughout text. Chapter XXI: *Gymnastics, Dancing,* &c. Chapter XXII: *Horsemanship.*

IMLAH, John. Huntsman rouse thee! Hark the horn! Song of the chase. The words by John Imlah, Esq. The music composed expressly for, and dedicated to John Braham, Esqr. By Joseph de Pinna. New York: T. Birch [1832].

Words and music. Fox-hunting lithograph on cover by Endicott & Swett. Reproduced in: Van Urk, J. Blan. *The story of American foxhunting.* . . . New York: 1940-1941, vol. 2.

INCIDENTS and sketches connected with the early history and settlement of the West. With numerous illustrations. Cincinnati: U. P. James, No. 167 Walnut Street, between Fourth and Fifth [ca. 1857]. RT

Paper covers, with woodcut. Cover title: *Sketches of incidents and adventures in the West. Twenty fine illustrations.* Frontispiece and 8 full page illustrations, and other small wood cuts. Contains: *Adventures of Captain Daniel Boon[e], Catching wild horses on a prairie,* etc.

INNOCENT poetry. New York: Published by Samuel Wood & Sons, no. 261, Pearl-street; and Samuel S. Wood & Co. no. 212, Market-street, Baltimore. [ca. 1825].

Frontispiece and seven plates, engravings in text. Moralistic poems. Illustrations of shooting, fishing, and shuttlecock.

[IRVING, John B.] The international cricket match played Oct., 1859, in the Elysian Fields, at Hoboken, on the ground of the St. George's Cricket Club . . . New York: Vinten . . . 1859. N

Dedication signed by John B. Irving.

[IRVING, John B.]. Local events and incidents at home. Charleston, S.C. Printed by A. E. Milller, [sic] 5 Broad-Street, 1850. Price 12½ cents. RT

Paper covers. Title from front cover, with border, frontispiece. *A fishing Excursion,* pp. 5-14. Not listed in Sabin, nor standard bibliographies of sporting books.

[IRVING, John B.] The South Carolina Jockey Club. Charleston, S.C.: Russell & Jones, 1857. RT

Sometimes *erroneously* attributed to E. P. Milliken, who signed *Preliminary Remarks. See: Harrison.*

IRVING, WASHINGTON. The sketch book of Geoffrey Crayon, gent. No. VII . . . New York: Printed by C. S. Van Winkle . . . 1820.　　　　　　　　　　　　　　　　　　N

Paper covers. *The Angler,* pp. 29-49. Other editions, of which there are many, are listed in: Williams, S. T. and M. A. Edge. *A bibliography of . . . Washington Irving* . . . New York: Oxford University Press, 1936.

IUCHO, Wilhelm. The sportsman's pleasure, a hunting rondo for the pianoforte. Composed and dedicated to Miss M. E. Penoyer, by Wilhelm Iucho. New York: Firth and Hall . . . [ca. 1834].

Music only. Stag-hunting lithograph by Brown on cover.

JAHN, F[riedrich] L[udwig]. A treatise on gymnastics. Taken chiefly from the German of F. L. Jahn. Northampton, Mass.: Published by Simeon Butler . . . 1828.　　　　　　　　RT

Translated by Charles Beck. 8 folding plates.

JEFFREYS, C. J. The merry days of old, the words by C. J. Jeffreys, Esq. The music by S. Nelson. New York: Published by James L. Hewitt, 239 Broadway . . . 1843.　　　RT

Words and music. Lithograph of medieval hawking scene by Thayer & Co.'s Lithography, Boston, on cover.

[JEFFREYS, George Washington.] Annals of the [Virginia] turf, by an Advocate for the Blood Horse. *In:* Petersburg Intelligencer, May, 1826.　　　　　　　　　　　　　　LC

The first form of an American stud book. Reprinted in *The Sporting Olio* column of *The American Farmer,* beginning with the issue of June 16, 1828 (Vol. 8, p. 102), and in the 1828 and later editions of Richard Mason's *The Gentleman's New Pocket Farrier. See: Harrison.*

JENKS, Joseph William. The rural poetry of the English language, illustrating the seasons and months of the year, their changes . . . pleasures. Topographically paragraphed, with a complete Index. Boston: John P. Hewitt & Co. . . . 1856.

Frontispiece, illustrations. Contains Longfellow's *Angler's Song.*

JESSE, Edward. Gleanings in natural history; with local recollections. To which are added Maxims and hints for an angler [by Richard Penn]. Philadelphia: Carey, Lea and Blanchard, 1833.
　　　　　　　　　　　　　　　　　　　　　　　　　LC

Paper label lettered: *First American Edition.* First published London, 1832. The *Maxims and Hints* were written for the album of a fishing club and signed "R.P. 31 May 1829." *See:* Penn, Richard.

JEWETT, Paul. The New England farrier; or, A compendium of Earriery [*sic*], in four parts . . . Being the result of many years experience and first production of the kind in New England. Intended for the use of private gentlemen and farmers. Newburyport: Printed by William Barrett . . . 1795. N

RT has copy with word *Earriery* corrected. Evans: 28901.

1802: Salem.

1806: Hudson, Printed by A. Stoddard. RT

1807: Second edition. Salem, Printed by Joshua Cushing . . . RT

1808: Newburyport, Printed; Edenton [N.C.], Reprinted.

1809: Leominster, Printed by Salmon Wilder.

1810: The farmer's farrier; or, A compendium of farriery . . . Correctly compiled from Jewett's New-England farrier. Concord, N.H., Published by G. Hough & D. Cooledge . . . AAS

1811: The New-England farrier; or A compendium of farriery . . . Augusta. Published by Ezekiel Goodale. . . . LC

1821: The New-England farrier; or a compendium of farriery, in four parts . . . Intended for the use of private gentlemen and farmers. By Paul Jewett. To which is added, An appendix, never before published, comprising many valuable recipes, prescriptions and rules compiled by a gentleman experienced in veterinary practice. Exeter: Printed by John J. Williams. RT

Paper wrappers.

1822: Second edition enlarged. Exeter, Printed by John J. Williams. RT

1824: Third edition. Woodstock, Printed by David Watson. RT

Published anonymously.

1826: New Edition, with valuable additions. Exeter, Published by Josiah Richardson. RT

JEWETT, Paul. *Continued:*

1827: Newport, Published by Aldrich & Barton.   RT

1828: *See:* Richardson, Josiah.

1834: The New England farrier; or Farmer's receipt book . . .
With copper-plate embellishments. Twenty-second edition. Boston, Published by Charles Gaylord.   AAS

Published anonymously.

1835: The New England farrier, Boston . . .   AAS

Identical with 1834 edition.

[JEWETT, Stephen]. Duelling incompatible with true honor.
A sermon delivered April 1820. Rutland: Printed by William
Fay, 1820.   RT

15 pp. RT copy has no cover. Refers to death of Stephen Decatur.

JOHN, Uncle. *See:* NOYCE, Elisha.

JOHNES, Merideth. The boy's book of modern travel and adventure. With eight illustrations by William Harvey. New York:
D. Appleton and Company . . . 1859.   RT

Illustrations: *The deer's leap, Chase of the eiderduck.*

JOHNSON, C[harles] B[ritten], M.D. Letters from the British
settlement in Pennsylvania. To which are added, The Constitutions of the United States, and of Pennsylvania; and extracts
from the laws respecting aliens and naturalized citizens. Philadelphia: Published by H. Hall, 209 Chestnut Street, and in
London, by John Miller, 1819.   N

Folded map frontispiece. Letter V: *Game,* pp. 42-44.

1820: A new edition. Philadelphia: Printed for H. Hall and
for John Souter, American Bookseller, 73 St. Paul's Church
Yard, London.   RT

Map lacking from RT copy. Letter V: *Game,* pp. 54-56.

JOHNSON, Jacob. *See:* The POCKET farrier. Philadelphia,
1807.

JONES. My bark is my courser Composed by Mr. Jones, and sung by him at the Park Theatre. The poetry selected from the *New York American*, and respectfully dedicated to the Gentlemen of the New York Boat Club. New York: Bourne, Broadway [1831]. RT

Words and music. Lithograph of boat on cover.

JONES, Arthur T. A horse story, by an Old Gray Horse, continued by Arthur T. Jones. New York: George F. Nesbitt & Co. . . . January 1856. N

JONES, Edward E., editor. *See:* AMERICAN turf register and racing & trotting calendar.

JONES, J[ohn] B[eauchamp]. Rural Sports: a tale in four parts. Philadelphia: C. Marshall, 1849. LC

In verse.

JONES, J[ohn] B[eauchamp]. Wild western scenes; a narrative of adventures in the Western wilderness, forty years ago, wherein the conduct of Daniel Boone is particularly described. Also, Minute accounts are given of bear hunts—deer and buffalo hunts —desperate conflicts with the savages—wolf hunts— fishing and fowling adventures—encounters with serpents, etc. etc. Number I [–VI]. By J. B. Jones, Editor of the Baltimore Saturday Visiter [*sic*]. Illustrations designed by Ruckle—engraved by Hinckley. New York: Samuel Colman, 14, John St. Baltimore: N. Hickman, 86, Baltimore St. Sherwood & Co., printers, Baltimore, 1841.

In six parts, paper wrappers. Not illustrated.

1845: . . . Also . . . Bear hunts . . . Bear and buffalo hunts . . . Fishing and fowling . . . By a Squatter. [*Pseud.* of John Beauchamp Jones.] Philadelphia, E. Ferrett & Co.

1849: Wild Western scenes: a narrative of adventures in the Western wilderness . . . Wherein the exploits of Daniel Boone, the great American pioneer are particularly described. Also, Minute accounts of bear, deer, and buffalo hunts . . . By Luke Shortfield. [*Pseud.* of John Beauchamp Jones.] . . . Beautifully illustrated. Philadelphia, Grigg, Elliot and Co. . . . N

Illustrations throughout text.

JONES, John Beauchamp. *Continued:*

1851: Philadelphia, E. Ferrett & Co.

1852: Wild Western scenes: a narrative of adventures in the Western wilderness. Wherein the exploits of Daniel Boone, the great American pioneer, are particularly described. Also, Accounts of bear, deer, and buffalo hunts . . . New stereotype edition, revised and corrected. By J. B. Jones . . . Illustrated with sixteen engravings from original designs. Philadelphia, Lippincott, Grambo & Co.   N

Illustrated paper covers. N copy has frontispiece, added illustrated title-page, and 4 plates.

1853: Wild Western scenes: a narrative of adventures in the Western wilderness, wherein the exploits of Daniel Boone, the great American pioneer, are particularly described. Also, Accounts of bear, deer, and buffalo Hunts . . . New stereotype edition, revised and corrected. By J. B. Jones . . . Illustrated with sixteen engravings from original designs. Philadelphia, Lippincott, Grambo & Co.   RT

RT copy has added illus. title-page and 7 plates.

1855: Philadelphia, Lippincott, Grambo & Co.   RT

RT copy has added illus. title-page, and 11 plates. A reprint of 1853 edition.

1857: Philadelphia, J. B. Lippincott & Co.   RT

RT copy has sixteen plates, including frontispiece and added illustrated title-page. A reprint of 1853 edition.

The JOURNAL of health. Conducted by an Association of Physicians. Philadelphia: Published at No. 108 Chesnut Street . . . 1830–1833.   N

Vol. 1-4: Sept. 9, 1829-Aug. 1833. Vol. 4 has caption title: *Journal of Health and Recreation.* Contains articles on exercise, etc. Vol. 1 has lithographed frontispiece of out-of-door recreations.

The JUVENILE forget me not; a Christmas, New Year's and birth day present for 1839. Philadelphia: Thomas T. Ash & Henry F. Anners [cop. 1838].   CU

Frontispiece and plates. *The riding school or, A cure for conceit,* pp. 59 ff.

JUVENILE pastimes; or Girls' and boys' book of sports. [Vignette and verse.] New Haven: Published by S. Babcock, 1849.
RT

Small cuts and full page illustrations. Vest pocket size. Includes illustration of game of baseball. Date on paper cover, 1850.

JUVENILE pastimes or Sports of the four seasons. Part I [–II]. Embellished with twenty-eight neat copper-plate engravings. Philadelphia: Published by Morgan and Yeager . . . [ca. 1815.]
N

Title on paper cover. Illustrations in color: "25 cents coloured, 18 plain."

1828: Juvenile pastimes or Sports for the four seasons. Part I. Embellish [sic] with twenty eight neat copper-plate engravings. Philadelphia. Published by Morgan and Yeager. 114 Chesnut St. first door below the Post Office.
N

Also Part II. Plates are colored. Title from covers. RT has copy of Part I, identical with N 1828 copy, except that paper cover is without title, and is blank. It seems to be contemporary, and is stitched in as though by publisher.

[1832:] Providence, Cory, Marshall and Hammond.
LC

JUVENILE pastimes, in verse. New-York: Printed and sold by Mahlon Day, At the New Juvenile Book-store, No. 376, Pearl-street [ca. 1830].
RT

Vest pocket size. Vignette and verse on title-page, small woodcuts throughout text. Pink paper wrappers, text as on title-page, but different woodcut (three boys skipping rope, same as on p. 16). Back cover lists "Three cent toys."

1847: Juvenile pastimes, in verse. New-York: S. M. Crane, 374 Pearl-street, 1847. Egbert, Hovey & King, Printers.
RT

Vest pocket size. Same cuts but type different from 1830 edition. Cuts on title-page and front blue paper wrappers new to this edition, and text of back cover differs. Verse on title-page not on cover.

JUVENILE sports. Philadelphia: W. Johnson, 1835.

Vest pocket size.

JUVENILE sports for boys and girls . . . See: KINGSTON Academy.

KEEPER'S travels in search of his master . . . See: KENDALL, Edward Augustus.

[KENDALL, Edward Augustus.] Keeper's travels in search of his master . . . Philadelphia: Printed by B. & J. Johnson, No. 147, High Street, 1801.   RT

First published London, 1798. Frontispiece.

1808: Keeper's travels in search of his master . . . Philadelphia, Published by Johnson & Warner, No. 147, Market Street.   RT

Frontispiece.

1833: Keeper's travels in search of his master. [Verse.] A new edition revised. Boston: Published by Lilly, Wait & Co. Portland: Colman, Holden & Company.   RT

Frontispiece and engravings throughout text.

[KENNEDY, John Pendleton]. The Blackwater chronicle. A narrative of an expedition into the land of Canaan, in Randolph County, Virginia . . . By "The Clerke of Oxenforde." With illustrations from life by Strother. New York: Redfield . . . 1853.   RT

Engraved title-page. This book has also been attributed to David Hunter Strothers, its illustrator, who was Kennedy's cousin. Also to Philip Kennedy, brother of John Pendleton Kennedy.

KENTUCKY Association for the Improvement of the Breed of Horses. Constitution of the Kentucky Association, for the Improvement of the Breed of Horses, &c. and Rules and regulations for the government of the course. Lexington, Ky.: T. Smith, Printer-Reporter office, 1831.   RT

RT, only known copy, has 7 blank pages at end ruled by hand, with ms. of "Rules proposed by Walter Dun and adopted, with others, on Thursday October 19, 1837."

KESTER, Jesse Y. *See:* The AMERICAN shooter's manual.

KINGSTON Academy. The book of games; or, A history of the juvenile sports practised at the Kingston Academy. Illustrated with twenty-four copperplates. Philadelphia: Published by Johnson & Warner, 147 Market Street. A. Fagan, printer, 1811.   RT

Binder's instructions lists 24 plates of games, including hockey, fives, trapball, cricket and football. RT copy has 16 plates only.

1821: The book of games; or, A history of the juvenile sports practised at the Kingston Academy. Illustrated with twenty-four copperplates. Philadelphia, B. Warner.   LC

1822: The book of games; or, A history on juvenile sports practised at the Kingston Academy. Illustrated with twenty-four copperplates. New York: Printed and published by George Long, No. 71, Pearl-Street.   RT

RT copy has 24 plates.

[ca. 1840:] Juvenile sports for boys and girls. With numerous engravings. Philadelphia: Published by M. Fithian, 61 North Second Street.   RT

Plates as in previous editions, but colored. Binder's instructions call for 24 plates, but RT copy has only 12. Another RT copy has 12 colored plates also, but 5 only are in both volumes.

1842: The book of games, or, A history on juvenile sports as practised at the different academies, and illustrated with coloured engravings. Philadelphia, Published by Crolius & Gladding. No. 341 Market Street, above North. Printed by King & Baird.   N

13 colored plates, including frontispiece.

KLAPP, H. Milnor, editor. *See:* KRIDER, John.

KNAEBEL, S. Pedestrian quick step. From a Tyrolean air. Arranged for the piano-forte and dedicated to Thomas Elworth. By S. Knaebel. Boston: Published by Henry Prentiss, 33 Court St. . . . [ca. 1839].   RT

Music only. Lithograph portrait of Thomas Elworth, famous pedestrian. *See:* ELWORTH, Thomas. *Sketches of incidents and adventures in the life of Thomas Elworth, written by himself.* Boston, 1844.

KNICKERBOCKER Base-Ball Club. By-laws, regulations and rules of the knickerbocker Base-Ball Club, of New-York. Organized September 23, 1845. New-York: Biglow & Bleecker . . . 1858.   N

KNIGHT, Joseph Philip. O swift we go. *See:* FIELDS, J. T.

KNOWLSON, John C. The complete farrier, or horse doctor. A treatise on the diseases of horses: written in plain language,

KNOWLSON, John C. *Continued:*

which those who can read may easily understand. The whole being the result of seventy years extensive practice of the author, John C. Knowlson. Many of the recipes in this book are worth one hundred dollars each, and the whole are new to the world. New-York: Wilson and Company, Brother Jonathan Press. 1845.

RT

Yellow paper covers, with title: *Knowlson's Complete farrier, or Horse doctor; being a plainly-written treatise on the diseases of horses, and the only proper mode of treatment. Price 25 cents.* At head of cover-title: *Brother Jonathan Monthly library. No. 15.*

1847: The complete farrier, or horse doctor. A treatise on the diseases of horses: written in plain language, which those who can read may easily understand. The whole being the result of seventy years extensive practice of the author. John C. Knowlson. Many of the recipes in this book are worth one hundred dollars each, and the whole are new to the world. New York: Wilson and Company, Brother Jonathan Press.

RT

Paper wrappers. Frontispiece: *From the stable of Gen. A. T. Dunham, West Troy, N. Y.* Cover title: *Knowlson's complete farrier.* [Cut of horses at drinking trough by F. Onwhyn] *or horse doctor. Price 25 cents.*

1848: The complete farrier, or horse-doctor. A treatise on the diseases of horses: written in plain language, which those who can read may easily understand. The whole being the result of seventy years extensive practice of the author, John C. Knowlson. Many of the recipes in this book are worth one hundred dollars each, and the whole are new to the world. Cincinnati: Stratton & Barnard. Printed by E. Shepard.

RT

Paper wrappers. Frontispiece: *The age of a horse by his teeth.* Verso of frontispiece: *The Horse. Terms denoting the external parts of the horse.* Cover title: *Price 25 cents. Knowlson's complete farrier,* [Cut of race horse.] *or horse doctor.* Cincinnati: Stratton & Barnard, 121 Main Street. Stereotyped by E. Shepard, 1849.

[ca. 1850:] The complete farrier, or horse-doctor. A treatise on the diseases of horses: written in plain language, which those who can read may easily understand. The whole being the result of seventy years extensive practice of the author, John C. Knowlson. Many of the recipes in this book are worth one hundred dollars each, and the whole are new to the world. Philadelphia: T. B.

KNOWLSON, John C. *Continued:*

Peterson, No. 98 Chesnut Street.   RT

Paper wrappers. Cover title. *All who own a horse sould possess this book.*
Knowlson's Complete farrier, [Cut of horse by F. Onwhyn as in 1847
edition.] *or horse doctor . . .*

[ca. 1850:] The complete farrier, or horse doctor. A treatise on
the diseases of horses: written in plain language which those who
can read may easily understand.—The whole being the result
of twenty years extensive practice by the author, John C. Knowlson. Many of the receipts in this book are worth one hundred
dollars each, and the whole are new to the world. Wooster, Ohio:
Published by George Howard.   RT

Paper covers. Verso title-page: *The age of a horse by his teeth,* same as
frontispiece of 1848 edition. Cover title: *All who own a horse should*
possess this book. Knowlson's complete farrier or [Cut of horse and
groom by W. T. Norman.] *horse doctor. A new and improved edition . . .*

[ca. 1850:] The complete farrier, or horse doctor; a treatise on
the diseases of horses: written in plain language, which those
who can read may easily understand. The whole being the result
of seventy years extensive practice of the author, John C. Knowlson. Many of the recipes in this book are worth one hundred dollars each, and the whole are new to the world. Cincinnati: Published by U. P. James, 167 Walnut Street.   RT

Paper covers. Cover title in border: *Price 25 cents. Knowlson's complete*
farrier [Cut of horse] *or horse doctor . . .* The cut of the horse has landscape with buildings behind. It was used in Sloan's *Complete farrier,*
Chicago, 1851 (front cover). Advertising matter verso front cover lists
first book: *The course of time.* First book listed verso back cover: *Ken-*
tucky tragedy.

[ca. 1850:] Cincinnati.   RT

Text and front cover identical with above, but verso front cover, and both
sides back wrapper vary. First book listed verso front cover: *Abednego.*
First item verso back cover: *Miss Eliza A. Dupuy's Novels.*

1851: The complete farrier, or horse-doctor. A treatise on the
diseases of horses: written in plain language, which those who
can read may easily understand. The whole being the result of
seventy years extensive practice of the author, John C. Knowlson.
Many of the recipes in this book are worth one hundred dollars

each, and the whole are new to the world. Cincinnati: Published by Lorenzo Stratton, No. 131 Main Street.   RT

Paper covers. Frontispiece: *The age of a horse by his teeth.* Verso frontispiece: *The horse. Terms denoting the external parts of the horse.* Cover title in border: *Price 25 cents. Knowlson's Complete farrier,* [Cut of race horse as in 1848 edition] *or horse doctor* . . .

[1858:] Taming or breaking the horse, by a new and improved method, as practiced with great success in the United States, and in all the countries of Europe, By J. S. Rarey. Containing rules for selecting a good horse, for feeding horses, &c. Also, The complete farrier, or horse doctor: a guide for the treatment of horses in all diseases to which that noble animal is liable . . . By John C. Knowlson . . . New York, Dick and Fitzgerald.   N

On cover: *The complete horse tamer and farrier. As practiced by Rarey and Knowlson.*

KOOGLE, J. D. The farmer's own book: a treatise on the numerous diseases of the horse, with an explanation of their symptoms, and the course of treatment to be pursued; also other useful information. By J. D. Koogle. Baltimore: Printed by McCoull & Slater, S. W. Corner of Baltimore and Sharp streets, 1857. RT

No copyright note. Two small woodcuts. R. G. Hayman Catalogue (1966) lists copy with copyright notice pasted on verso of title-page.

1858: The farmer's own book: a treatise on the numerous diseases of the horse, with an explanation of their symptoms, and the course of treatment to be pursued; also a treatise on the diseases of horned cattle. Middletown, Maryland: Published by J. D. Koogle.   RT

Entered according to the Act of Congress in the year 1857 by J. D. Koogle. 2 woodcuts as in 1857 edition. Supplement with separate title-page, and separate pagination: *A supplement to the farmer's own book: a treatise on the diseases of horned cattle, with an explanation of their symptoms, and the course of treatment to be pursued.* Middletown, Maryland: Published by J. D. Koogle, 1858.

KRIDER [John]. Krider's sporting anecdotes, illustrative of the habits of certain varieties of American game. Edited by H. Milnor Klapp. Philadelphia: A. Hart . . . 1853.   RT

Engraved frontispiece.

KRIDER, John. Sportsmens depot established in 1826. John Krider, gun maker, dealer in fishing tackle and all kinds of sporting apparatus. N.E. cor. 2nd & Walnut Sts. Philadelphia Pa. [ca. 1850.]   RT

Broadside advertisement. Heavy border with sporting scenes.

KRUMMACHER, F[riedrich] A[dolf]. The little dove. From the German of F. A. Krummacher. Boston: Weeks, Jordan & Company, 1839.   CU

Frontispiece. *The hunter*, p. 30 ff.

Eine KURTZGEFASSTE neue Sammlung in sich haltend mehrentheils wunderseltsamen auserlesenen nütlichen und bemährten Recepten und Kunst-Stücke, erste Abhandlung ueber die Jagd, die dem Landmanne so schädliche Thiere, als Füchse, Wolfe, und Hasen, als auch Hirsche, Fische und Vögel zu fangen. Zweyte Abhandlung ueber andere zur Hausshaltung . . . Dritte Abhandlung . . . Nothwendigsten Mitteln und Recepte für Pferde, Hornvieh, Schaafe, und Schweine . . . [Reading, Pa.: H. B. Sage.] Auf Kosten des Liebhabers herausgegeben, im Jahr 1815.   RT

Printed on paper and type imported from Germany. Sage published other books on same paper, with same type.

KURTZGEFASSTES Arzney-Büchlein für Menschen und Vieh, Darinnen CXXX auserlesene Recepten. Ephrata: Klosterpresse, 1790.   HTP

Evans: 22604.

1791: In Wien Gedruckt. In Ephrata Nach-gedruckt.   RT

Evans: 23483.

1791: . . . Darinnen CXXVIII auserlesene Recepten, nebst einer prognostischen Tafel. Wien gedruckt, Ephrata nachgedruckt. RT

1792: [Vierte Auflage.] Ephrata, Klosterpresse.

Evans: 24449.

1794: Reading, Gedruckt bey Jungmann und Gruber.

KURTZGEFASSTES. *Continued:*

Evans: 27190.

1795: Ephrata. Zum sechten Mal gedruckt.   RT

1797: Ephrata, Benjamin Meyer.

Evans: 32343.

1798: Ephrata.

1803: Hagerstown, Md.

See: COWEN, David L. *America's pre-pharmacopoeial literature.* Madison, Wis., 1961.

KURZ gefasztes Ross-Arzney Buchlein. Ephrata: Gedruckt bey T. Baumann, 1802.

Wrappers, sewn. Woodcut of horse on title-page. 23 pp. Noted in James Lewis Hook, Catalogue 354, 1955, no. 273.

1803: Kurz gefasztes Ross-Arzney Buchlein. Ephrata.

24 pp. Noted in James Lewis Hook, Catalogue 354, 1955, no. 274.

1805: *See:* Schneyder, John. Nutzliches. . . .

[LADD, William.] A letter to Aaron Burr, Vice-President of the United States of America, on the barbarous origin, the criminal nature and the baneful effects of duels; occasioned by his late fatal interview with the deceased and much lamented General Alexander Hamilton. By Philanthropos. [*Pseud.* of William LADD.] *Ne occidas.* New-York: Printed for the author, and sold by John Low, No. 33 Chatham-Street . . . 1804.   N

LADY of Lexington. *See:* LITTLEFORD, Mrs.

The LADY'S book. Philadelphia: Louis A. Godey, 1839. Vol. 19. October 1839.   N

Article: *Riding,* pp. 145-152. One full page plate, and several small cuts in text.

The LADY'S Equestrian manual. *See:* The YOUNG lady's equestrian manual.

LAMB, Cornelius. The Western farrier: in which the principal diseases of horses are described, and The mode of treatment for the cure of the same. Remarks on stable management, feeding, exercise, etc. . . . Illustrated by a finely engraved anatomy of the horse. By Cornelius Lamb, Esq. the great farrier of the West. Arranged and published by George C. Snow. Terre Haute, [Indiana], George A. Chapman, Printer, 1841.

Described in Catalogue of Robert G. Hayman, September 1965, as follows: Apparently the only known copy being the one cited by Byrd and Peckham 937 and located as at the St. Louis Medical Society Library. Walker picked up the title from the copyright entry but was unable to locate a copy. The title page of the present copy differs very slightly from the entry as given by Byrd and Peckham but the difference may be the result of careless transcription. The compilers . . . stated that no plate is present in the one copy located although called for on the title page; the plate, in fact, appears on page 139 and has page text on the verso.

LAMB, J. The dog. Burlington [Vt.]: Smith and Harrington, 1836.   RT

Wrappers small woodcuts throughout text and on title-page. Back cover lists *Books for children,* and front cover, with border reads: *No. 10.* Vest pocket size.

LANMAN, Charles. Adventures in the wilds of the United States and British American Provinces. Illustrated by the author and Oscar Bessau . . . With an Appendix by Lieut. Campbell Hardy. In two volumes. Philadelphia: John W. Moore . . . 1856.   RT

Plates. Vol. I includes reprints of: *A Summer in the Wilderness,* New York, 1847; *A Tour of the River Saguenay,* Philadelphia, 1848; *Letters from the Alleghany Mountains,* New York, 1849. First published in London by Longman, Brown, Green and Longmans, 1854, as *Adventures in the Wilds of North America;* numbers 55 and 56 of *The Traveller's Library,* in 2 parts, paper wrappers.

LANMAN, Charles. Essays for summer hours. Boston: Hilliard, Gray & Company, 1841.   N

1842: Second edition. Boston, Hilliard, Gray and Company.   RT

Frontispiece and tailpiece.

1853: Third edition. New York, M. W. Dodd.   LC

Omits some articles in earlier editions.

LANMAN, Charles. Haw-Ho-Noo; or, Records of a tourist. Philadelphia: Lippincott, Grambo & Co., 1850.   LC

Reproduced as: *The Sugar Camp and other Sketches.*

LANMAN, Charles. Letters from the Alleghany Mountains. New York: Geo. P. Putnam, 155, Broadway. 1849.   N

Letter VI. *The hunter of Tallulah.*

1856: *Reprinted in his:* Adventures in the Wilds of the United States. Philadelphia, John W. Moore.   N

[LANMAN, Charles]. Letters from a landscape painter. By the author of "Essays for summer hours." Boston: James Munroe and Company, 1845.   RT

Part of this is reprinted in his: *Haw-Ho-Noo.* Chapters include: *Trouting among the Catskills, A week in a fishing smack, Moosehead Lake and the Kennebeck.*

LANMAN, Charles. A summer in the wilderness; embracing a canoe voyage up the Mississippi and around Lake Superior . . . New York: D. Appleton & Company . . . Philadelphia: Geo. S. Appleton . . . 1847.   RT

Also appeared with different title-page: *A Canoe Voyage up the Mississippi and around Lake Superior.* Same year and publisher. Reprinted in his: *Adventures in the Wilds of the United States,* Philadelphia, 1856.

LANMAN, Charles. A tour of the river Saguaney, in Lower Canada. Philadelphia: Carey and Hart, 1848.   RT

First published in London, 1848.

1856: *Reprinted in his:* Adventures in the wilds of the United States. Philadelphia, John W. Moore.   N

LAWRENCE, John. The horse in all his varieties and uses; his breeding, rearing and management . . . with Rules . . . for his preservation from disease . . . Philadelphia: E. L. Carey and A. Hart . . . 1830.   RT

First published London, 1829.

LEBANON County Horse Company. Charter of the Lebanon County Horse Company, for the Detection of Horse Thieves and the Recovery of Stolen Horses. Incorporated April 14th, 1853.

Broadside. Includes: *Charter, rules and by-laws, and list of members.* RT

LEBEAUD. The principles of the art of modern horsemanship, for ladies and gentlemen . . . Translated from the French, By Daniel J. Desmond, Esquire. Philadelphia: E. L. Carey & A. Hart . . . 1833.   RT

LEE, Alex[ande]r. The hunter's signal horn. Tyrolese song. Sung by Mrs. Knight, the music arranged by Alexr. Lee. Philadelphia: Published and sold by G. E. Blake, N. 13 South and 5th Street [ca. 1830].   RT

Words and music. Deer hunting.

LEIB, Isaac. Wohlerfahrner Pferde-Arzt; enthaltend Mittel für die Heilung aller Bekannten und Verschiedenartigen Krankheiten und Seuchen der Pferde . . . Libanon: Gedruckt bey Jos. Hartman, 1842.   RT

Frontispiece.

LEIBLING. The gallop waltz. Composed for the piano-forte by Leibling. New York: E. S. Mesier, no. 28 Wall Street . . . [ca. 1820].   RT

Music only. At head of music: Lithograph of lady acrobat circus rider.

LESHER, C. D. *See:* MARKHAM, J.

LETTER to a friend against gaming for money. Boston, 1720.

Evans: 2127.

LETTER to a gentleman, on the sin and danger of playing cards and other games. Boston: 1775.

Evans: 7448.

LETTERS from a landscape painter. *See:* LANMAN, Charles. Letters from a landscape painter.

LEWIS, E[lisha] J[arett]. Hints to sportsmen, containing notes on shooting; the habits of the game birds and wild fowl of America; the dog, the gun, the field, and the kitchen. Philadelphia: Lea & Blanchard, 1851.   RT

LEWIS, Elisha Jarett. *Continued:*

Frontispiece, illustrations.

1855: The American sportsman. Philadelphia, Lippincott, Grambo & Co.   RT

Added engraved title-page.

1855: The American sportsman. Philadelphia, Lippincott, Grambo & Co.   VW

An *edition de luxe* from same plates as 1855 edition, except that frontispiece and engraved added title-page are tinted. Added title-page has variant imprint. Heavy binding, cloth, with bevelled edges, and extra blind tooling.

1857: The American sportsman . . . Philadelphia, J. B. Lippincott & Co.   RT

Frontispiece and added engraved title-page, tinted, and illustrations. Variations of 1857 edition: Philadelphia, Lippincott, Grambo & Co., 1855 on title-page, but J. B. Lippincott & Co., 1857 on engraved title-page. Another has: J. B. Lippincott & Co., 1857 on title-page, but no date on engraved title-page. N has a copy with: J. B. Lippincott & Co. on both title-pages. *See: Phillips.*

LIFE and battles of Yankee Sullivan, embracing full and accurate reports of his fights with Hammer Lane, Bob Caunt, Tom Secor, Tom Hyer, Harry Bell, John Morrisey, together with a Synopsis of his minor battles . . . Philadelphia: A. Winch . . . [1854.]

Paper covers.   LC

LIFE of William Poole, with a full account of the terrible affray in which he received his death wound. Containing also sketches of Tom Hyer, James Sullivan and John Morrissey. New York: Clinton T. de Witt, publisher, 33 Rose Street [1855].   RT

Paper wrappers, portrait vignette of William Poole on title-page.

LING, P. H. The gymnastic free exercises of P. H. Ling, arranged by H. Rothstein. Translated, with additions, by M. Roth, M.D. . . . A systematized course of gymnastics without apparatus, for the development and strengthening of the body and improvement of the figure . . . Boston: Ticknor, Reed and Fields, 1853.   AAS

Folding plate.

LINLEY, Geo[rge]. Morning's ruddy beam. Song of the Alpine hunters. Written and composed by Geo. Linley, Esq. New York: Published by Firth & Hall . . . 1839. RT

Words and music. First line: *Morning's ruddy beam tints the eastern sky.*

LINSLEY, D[aniel] C[hipman]. Morgan horses: a premium essay on the origin, history, and characteristics of this remarkable American breed of horses. With numerous portraits. New York: C. M. Saxton and Company . . . 1857. RT

1858: New York, A. O. Moore & Co. HPL

1859: New York, A. O. Moore & Co. RT

LIPPINCOTT, Sara Jane (Clarke). Greenwood leaves: a collection of sketches and letters by Grace Greenwood [pseud]. Boston: Ticknor, Reed, and Fields, 1850. RT

Extra engraved title-page. *My first hunting and fishing,* pp. 28–37. Verso title-page: Entered according to act of Congress . . . 1849, by Sara J. Clark. Brown cloth, gilt-embossed spine.

1850: same as above.

Green cloth, gilt-embossed spine and covers.

LISLE, Estelle de. Undine mazourka. Composed for, and respectfully dedicated to, the Undine Barge Association of Philadelphia by Estelle de Lisle. Philadelphia: Published by Beck & Lawton, 166 Chestnut St., cor. of 7th . . . [cop. 1857]. RT

Music only. Lithograph on cover by T. Sinclair's Lith., Philadelphia, of four-oared barge with Undine pennant.

LITTLE Charley's games and sports. Philadelphia: C. G. Henderson & Co., no. 164 Chestnut Street, 1852. RT

Thirty-two pp. printed on one side only, frontispiece. At end: *A catalogue of entertaining and instructive juvenile books . . . ,* pp. [1]–11. Page numbers on inside margins.

1856: Philadelphia, C. G. Henderson, & Co., N w. Corner Arch and Fifth Streets RT

Text same, but page numbers at center bottom of each page. At end: *A catalogue of popular and instructive juvenile and other valuable works,* pp. [1]–16.

LITTLE Charley's games and sports. *Continued:*

1857: Little Charley's picture home book: or Treasury of amusement and pleasing instruction. Numerous engravings. Philadelphia: C. G. Henderson & Co. N

Little Charley's Games and Sports is included.

1858: Philadelphia, C. G. Henderson & Co. . . . RT

Text same as 1856 ed. At end: *A catalogue of popular and instructive juvenile and other valuable works,* pp. [1]-16.

The LITTLE fisherman. New York: Printed and sold by Mahlon Day, At the New Juvenile Book-store, No. 374, Pearl-street [1844]. RT

Vest pocket juvenile. Vignette and verse on title page, small cuts throughout text. Gilt paper cover.

The LITTLE keepsake; or, Easy lessons in words of one syllable. New Haven: S. Babcock [ca. 1835].

Cut of game of cricket.

A LITTLE pretty book, intended for the instruction and amusement of Little Master Tommy, and Pretty Miss Polly. With two letters from Jack the Giant-Killer. New York: Printed by Hugh Gaine, 1762.

Small woodcuts of games, including baseball and angling. First published London, 1744. First mention of baseball in United States. No copy known. Evans: 20459.

1787: A little pretty pocket-book . . . The first Worcester edition. Worcester, Massachusetts, Isaiah Thomas. N

London edition has this title. Originally issued in gilt-stamped paper, with edges cut. Uncut copies were later made up from sheets and bound in boards. *See:* Henderson, Robert William. *Ball, bat and bishop.* New York, Rockport Press, 1947, or Detroit, Gale Research Co., 1974.

[LITTLEFORD, Mrs.]. The Wreath: or, Verses on various subjects. By a Lady of Lexington. Lexington, Kentucky: Printed by D. Bradford, 1820.

Boards, calf back. *The Hunter's Call,* pp. 9-12. First edition of one of the earliest volumes of Western verse. Wegelin (#1041) records only the second edition of 1828. Noted in: Howard S. Mott Catalogue. October, 1959.

LIVERMORE, A. A. Physical education; a lecture delivered before the teachers of Hamilton and Butler Co. Ohio, on several different occasions. Published by request. Cincinnati: Stanhope S. Rowe . . . 1855.   RT

Paper covers.

[LONGSTREET, Augustus Baldwin.] Georgia scenes, characters, incidents &c., in the first half century of the Republic. By a native Georgian. Augusta, Ga.: Printed at the S.R. Sentinel Office, 1835.   N

Boards, cloth back, paper label. A series of newspaper sketches, including: *The fox hunt, The shooting match,* etc. Of considerable influence in American literature, and frequently imitated. *See:* Wade, John David. *Augustus Baldwin Longstreet* . . . New York, Macmillan, 1924. Though Longstreet attempted to suppress *Georgia Scenes* when he entered the Methodist ministry, fifteen printings were made before 1860. Wright's *American Fiction* 1774-1850, revised edition, 1948, locates eight copies.

1840: Second edition, with original illustrations. New York, Harper & Brothers.

1842: Second edition. New York, Harper & Brothers.   LC

1843: Second edition. New York, Harper & Brothers.   RT

1845: Second edition. New York, Harper & Brothers.

1846: Second edition. New York, Harper & Brothers.   LC

1847: Second edition. New York, Harper & Brothers.   N

1848: Second edition. New York, Harper & Brothers.

1850: Second edition. New York, Harper & Brothers.   N

1851: Second edition. New York, Harper & Brothers.   N

1852: Second edition. New York, Harper & Brothers.   N

1854: Second edition. New York, Harper & Brothers.   LC

1856: Second edition. New York, Harper & Brothers.   N

1857: Second edition. New York, Harper & Brothers.   LC

1858: Second edition. New York, Harper & Brothers.

1859: Second edition. New York, Harper & Brothers.   LC

Editions 1840 to 1859, all called *Second edition,* are identical, except for dates on title-pages.

LOVER, Samuel. Slaying the deer. No. 2 of the Songs of America, written and composed by Samuel Lover. New York: Published by Firth, Hall & Pond . . . 1847.　　　　　　　　　　　　RT

Words and music. Two lithographs on cover by C. Parsons: One a deer-hunting scene, the other, "Sleighing the Deer." Verso of title-page blank.

1847: New York.　　　　　　　　　　　　　　　　　RT

A variant of the above, with the text beginning on verso of title-page.

LOW, Samuel. Poems . . . In two volumes. Vol. 1 [–2]. New York: Printed by T. & J. Swords, No. 99 Pearl-Street, 1800.　N

On a small fish caught by angling. Vol. 2, pp. 152-154.

LYON, C. B. My bonnie steed. Ballad, music composed and respectfully dedicated to Mrs. Mary R. F. Lyon, by C. B. Lyon. Boston: Published at Keith's Music Publishing House, 67 & 69 Court Street, 1845.　　　　　　　　　　　　　RT

Words and music. Lithograph on cover of lady equestrian, dog in fore-ground, by E. W. Bouvé.

M'DOWELL, John. Sermon on horse racing; preached in the Presbyterian Church, Elizabeth-Town, September 17, 1809 by the Rev. John M'Dowell, A.M. Pastor of the said Church. Published by request of several who heard it. Elizabeth-Town, N.J.: Printed by Isaac V. Kollock, 1809.　　　　　　　　　AAS

Paper covers.

McLELLAN, Isaac. The angler's song. *See:* The MEMORIAL, a Christmas and New Year's offering.

MAEDER, James G. Gymnastic galopade. Composed & dedicated to John Sheridan, Esq. by James G. Maeder. Boston: Published by Wm. H. Oakes . . . [cop. 1843].　　　　RT

Music only. Lithograph on cover shows games: boxing, fencing, cricket, skating, etc.

[MANT, Alicia Catherine.] Ellen and George: or, The game at cricket. By the author of "Ellen, the young godmother;" "The young naturalist;" &c. &c. Boston: Published by Munroe and Francis. No. 123 Washington-Street; and C. S. Francis, 252 Broadway, New-York [1827].　　　　　　　　　　N

Vignette title-page, frontispiece, and 1 pl. showing game of cricket. Bound with her: Tales for Ellen. By the author of "Ellen, the young godmother;"

MANT, Alicia Catherine. *Continued:*

"The young naturalist;" &c. &c. Vol. 1, Containing Harry, the peasant; Ellen & George, or The game at cricket; The little blue bag. Boston: Published by Munroe and Francis, No. 128 Washington-Street; and C. S. Francis, 189 Broadway, New York [1827]. Boards, with title on cover, and vignette. Back cover has seal: *Munroe & Francis' Juvenile Library.* Boston State House in center.

MANUAL of the arts, for young people . . .
      See: The YOUNG lady's book: a manual
            of elegant recreations . . .

A MANUAL of cricket and base ball, containing plans for laying out the grounds, plans for forming clubs, &c., &c.; to which are added Rules and regulations for cricket, adopted by the Marylebone Club; also, Rules and regulations which govern several celebrated base ball clubs. Illustrated. Boston: Mayhew & Baker . . . 1858.   RT

The second edition of this work appeared under two separate titles:

1859: The base ball player's pocket companion: containing Rules and regulations for forming clubs, directions for playing the "Massachusetts game," and the "New York game," from official reports. Boston, Mayhew & Baker . . .   RT

Illustrated. Advertisement on p. [35] reads: *Uniform with Base ball player's companion. The cricket player's pocket companion . . .*

1859: The cricket player's pocket companion. Containing plans for laying out the grounds, forming clubs, &c., &c., to which are added Rules and regulations for cricket, Adopted by the Maryle-Bone Club. Boston: Mayhew & Baker . . .   RT

Illustrated. Verso of title: "Announcement. This work is really the Second Edition of a book issued by the present publishers in the Spring of 1858, under the title of "A Manual of Cricket and Base Ball," containing, however, only the matter relating to Cricket, Base-ball being treated in another book of the same size and style . . ."

1860: The cricket player's pocket companion. Containing plans for laying out the grounds, forming clubs, &c., &c., to which are added Rules and regulations for cricket, Adopted by the Maryle-Bone Club. Boston: Mayhew & Baker, 208 Washington Street.   RT

Illustrated. Text same as 1859 edition, but with slight variations in setting. Advertisement on p. [35] is identical with 1859, but that on p. [36] is different.

MARKHAM, [J. and others]. The citizen and countryman's experienced farrier. Containing, I. The most approved method of ordering . . . so as to strengthen wind, and give large breath to the running or race-horse . . . By J. Markham, G. Jefferies, and discreet Indians. London, Printed; — and, Wilmington, Reprinted, and sold by James Adams . . . 1764.   RT

Edited by John Millis. Evans: 9718.

1797: Baltimore, Printed by Samuel Sower.   RT

Evans: 32419.

1798: Baltimore.

1803: By J. Markham, G. Jefferies, and experienced Indians. Baltimore, Printed and sold by Samuel Sower.   RT

1839: The citizen and countryman's experienced farrier: containing, I. The most and best approved method of ordering, dieting, exercising . . . horses . . . II. A certain sure method to know the true state of any horse's body . . . By J. Markham, G. Jefferies, and experienced Indians. Chambersburg, Printed by Thomas J. Wright.   RT

Introduction signed: C. D. Lesher. *See: James Adams: the first printer of Delaware. In:* Bibliographical Society of America. *Papers.* Vol. 28, pt. I, 1934.

[ca. 1840:] The citizen and countryman's experienced farrier, containing a description of the symptoms and causes of the various diseases to which the horse is liable, and the most approved remedies, employed for cureing of the same . . . By J. Markham, G. Jefferies, and experienced Indians. Chambersburg, Printed by Thomas J. Wright.   AAS

1841: Chambersburg.

MARRYAT, F[rederick]. Snarleyyow; or, The dog fiend. An historical novel. By Capt. F. Marryat, author of "Peter Simple," "Japhet, in search of a father," "Mr. Midshipman Easy," &c. &c. Complete in two volumes. Vol. I [–II]. Philadelphia: E. L. Carey and A. Hart, 1837.   RT

First published London, 1837.

1837: New York, W. H. Collyer.   N

MARSH, George P. Reports, made under authority of the Legislature of Vermont on the artificial propagation of fish. Burlington: Free Press Print, 1857.   RT

Paper covers. Reprints: Massachusetts. *Report of Commissioners . . . Concerning the Artificial Propagation of Fish, Boston,* 1857.

MARSHALL, Josiah T. The farmer's and emigrant's hand-book: being a full and complete guide for the farmer and the emigrant. Comprising the clearing of forest and prairie land—gardening—farming generally—farriery—cookery—and the prevention and cure of diseases. With copious hints, recipes, and tables. By Josiah T. Marshall, author of The emigrant's true guide. Chicago: Hopkins, Douglas & Co., 1853.   RT

MARSHALL, L. G. The Arabian art of taming and training wild and vicious horses. *See:* RAREY, John Solomon.

MARSHALL, Leonard. Hunter's glee. Words from the German. Music composed and respectfully dedicated to his brother Wyzeman Marshall by Leonard Marshall . . . Boston: Geo. P. Reed & Co., 13 Tremont St. [cop. 1854].   RT

Words and music. Stag and game-bird shooting.

MASON, Richard. The gentleman's new pocket companion, comprising a general description of the noble and useful animal, the horse; together with the quickest and simplest mode of fattening; necessary treatment while undergoing excessive fatigue, or on a journey; the construction and management of stables; different marks for ascertaining the age of a horse, from three to nine years old. With a concise account of the diseases to which the horse is most subject, with such remedies as long experience has proven to be effectual. By Richard Mason of Surry County, Virginia. Petersburg: Printed by John Dickson, Bollingbrook Street, 1811.

Five plates, leaf of *Errata,* and *List of Subscribers.* Copy in Duke University Library. Of importance because it "eventually [became] the vehicle which brought into the world the first Stud Book printed in America." The copyright was acquired by Peter Cottom, of Richmond, Va., who changed the title in subsequent editions to: *The Gentleman's New Pocket Farrier. . . .*
The *Richmond Daily Compiler* of May 11, 1813, advertised an edition *Embellished with Six Elegant Engravings,* "Just Published and for sale by Samuel Pleasants." Possibly this is a second Petersburg edition of 1813.

The Virginia Argus of March 19, 1814, advertised an edition also *Embellished with Six Elegant Engravings,* "Just Published and for sale at S. Pleasant's Book Store, Richmond." Possibly this is a third Petersburg edition of 1814. No copies of the 1813 and 1814 editions have been located. The first Richmond edition is that of 1820. *See* p. xxiii.

1820: Second edition. The gentleman's new pocket farrier . . . Richmond, Printed by Peter Cottom. N

1825: Third edition. Richmond, Printed by Peter Cottom. RT

1828: Fourth edition. . . . To which is added an Appendix, containing observations and receipts . . . Also, Annals of the turf, or Virginia stud book. [By George W. Jeffreys.] Richmond, Printed by Peter Cottom. LC

First appearance in America, in book form, of a Stud Book. *See:* Jeffreys, G. W.

1828: Appendix to Mason's Farrier, containing observations and receipts for the cure of most of the common distempers incident to horses, oxen, cows, calves, sheep, lambs, swine, dogs, &c. &c. Selected from different authors. Richmond: Printed by Peter Cottom, and for sale at his law and miscellaneous book-store, near the Eagle Hotel. RT

Title page, pp. [159]–300, Table of contents, pp. [1]–4. Undoubtedly issued separately. An adqvertisement of 1828 reads: *The Appendix to Mason's Farrier (Bound separate) Containing . . . Annals of the turf, or Virginia stud book . . . Price 75 cents, bound.* Only known copy.

1830: Fifth edition, with additions. To which is Added A prize essay on mules [By Samuel Wyllys Pomeroy], and an Appendix containing observations and receipts . . . Also, an Adenda [*sic*], containing Annals of the turf, American stud book, Rules for training, racing, &c. Richmond, Printed by Peter Cottom . . . RT

Earliest example of an alphabetical Stud Book printed in America. Pomeroy's *Essay on Mules* is from *The American Farmer,* 1825, Vol. 7, pp. 169–173.

1833: Sixth edition. Richmond, Printed by Peter Cottom. RT

1835: Sixth edition. Richmond, Printed by Peter Cottom. RT

1836: Seventh edition. Richmond, Printed by Peter Cottom. LC

MASON, Richard. *Continued:*

1838: Eighth edition. Richmond, Printed by Peter Cottom. RT

1841: Eighth edition. Philadelphia, Grigg & Elliott. RT

1842: Philadelphia, Grigg & Elliott.

1845: Eighth edition. Philadelphia, Grigg & Elliot . . . RT

1846: Eighth edition. Philadelphia, Grigg & Elliot . . . RT

1847: Eighth edition. Philadelphia, Grigg, Elliot & Co. . . . RT

1848: Mason's Farrier and stud book—New edition . . . By J. S. Skinner. Philadelphia, Grigg, Elliott & Co. LC

1849: Mason's Farrier and stud book—New edition . . . By J. S. Skinner. Philadelphia, Grigg, Elliott & Co. JLO

1850: Mason's Farrier and stud book—New edition . . . By J. S. Skinner. Philadelphia, Lippincott, Grambo & Co. VA. STATE LIB.

1852: Mason's Farrier and stud book—New edition . . . By J. S. Skinner. Philadelphia, Lippincott, Grambo & Co. DEPT. AGRIC.

1853: Mason's Farrier and stud book—New edition . . . By J. S. Skinner. Philadelphia, Lippincott, Grambo & Co. DEPT. AGRIC.

1854: Mason's Farrier and stud book—New edition . . . By J. S. Skinner. Philadelphia, Lippincott, Grambo & Co. RUTGERS

1855: Mason's Farrier and stud book—New edition . . . By J. S. Skinner. Philadelphia, J. B. Lippincott & Co. RT

1856: Philadelphia.

1857: Mason's Farrier and stud book—New edition . . . By J. S. Skinner. Philadelphia, J. B. Lippincott & Co. JLO

1858: Mason's Farrier and stud book—New edition . . . By J. S. Skinner. Philadelphia, J. B. Lippincott & Co. RT

MASSACHUSETTS Bay Colony. At a Council held at Boston the 9th of April, 1677. [Cambridge: Printed by Samuel Green, 1677.] BA

An order against horse racing as "occasioning much mispence of time, and the drawing of many persons from the duty of their particular callings, with the hazard of their limbs and lives." Evans: 234. Notices of horse races appear in: *Boston News Letter,* Aug. 22-29, 1715. Nov. 11-28, 1717. May 15-22, 1721. March 23-30, 1732. *Boston Gazette,* April 19-26, 1725.

MASSACHUSETTS Bay Colony. The book of the general lawes and libertyes concerning the inhabitants of the Massachusetts, collected, out of the records of the General Court. Cambridge, printed according to order of the General Court, 1660.

Earliest printed copy of the 1641 "Liberties" [1641-47]. Established fishing and fowling rights to inhabitants of Massachusetts. *See: Goodspeed.*

MASSACHUSETTS Bay Colony. [The liberties of the Massachusets Colonie in New England. Drawn up by Nathaniel Ward, 1641.]

Established fishing and fowling rights to the inhabitants of Massachusetts. The code was not printed, but nineteen copies were transcribed for the use of officials requiring them. The Boston Athenaeum has only existing copy. Evans: 6.

MASSACHUSETTS Bay Province. Acts and laws, passed by the Great and General Court or Assembly of His Majesty's Province of the Massachusetts-Bay in New-England, begun and held at Boston, upon Wednesday the thirty-first day of May, 1727. And continued by adjournment to the sixteenth day of August following. [Boston: Printed by B. Green, printer to His Honour the Lieut. Governour & Council, for Benjamin Eliot. 1727.] pp. 371–373. RT

Chap. II. *An act to prevent the destruction of wild fowl,* p. 373. These acts were printed as they were enacted, the public printer signaturing and paging so that they could be bound together.

MASSACHUSETTS Bay Province. Acts and laws, passed by the Great and General Court or Assembly . . . upon Wednesday the twenty-seventh Day of May, 1772 . . . [Boston: Printed by Richard Draper . . . 1773.] pp. 479–500. RT

Chap. IV. *An Act to Prevent the Destruction of Salmon and Other Fish in Merrimack River.*
Chap. V. *An Act to Impower the Inhabitants of the Town of Rochester . . . to Regulate the Taking of Fish.*
Chap. VII. *An Act to Regulate the Alewife Fishery in the Town of Halifax . . .*

Chap. X. *An Act to Prevent the Destruction of Alewives and Other Fish in Ipswich River* . . .
Evans: 12849.

MASSACHUSETTS Bay Province. Acts and laws, passed by the Great and General Court or Assembly . . . upon Wednesday the twenty-sixth day of May, 1773 . . . [Boston: Printed by Richard Draper . . . 1774.] pp. 509–516.   RT

Chap. II. *An Act Making Further Provision for Regulating the Alewives Fishery in the Town of Bridgwater.*
Chap. V. *An Act in Addition to* . . . *"An Act . . . to Prevent the Destruction of Salmon and Other Fish in Merrimack River . . ."*
Chap. VI. *An Act for Continuing an Act Intitled, "An Act to Impower the Inhabitants of the Town of Dartmouth to Regulate the Taking of Fish . . ."*
Not in Evans.

MASSACHUSETTS Bay Province. Acts and laws passed by the Great and General Court or Assembly of the Province of the Massachusetts-Bay in New England: begun and held at Boston the twenty-ninth of May, 1700 . . . pp. 193–204. [Boston: Printed by Bartholomew Green, and John Allen . . . 1700.]
                                                                          N

An act for tolling horses that are to be exported. For the better preventing the stealing of horses and horse-kind . . . pp. 195-196.

MASSACHUSETTS Bay Province. Temporary acts and laws of His Majesty's Province of the Massachusetts-Bay in New England. Boston; New England: Printed by Order of His Excellency the Governor, Council and House of Representatives: and sold by Green and Russell in Queen-Street. 1763.   RT

Eight acts, extending to p. 179, including *The Table,* pp. [i]-x, and *The Titles of the Acts,* pp. [i]-viii. Later acts, through 1768 are bound in, and continuously paged to p. 274.
Contains:
An act for preventing mischief by unruly dogs. 1743.
An act to prevent mischief being done by unruly dogs, 1744.
An act to prevent the destruction of wild fowl, 1747.
An act to prevent firing the woods, 1753.
An act to prevent any persons obstructing the fish in their passing up into Monatiquot-River.
An act to prevent damage by horses going at large.
An act for the preservation and increase of moose and deer, 1763.

An act for the effectual preventing of horses . . . from running at large.
An act to prevent gaming for money or other gain. [*Mentions tennis*] *1763.*
An act to prevent the destruction of salmon and other fish in Merrimack-River, 1765
An act to prevent damage being done in the woods, 1765.
An act for amending . . . An act to prevent the destruction of salmon and other fish in the Merrimack River, 1766

MASSACHUSETTS Shooting Club. Constitution and by-laws of the Massachusetts Shooting Club. Boston, **1848**.

Paper covers. Perhaps the first organization for the conservation of game birds.

MASSACHUSETTS Society for Encouraging the Breed of Fine Horses. Articles of the Massachusetts Society for Encouraging the Breed of Fine Horses. Boston: Printed for the Society. J. Belcher, Printer, 1810. N

Paper covers.

MASSACHUSETTS State. Report of Commissioners appointed under Resolve of 1856, Chap. 58, Concerning the artificial propagation of fish, with other documents. Boston: William White . . . **1857.** RT

Reprints: *Pisciculture,* by Jules Haime, translated from *Revue des Deux Mondes,* June, 1854. This report was reprinted in: Marsh, George P., *Report . . . on the Artificial Propagation of Fish,* Burlington, 1857.

MATSELL, George W. Vocabulum; or, The rogue's lexicon. Compiled from the most authentic sources. New York: Published by George W. Matsell & Co. . . . [1859]. N

Portrait frontispiece. Includes list of words: *The Gambler's Flash, Billiard Players, Pugilists.*

[MAXWELL, William Hamilton.] Wild sports of the West. With legendary tales and local sketches. By the author of "Stories of Waterloo" . . . In two volumes. New York: Printed and published by J. & J. Harper . . . 1833. N

First published London, 1832. "The West," i.e., Western Ireland.

1847: Third edition. New York, Harper & Brothers. 2 vols. LC

MAYHEW, Edward. Dogs: their management. Being a new plan of treating the animal, based upon a consideration of his natural temperament. Illustrated by numerous woodcuts . . . London: G. Routledge & Co. . . . New York, 1854.   RT

Reprinted in the 1856 edition of Jonathan Peel's *The Sportsman's Vade Mecum.*

MAYO, W[illiam] S[tarbuck]. Kaloolah, or Journeyings to the Djébel Kumri: an autobiography of Jonathan Romer. Edited by W. S. Mayor, M.D. New-York: George P. Putnam, 155 Broadway. London: David Bogue, 86 Fleet-Street, 1849.   RT

Extra engraved title-page. Chapter VI. A *hunting expedition* [on the Raquette River, Adirondacks, N. Y.].

MAZZINGHI, J. *See:* SCOTT, Sir Walter. Huntsman rest! Thy chace is done.

The MEMORIAL, a Christmas & New Years' offering . . . Edited by F. S. H. Boston: Published by True & Greene [1826].   RT

Gold and blind-tooled leather, gilt edges. Contains *Scenes in America,* by Hermano, describing a hunting party in West Tennessee, 1815. Also, *The angler's song,* attributed to Isaac McLellan. Engraved title-page with vignette, and three engravings, full page. Editor: F. S. Hill.

MERRYMAN, Grandfather, *pseud. See:* GRANDFATHER Merryman.

METAIRIE Jockey Club. Rules and regulations of the Metairie Jockey Club. New Orleans, 1838.   H

A METHOD of raising and training pointers, with instructions and precautions in selecting them; an account of the several disorders to which they are subject, and the proper treatment and medicines in such cases. Translated from a celebrated Italian author . . . Charleston: No. 260, King Street, 1799.

Evans: 35817.

METHODIST Episcopal Church. Tract Society. No. 120. On gambling. "Touch not, taste not, handle not."—Bible. [New York:] Published by J. Emory and B. Waugh, for the Tract Society of the Methodist Episcopal Church, at the Conference Office, 14 Crosby-street. J. Collord, Printer [ca. 1840.]   RT

No title page. Title from colophon.

MILES, William. The horse's foot and how to keep it sound. With illustrations. From the third London Edition. New York: D. Appleton & Company; Philadelphia: G. S. Appleton, 1847.

LC

First published London, 1845.

1853: *In:* Stewart, J. Stable economy. New York: D. Appleton & Company.

N

1856: New York: C. M. Saxton & Company.

RT

MILES, William. A plain treatise on horse-shoeing. With illustrations. Philadelphia: Henry Carey Baird, (successor to E. L. Carey,) no. 7 Hart's Buildings, Sixth St. above Chestnut, 1856.

RT

Eight plates, but plate VIII comes between III and IV.
48 pp. with *Publications of Henry Carey Baird* at end, pp. 1–16.

MILLER, David. The practical horse farrier. Containing a treatise on the different diseases of horses, and the cures for the same. Hamilton, Ohio: Printed for the publisher by E. Shaeffer, 1830.

RT

MILLER, James William. Poems and sketches, by the late James William Miller. Boston: Published by Carter & Hendee, Eastburn's Press, 1830.

RT

Highland ballad. The Hunter, pp. 40–41, *Angler's reminiscences, White Island* [deer hunting], pp. 114–121, *Angler's reminiscence, The floe fishing,* pp. 130–33.

MILLER, Thomas. The boy's winter book descriptive of the season, scenery, rural life, and country amusements. By Thomas Miller, author of "Beauties of the country," "Rural sketches," etc. With thirty-six illustrations. New York: Harper & Brothers, publishers, 82 Cliff Street, 1847.

RT

Colored frontispiece and extra title-page, small engravings throughout text. Includes short articles on wild fowling, football, fox hunting etc. Blind and gilt tooling on binding, with title: *The boy's own library. Winter book.*

MILLER & FOX. Strong documents in regard to the "Fox Morgan." Owned by Miller & Fox, New Ipswich, N.H. Fitchburg: Printed by E. & J. F. D. Garfield, No. 176 Main Street [1856].

Engraving of horse by S. S. Brown on title-page.

MILLIKEN, E. P. *See:* IRVING, John B.

MILLIS, John, editor. *See:* MARKHAM, J.

MILLS, James. The horse-keeper's guide. With engravings. New York: Mowatt, 1844.　　　　　　　HCL

First published London, 1843.

1847: The horse-keeper's guide. Philadelphia, G. B. Zieber & Co.

3 plates and illustrations in text.　　　　　　　RT

MILLS, John. The modern system of farriery: showing the most approved methods of breeding, rearing, and fitting for use, all kinds of horses . . . To which is added, A successful method of treating the canine species in that destructive disease called the distemper. Boston: Printed and sold by William Spotswood, 1796.　　　　　　　RT

Evans: 30797. *See also:* Taplin, William.

MILLS, John. The sportsman's library; or, Hints on the hunter—hunting-hounds—shooting—game—sporting-dogs—fishing　　&c. &c. Philadelphia: Lea & Blanchard, 1846.　　　　　　　RT

First published Edinburgh, 1845.

[MILNOR, William, Jr.] An authentic historical memoir of the Schuylkill Fishing Company in the State in Schuylkill. From its establishment . . . in the year 1732, to the present time. By a member . . . Philadelphia: Published by Judah Dobson, 1830.

First issue of the first edition, without the paragraph on p. viii beginning: *The accompanying miniature of Governor Morris* . . . and without the portrait of Governor Morris by St. Memin. Frontispiece and one portrait; frontispiece, *Castle of the State in Schuylkill,* also in *American Turf Register,* vol. 1, pt. 5, 1830. The author's: *Memoirs of the Gloucester Fox Hunting Club* is usually bound with the *Memoir of the Schuylkill Fishing Company. See:* GEE.　　　　　　　Y

1830: An authentic historical memoir of the Schuylkill Fishing Company of the State in Schuylkill. From its establishment . . . in the year 1732, to the present time. By a member . . . Philadelphia: Published by Judah Dobson, 1830.　　　　　　　RT

First edition, later issue. Frontispiece and two portraits, including the "miniature of Governor Morris" mentioned in the paragraph added to the *Introduction* on p. viii.

[MILNOR, William, Jr.] Memoirs of the Gloucester Fox Hunting Club, near Philadelphia . . . Philadelphia: Published by Judah Dobson, 1830. RT

Frontispiece, and portrait of Jonas Cattell. Usually bound with his: *An Authentic Historical Memoir of the Schuylkill Fishing Company . . . ,* but also issued separately. *See: Gee.*

MILTON Society for the Apprehending of Horse Thieves. Constitution of a Society in Milton for apprehending horse thieves. Dedham [Mass.]: Printed by H. Mann . . . High Street, 1848. RT

8 pp. Not bound. RT copy uncut.

MISSOURI Association for the Improvement of the Breed of Horses. Constitution of the Missouri Association for the Improvement of the Breed of Horses. St. Louis: C. Keemle, Book and Job Printer, 1835. N

Paper covers.

MITCHELL, Samuel L. Reports, in part, of Samuel L. Mitchell, M.D. Professor of Natural History, &c. on the fishes of New-York . . . New-York: Printed by D. Carlisle—no. 301 Broadway, Jan. 1, 1814.

Probably published with paper wrappers. Copy in New York Historical Society.

MITFORD, Mary Russell. Our village: sketches of rural character and scenery. New York: E. Bliss, 1828. 2 vols.

First published London, 1824. Reference to game of baseball, vol. 2, p. 23. "Better than playing with her doll, better even than base-ball, or sliding or romping, does she like to creep of an evening to her father's knee."

MOORE, B. W. The horseman's friend, or pocket counsellor, by D. B. W. Moore, of New York. A complete practical system. With the causes and remedies for all the diseases the horse is subject to, and all of the jockey tricks that is practiced, with a complete system of farriering horses. [New York? ca. 1840.] RT

Wrappers. Vignette of horse on title-page.

MOORE, Edward. The gamester, a tragedy, as performed by the Old American Company. At the Theatre, in Southwark, Philadelphia . . . Philadelphia: Printed and sold by E. Story . . .

MOORE, Edward. *Continued:*

[1790]. (The American theatre . . . Philadelphia, 1792. Vol. 1,
No. 1.)   RT

At head of title: *American Edition.* First published London, 1753. Evans:
22675.

1791: Philadelphia, Printed and sold by Henry Taylor.   N

Not in Evans.

1806: New York, D. Longworth.   N

1820: Baltimore, Printed and published by J. Robinson.   N

1825: New York, C. Wiley.   N

1846: New York, W. Taylor; Baltimore, Taylor, Wilde & Co.
(Modern standard drama. Edited by Epes Sargent. [Vol. II.]
(No. XIII.)   LC

[1856:] New York, S. French. (French's standard drama. No.
13.)   RT

MOORE, [Thomas]. The gazelle. From Moore's National
Melodies. The accompaniments by Sir Henry R[owley] Bishop.
Philadelphia: Published & Sold by Geo. Willig, 171 Chestnut
St. [ca. 1830].   RT

Words and music. Lithograph of gazelle at head of text.

MOORE, T[homas]. The rapids, a Canadian boat song. Written
and composed by T. Moore, Esqr. Philadelphia: G. E. Blake
[ca. 1800].

A popular rowing song. Many later editions were published: by G. Graupner, Boston between 1802-1817; Carr & Schetky, Philadelphia, 1806 and
1807(?); J. Hewitt, New York between 1801 and 1810; and E. Riley & Co.,
New York, ca 1825.

[MOORE, Thomas.] Tom Crib's memorial to Congress. With a
preface, notes and appendix. By One of the Fancy: author of
Fudge family, &c. &c. . . . London printed,—1819. New-York:
Reprinted for Kirk and Mercein, C. Wiley and Co. W. B. Gilley,
and A. T. Goodrich and Co. William A. Mercein, printer, 1819.

First published London, 1819. A pugilistic-political poem.   RT

MOORE, Thomas. Wind thy horn my hunter boy, a favorite German air. Sung with the most unbounded applause at the Park Theatre by Charles E. Horn. Written by Thomas Moore, Esq. Arranged by Henry R. Bishop. New York: Published by Firth & Hall, 1, Franklin Sq. [ca. 1836].   RT

Words and music. Hunting wild boar.

[MOREAU DE SAINT-MÉRY, Médéric Louis Elie.] Essai sur la manière d'ameliorer l'éducation des chevaux en Amerique. A Philadelphie: De l'Imprimerie de Moreau de Saint-Méry, 1795.

Evans: 29108.   LCP

1795: An essay on the manner of improving the breed of horses in American. Philadelphia, Printed and Sold by Moreau de Saint-Méry . . .   N

Evans: 29109.

The MORNING walk; with other stories for girls and boys. Embellished with cuts. Providence: Published by Cary and Daniels, 1835.   N

Angling, pp. [17-] 18, with cut. Vignette title-page, frontispiece and small cuts. Yellow paper covers, lettering same as title-page, but with different vignette and borders.

MORRIS, George P. Cheerly o'er the mountains. A popular southern refrain, the poetry written and respectfully dedicated to Major James Phalen by George P. Morris. Music . . . by George Loder. New York: Atwill, Publisher, 201 Broadway [1844]. RT

Words and music. Hunting lithograph by Thayer & Co., Boston, on cover.

MORRIS, George P. A life in the woods. [Verse.] A hunting song. As sung with great applause by Mr. Russell, Mr. Seguin and Mr. F. H. Brown. The words . . . by George P. Morris. The music composed by Francis H. Brown. New York: Published by Atwill, 201 Broadway [cop. 1841].   RT

Words and music. At head of title: New edition. Lithograph of mounted deer hunters by Lewis & Brown, New York, on cover.

1850: New edition. Boston: Published by Oliver Ditson, Washington St. [cop. 1850].   RT

Cover not illustrated.

MOSCHELLES, I. The Swiss hunter. A ballad as sung by Mr. Braham, the music arranged by I. Moschelles. Philadelphia: Kreischmar & Nunns, no. 70 So. Third St. [ca. 1834].   RT

Words and music. RT copy lacks cover.

The MOTHER'S gift, or Remarks on a set of cuts for children . . . Philadelphia: Published by Johnson & Warner . . . 1809.
                                                                          N

Woodcuts of *A net, A bow, A dog*, etc. Companion to: *The father's gift.*

MOXLEY, Alfred. The sports of the village. A new ballad arranged for the pianoforte by Alfred Moxley. Boston: Published by G. Graupner & Co., no. 15, Marlboro' St. [ca. 1835].   RT

Words and music. Reference to fox hunting.

MULLER, Julius E. The merry sleigh-ride galopade, composed for, and as a token of friendship, inscribed to Charles Grobe, by Julius E. Muller. Baltimore: Published by W. C. Peters . . . [cop. 1850].   RT

Music only. Cut of horse-drawn sleigh on cover.

MUNCK, Johann. The coster polka. Composed by Johann Munck. New York: William Hall & Son, [cop. 1853].   RT

Sheet music. On cover: Tinted lithograph by Sarony & Major. Lady on horseback, side-saddle, in riding habit. At head of title: *To Mrs. Henry Chadwick.*

MUNCK, Johann. The stag leap polka redowa. New York: Wm. Hall & Son [cop. 1852].   RT

Music only. Full-page colored lithograph of stag on cover.

[MURRAY, Sir Charles Augustus]. The trapper's bride: or Spirit of adventure. By the author of The Prairie Bird . . . Cincinnati: Published by Stratton and Barnard, 1848.   N

Brown-paper covers. Title within borders. Plate with two woodcuts of buffalo hunting, p. 76. Very doubtful if by Murray. Probably issued to take advantage of the popularity of *The Prairie Bird.*

MURRAY, John. To the citizens of the United States of America. New York, 1803.   RT

Quaker pamphlet, signed John Murray. Anti-horse-racing, cockfighting, etc.

MY dog and my gun. Boston, [1818?].   RT

Broadside, RT copy clipped to 24.3 cm. x 18.7 cm. 4 small woodcuts at head.
A romantic hunting poem. Verso: Obolition of slavery!!!! Grand sele-
brashum by de Africum Shocietee!!!!!! Bosson, Uly, 18180. Woodcut of
uniformed blacks marching. Clipped at bottom, breaks into text.

NAPIER, [Edward Delaval Hungerford] Elers. Wild sports in
Europe, Asia and Africa. Philadelphia: E. Ferrett & Co. . . .
1846.   HCL

First published London, 1844.

NARRAGANSET Boat Club. Constitution, by-laws and drill
of the Narraganset Boat Club, Providence, R.I. Instituted July
4, 1837. Providence: Wm. Simons, Jr., Printer. 1838.   RT

Blue paper covers.

NASH, E[phraim]. The farmer's practical horse farriery. Containing practical rules on buying, breeding . . . To which is
prefixed An account of the breeds in the United States. With
numerous illustrations. Compiled by E. Nash . . . Auburn and
Buffalo: Ephraim Nash [1857].   LC

At head of title: *A Book for Every Farmer*, 14th thousand, revised.

1858: Auburn, Ephraim Nash.   RT

1858: The farmer's practical horse farriery. Containing practical
rules on buying, breeding, breaking, lameness, . . . To which is
prefixed An account of the breeds in the United States. With
numerous illustrations. Compiled by E. Nash . . . Auburn, H. A.
Yates.   RT

At head of title: *A book for every farmer.*

1859: Auburn, Ephraim Nash: New York, C. M. Saxton.   JLO

1859: The farmer's practical horse farriery. Containing Rarey's
Art of taiming [sic] vicious horses, with illustrated instructions,
practical rules on buying, breeding . . . To which is prefixed An
account of the breeds in the United States. With numerous illustrations. 10th thousand revised. [By Ephraim Nash.] Copy right
secured. Goshen; Dr. J. H. Reevs.   RT

At head of title: *A book for every farmer.* Chapter III of earlier editions
is: *B. F. Davis' new method of taming wild horses,* which is a piracy of

J. S. Rarey's *Modern art of taming wild horses.* In the Reevs' 1859 edition, Chapter III is: *The American art of taming, and breaking horses. Originally systematized by John S. Rarey,* which although credited to Rarey, is undoubtedly pirated. Most of the pages of the chapter are from the same plates as the earlier editions.

NEFF, Henrich. Das durch viele Curen bestatigte, und sicher befundene Pferdarzney-Buchlein . . . Ephrata: Gedruckt bey Bauman und Cleim, 1804.

Wrappers, sewn. 52 pp. Noted in James Lewis Hook, Catalogue 354, 1955, no. 275, which states "possibly unique copy."

NELSON, S., composer. *See:* JEFFREYS, C. J. The merry days of old.

NETTLE, Richard. The salmon fisheries of the St. Lawrence and its tributaries. Montreal: Printed by John Lovell . . . 1857.

N

Chapters: *Artificial Fly Fishing,* and *Trout Fishing.*

NEUER erfahrner, Amerikanischer, Haus- und Stallarzt, mit den natürlichsten, und leichtesten Mitteln, wider alle Kranckheiten, und Schwachhetien, der Menschen und Viehe. Zum Nutzen der Deutschen Nation in den Vereinigten Staaten . . . Friederich-Stadt [Md.]: Gedruckt, verlegt und zu haben bey Matthias Bärtgis, 1794.

Second title:

Zweyter Theil des neuen erfahrnen, amerikanischen Haus- und Stallarztes. Zum Nutzen der Deutschen Nation in den Vereinigten Staaten. Copy-Right secured according to Law. Friederich-Stadt [Md.]: Gedrucht bey Matthias Bärtgis, 1794. RT

2 v. in 1. Evans: 27362.

NEUKOMM, S. The daring huntsman, composed by Chevalier S. Neukomm. Arranged for four voices by I. B. Woodbury. Boston: Published by C. Bradlee & Co., 184 Washington Street. 1846. RT

Words and music. Chamois hunting.

The NEW American pocket farrier and farmer's guide in the choice and management of horses . . . From the writings of Youatt, Lawrence, Hines, White, Clayter [*sic*], and others . . . Philadelphia: John B. Perry . . . New York: Nafis & Cornish . . . [1845].   LC

[Cop. 1845:] Philadelphia, Published by Leary & Getz . . .   RT

NEWBURGH Base Ball Club. By-laws, and rules and regulations of the Newburgh Base Ball Club. Instituted September 1858. Newburgh [N.Y.]: Gray & Lawson, Printers, 1858.   RT

22 pp. Rules and Regulations of the game of Base Ball, Adopted by the National Convention of Base Ball Players, held in New York, March 10, 1858.

NEWDEGATE, C. V. Sketches from the Washington races in October 1840. By an eye witness. [ca. 1840.]

Three colored lithographic plates by C. V. Newdegate. 4-line stanza beneath each plate. Oblong folio, in wrappers. A very rare series of American humorous racing plates. The title-page is slightly narrower than the plates. The plates are without dates or watermarks. Title from Parke-Bernet Catalogue No. 608: Widener sale, November 29, 1944.

The NEW England farrier. *See:* JEWETT, Paul.

NEW HAMPSHIRE. Report of the Special Committee on the Propagation and Preservation of Fish, June, 1857. Concord [N.H.]: George F. Fogg, 1857.   RT

Paper covers.

NEW JERSEY. Acts of the General Assembly of the Council of New-Jersey . . . Compiled . . . by Samuel Allinson. Burlington, [N.J.]. Printed by Isaac Collins . . . 1776.   N

An Act for the better preservation of deer in the Township of Morris. Passed September 26, 1772, p. 384.

NEW JERSEY. [Acts of the General Assembly.] February 20, 1835.

Manuscript, two pages, folio. An original legislative act of the State of New Jersey, prohibiting "prize-fighting," even spectators are "regarded as guilty." Listed in Catalog 8 of Charles Hamilton, New York.

NEW JERSEY. Acts of the twenty-first General Assembly of the State of New Jersey. At the session begun at Trenton on the twenty-fifth day of October, seventeen hundred and ninety-six, and continued by adjournment. Being the first sitting. Trenton: Printed by Matthias Day, Printer to the State M,DCC, XCVI.   N

An Act to prevent gaming, February 8, 1797, pp. 149-51. Prevents gaming at cards, dice, billiards, bowls, tennis, cockfighting, etc. RT has original manuscript. An Act to prevent horse racing waas passed in February, 1811.

NEW-YORK Association for the Improvement of the Breed of Horses. Articles and rules of the New-York Association for the Improvement of the Breed of Horses. New-York: Printed by J. Seymour . . . 1823.   HTP

Racing vignette on title-page, See p. xxiv.

[NEW YORK CITY.] Document no. 41, Board of Assistants, July 2, 1832. The Police Commissioner presented the following report, together with a law regulating hackney coaches, carriages, and stage coaches . . . [New York,] 1832.   JLO

NEW YORK CITY. A law for preserving the fish in Fresh-water Pond [New York, 1734.]   H

Broadside, dated May 28, 1734. Not in Evans.

NEW YORK Clipper. Sporting and theatrical journal. New York, 1853–1924.   N

NEW YORK Jockey Club. Rules and regulations adopted by the New-York Jockey Club, April 9th, 1836. [New York, 1836.] N

11 pp., pink paper covers. Front cover, probably with title, missing from N copy. Rules for races "at the Union Course".

The NEW YORK monthly. Vol 1, no. 1–4. New York, 1854.

All published. Includes: *The game bag of sportsman, A pigeon hunt on the Ohio, A wild-hog hunt in Texas, Swan-shooting by torchlight, A coon chase in Kentucky, Sparing the musquash,* etc. Noted in letter from Richard G. Wormser, 1955.

The NEW YORK primer; or Second book . . . New York: Published by Samuel Wood & Sons, No. 261 Pearl-Street; and Samuel S. Wood & Co., No. 212, Market-Street, Baltimore, [1823].   AAS

The NEW YORK primer. *Continued:*

Woodcut: *Playing Ball* on back cover, shows a game closely resembling baseball. Not in earlier editions, but first used in: *Children's amusements.* Baltimore, 1820.

The NEW-YORK sporting magazine, and Annals of the American and English turf: a work entirely dedicated to sporting subjects and fancy pursuits; containing the sports of the day, and every thing worthy of notice in relation thereto, occurring in the United States, Canada, or Europe. [List of sports]. Illustrated with engravings and striking representations of the various subjects. Vol. 1, no. 1, March 1833. New-York: Printed for the editor and proprietor, C. R. Colden, by Jared W. Bell Franklin-Hall, no. 17 Ann-Street, near Broadway, MDCCCXXXIII.   RT

Founded and edited by Cadwallader R. Colden in March 1833 as a monthly magazine. Vol. I ran from March 1833 to Vol. I, no. 12, February 1834. Vol. 2, pt. 1 was published in July 1834, and it ceased publication with Vol. 2, no. 6 in December 1834. Undistributed numbers were destroyed by fire, hence complete sets are extremely rare. The MS of the index to Vol. 1 was destroyed in the fire, and never published. Plates are colored by hand: the colors vary on the costumes. *The United States sporting magazine* was "intended as a continuation" of *The New-York sporting magazine.* The following collation was made from the bound copy in the Racquet & Tennis Club.

1 p. l., title-page, v.b., Introduction [etc.], pp. [iii]-xiv. Size: 20 x 27.8 cm. Vol. 1.

No. 1. March, 1833. pp. [1]-42, 2 colored plates and 1 engraved plate.
    p. 1. Col. pl. *Chorister.*
    p. 20. pl. *Riddlesworth.*
    p. 31. Engr. pl. *Hedgeford.*
No. 2. April, 1833. pp. [43]-90, 2 colored plates and 1 engraved plate.
    p. 43. Col. pl. *Birmingham.*
    p. 66. Col. pl. *Priam.*
    p. 76. Engr. pl. *How to train a bull dog.*
No. III. May, 1833. pp. [91]-138, with 2 folded colored plates.
    p. 91. Fold. col. pl. *Extraordinary match by George Osbaldeston, Esqr.*
    p. 117. Fold. col. pl. *The proportions of a horse, by G. H. Laporte.*
No. 4. June, 1833. pp. [139]-194, with 2 colored plates.
    p. 141. Col. pl. *Orville.*
    p. 164. Col. pl. *St. Giles . . . Engraved by J. Bowen . . .*
No. 5. July, 1833. pp. [195]-250, with 2 colored plates.
    p. 195. Col. pl. *Mary Randolph. By Gohanna Dam . . .*
    p. 205. Col. pl. *Valentine. Bred by Mr. Houldsworth . . .*
No. 6. August, 1833. pp. [251]-298. p. 251/2 misnumbered 253/4, pp. 255/6 bis, with 2 colored plates.

The NEW-YORK sporting magazine. *Continued:*

    p. 253. Col. pl. *Mercury.*

    p. 275. Col. pl. [Persian Greyhound *Dudu.*] [Lacking from RT].

No. 7 September, 1833. pp. [299]-346, with 2 colored plates.

    p. 299. Col. pl. *O'Kelly.*

    p. 321. Col. pl. *Tormentor.*

No. 8. October, 1833. pp. [347]-396, with 2 engraved plates.

    p. 347. Engraved plates, *Plate 1, Plate 2,* of horse's leg and feet.

No. 9. November, 1833. pp. [397]-444, with 2 engravings.

    p. 397. Engraved plates, *Plate III, Plate IV,* with 4 engravings of horse's feet on each.

No. 10. December, 1833. pp. [445]-492, with 1 engraved plate.

    p. 477. Engr. pl. *Rockingham.*

No. 11. January, 1834. pp. [493]-540, with 2 engraved plates.

    p. 493. Engraved plates, *Plate V, Plate VI,* of horse's feet. Plate VII evidently not issued.

No. 12. February, 1834. pp. [493]-540. Erroneously duplicating numbering of No. 11, with 2 engravings and errata slip.

    p. 493. Errata slip.

    p. 493. Engraved plate. *Plate VIII.* [Steel tablet expansion shoe.]

    p. 515. Engraved portrait of *W. Crockford.*

Volume 2.

No. 1. July, 1834. pp. [1]-28, [1]-20, with 2 engraved plates. Separate pagination at end is *Racing Calendar.*

    p. 1. Engr. pl. *Henry. Painted by E. Troye, 1834.*

    p. 1. Engr. pl. *Plate IX,* of horseshoes, faced by page: *Explanation of Plate IX.*

No. 2. August, 1834. pp. [29-74]. P. 73/4 misnumbered 75/6, 21-22, with 2 engraved plates.

    p. 29. Engr. pl. *Plate X.* Horseshoes, with page: *Explanation of Plate X.*

    p. 29. Engr. pl. *Woodcock shooting with springers.*

No. 3. September, 1834. pp. [77]-122, 23-24, with 2 engraved plates.

    P. 77. Engr. pl. [Outline] *Portrait of Plenipotentiary, the winner of the Derby, 1834.*

    p. 77. Engr. pl. *Eclipse.*

No. 4. October, 1834. pp. [125]-166, 25-30, with 2 engraved plates.

    p. 125. Engr. pl. [*Portrait of . . . Jem Bland.*]

    p. 125. Engr. pl. *Busiris;* at p. 133 in another copy.

No. 5. November, 1834. pp. [167-202]. pp. 199-202 misnumbered 195-198, 31-42, with 2 engraved plates.

    p. 167. Engr. pl. [Outline of] *Dangerous. Painted by Herring.*

    p. 180. Engr. pl. *Nimrod.*

No. 6. December, 1834.. pp. [199]-242, 43-46, with 2 engraved plates.

    p. 199. Engr. pl. *Chateau Margaux.*

    p. 238. Engr. pl. [Portrait of] *W. Tattersal.*

[NEWTON, Augustus.] An authentic account of the fatal duel fought Sunday the 21st March 1830, near Chester, Penna. be-

NEWTON, Augustus. *Continued:*

tween Mr. Charles G. Hunter, late midshipman of the U.S. Navy, and Mr. William Miller, Jun. late attorney at law of Philadelphia; containing an impartial investigation . . . Washington City: Published by Jonathan Elliot, Bookseller, 1830.   RT

NILES, M. A. H. The sin of duelling. A sermon preached at Marblehead on the fifth of April, 1838; by M. A. H. Niles. Newburyport, 1838.

NIMROD, *pseud. See:* APPERLEY, Charles James.

NORRIS, Charles, & Co. School books. Exeter, N.H. [1813].   RT
Index-note book with cut of two boys playing tops on cover.

NORTH Woods Walton Club. 'O for a lodge in some vast wilderness.' Utica, N.Y.: Curtiss & White [1858].

See: Goodspeed.

[NOYCE, Elisha]. Boy's Own book of sports, birds and animals. New York, Leavitt & Allen . . . [1848].   RT

[NOYCE, Elisha]. The boy's book of sports and games . . . By Uncle John. With illustrations. Philadelphia, G. S. Appleton, 1851.

1852: New York, G. S. Appleton.   RT

1858: New York, Leavitt & Allen.   RT

[NOYCE, Elisha]. Uncle John's panorama. Games and sports. Philadelphia, C. G. Henderson & Co., 1854.

P. 3–26 in accordian form. 19 colored cuts of games in text. Games of ball: colly ball, cricket, "base ball", football, bat ball.

OFFUTT, Denton. Denton Offutt's Method of gentling horses, their selection, and curing their diseases. [Lexington, Fayette Co., Ky. 1846 cop.]   RT
No text on paper covers. Verso title-page reads: Persons having received instructions of me, and one of these books, are expected not to divulge the secrets or lend the book out of their families. Copyright note reads in part: . . . on the twelvth day of October, Anno Domini one thousand eight hundred and forty-six, Denton Offutt, of the said District, hath deposited in this office the Title of a Book . . . Denton Offutt claimed that John Solomon Rarey stole his system of gentling horses.

189

OFFUTT, Denton. A new and complete system of teaching the horse, on phrenological principles: also, A rule for selecting the best animals, and mode of teaching all beasts your will, breeding of horses, and cure of part of their diseases. Cincinnati: Appleton's Queen City Press, 1848.   RT

Illustrations.

1854: The educated horse: teaching horses and other animals to obey at word, sign, or signal, to work or ride; also, The breeding of animals, and discovery in animal physiology, and the improvement of domestic animals. Washington, March, 1854. RT

Illustrations, plates. Offutt was an early associate of Abraham Lincoln. It is known he possessed the ability to calm a fractious horse with a few strokes of his hand, and some gentle words. He left Illinois and travelled through the country; selling the book which was supposed to contain his secret.—Ernest J. Wessen. Letter June 6, 1940.

The OLD American comic almanac. *See:* The AMERICAN comic almanac.

The OLIO: collected by a literary traveller . . . Boston, 1833.
                                                                    RT

Contains: *The Principal Matches and Sweepstakes over the Union Course, L.I.*, a reprint from *The American Turf Register*, Vol. 2, pp. 553-558, July, 1831.

OLIPHANT, George Henry Hewit. The law concerning horses, racing, wagers, and gaming: With an Appendix containing recent cases . . . Philadelphia: T. & J. Johnson, 1847.   DCL

The Law Library. Volume 58, No. 2.

OLNEY, J[esse]. The easy reader; or, Introduction to the national preceptor: consisting of familiar and progressive lessons designed to aid in thinking, spelling, defining and correct reading. New-Haven: Burrie & Peck [cop. 1833].   CU

Illustrations throughout text. *Lazy Lawrence*, p. 59, mentions "playing ball", with woodcut. Game uncertain. Same cut on front cover.

[ONTARIO.] Public Instruction, Department of. Physical training in schools, in a series of gymnastic exercises. Illustrated by upwards of one hundred engravings of the different positions of the gymnast; with an introductory sketch of the athletic games of antiquity. Toronto: Educational Depository, Department of Public Instruction for Upper Canada, 1852.   RT

Paper wrappers. Title also on cover.

ORDWAY, J. P. Athletic waltz, composed & dedicated to John Sheridan, Esq. (Professor of gymnastics) and the athletæ of Boston. By J. P. Ordway. Boston: Published by the Author . . . [cop. 1844].   RT

Lithograph on cover showing interior of gymnasium.

O'ROURK, Samuel. The art of pugilism, by Samuel O'Rourk, the celebrated Irish champion, being a short system of acquiring the art of self defence, without the aid of a professed pugilist. Philadelphia: Printed by John Brereton, Commerce-Street, 1835.   RT

Blue-paper covers, title from cover. Verso of cover has copy of title-page of Dublin edition: Dublin: Printed by C. Crookes, 85, Capel-St., 1834. Title-page missing. *An Abstract of the life of Mr. Samuel O'Rourk* pp. [5]-48; p. [49] has separate title same as cover title. This section covers pp. [49]-60. Small cuts in text.

ORR'S Book of swimming: as practised and taught in civilized and savage nations, and used for the preservation of health and life. Illustrated. New York: J. W. and N. Orr, 1846.   RT

Frontispiece wood engraving and small wood engravings throughout text. RT copy contemporary cloth.

1849: Science of swimming as taught and practiced in civilized nations . . . By an experienced swimmer. New York.   RT

Paper covers, with wood engraving frontispiece of 1846 edition used on cover. No frontispiece, but wood engravings as in 1846 edition except that J. W. & N. Orr's trade vignette is omitted on p. 36.

PADDOCK, Jonathan R. *See:* CLASSICAL and Scientific Academy.

PALLISER, John. The solitary hunter; or, Sporting adventures in the prairies. By John Palliser, Esq. With illustrations. London: G. Routledge & Co. Farringdon Street; New York: 18, Beekman Street, 1856.   RT

PALLISER, John. *Continued:*

Engraved title-page, frontispiece and 6 plates. Printed in England. First published London, 1853 as: *Solitary rambles and adventures of a hunter in the prairies.*

1856: The solitary hunter: or, Sporting adventures in the prairies. The eighth thousand, with illustrations. London, New York, G. Routledge & Co.   Y

[1856:] The solitary hunter; or, Sporting adventures in the prairies. By John Palliser, Esq. With illustrations. New York, R. M. De Witt (Late De Witt & Davenport), publisher, 160 & 162 Nassau Street.   RT

Paper covers. Illustrations throughout text.

[PARIS, J. A.] Philosophy in sport made science in earnest, being an attempt to illustrate the first principles of natural philosophy by the aid of the popular toys and sports of youth. Philadelphia: Lea and Blanchard, 1847.

Title noted in *The Spirit of the Times,* vol. 16, no. 50, February 6, 1847. "From the sixth and greatly improved London edition." First published in London, 1827.

1853: Philosophy in sport made science in earnest: being an attempt to implant in the young mind the first principles of natural philosophy by the aid of the popular toys and sports of youth. Eighth edition, revised and considerably enlarged . . . New York: Clark, Austin & Smith.   RT

Contains references to ball games, including tennis.

PARKINSON, Richard. The experienced farmer, an entire new work, in which the whole system of agriculture, husbandry, and breeding of cattle is explained . . . In two volumes. Philadelphia: Printed by Charles Cist . . . 1799.   AAS

Chapters on the raising of horses. Made up from the sheets of the English edition, with titles only printed in the United States.

PATERSON, Alexander D. The manual of cricket; with numerous illustrations, comprising the laws of the game . . . The whole being intended as a complete cricketer's guide: to which is added the body, and all that is important of "Felix on the bat." By Alexander D. Paterson. New York: Published by Berford & Co., No. 2 Astor House, 1847.   N

13 plates and cuts in text.

PATTIE, James O[hio]. The personal narrative of James O. Pattie, of Kentucky, during an expedition from St. Louis, through the vast regions between that place and the Pacific Ocean, and thence back through the City of Mexico to Vera Cruz . . . Edited by Timothy Flint. Cincinnati: Printed and published by John H. Wood, 1831.

Five engraved plates. Contains some account of bear, deer, and beaver shooting.

1833: Cincinnati, E. H. Flint.

Five engraved plates. Second edition, but using same plates as 1831 edition. Parke-Bernet Catalogue notes: In 1833 Flint's nephew came into possession of unsold copies, printed a new title page, and recopyrighted the book in his own name. This copy has the appendix *Inland Trade with New Mexico.*

1847: The hunters of Kentucky; or The trials and toils of trappers and traders, during an expedition to the Rocky Mountains, New Mexico, and California. "O Kentucky, the Hunters of Kentucky." New York: Wm. H. Graham, Tribune Buildings, 161 Nassau Street.   RT

Purports to be an account of the adventures of "Ben Bilson" and his son, written by the latter, but is a slightly altered and abridged reprint of *The Personal Narrative of James O. Pattie of Kentucky,* Cincinnati, 1833. The three sketches appended in the original are omitted from this reprint. Brown-paper wrappers. Title within borders reads: *The hunters of Kentucky; or, The trials and toils of trappers & traders.* By the captain of an expedition to the Rocky Mountains. New-York: Published by William H. Graham, Tribune Buildings, 1847. Price: 25 cents.

PATTON, Rev. W. W. Duty of Christians to suppress duelling. A sermon preached on the Annual Fast, April 4, 1844, at South Boston. [Boston: Leavitt & Alden, 7 Cornhill, 1844.]   RT

Cover title: Patton on duelling. At head of title: no. 14. RT copy lacks paper covers.

PAXTON, Philip. *See:* HAMMETT, Samuel Adams.

PECK, John M. Life of Daniel Boone. *See:* SPARKS, Jared. The library of American biography.

[PEEL, Jonathan.] The sportsman's vade mecum; by "Dinks." [*Pseud.* of Jonathan Peel.] Edited by Frank Forester. [*Pseud.* of Henry William Herbert.] Containing full instructions in all that relates to breeding, rearing, breaking, kennelling, and conditioning of dogs . . . As also a few remarks on guns—their loading

PEEL, Jonathan. *Continued:*

and carriage . . . New York: Stringer & Townsend . . . 1850.

Frontispiece and 3 plates by Herbert.   N

1853: New York, Stringer & Townsend.   Y

1856: The sportsman's vade mecum . . . and Dogs, their management, by Edward Mayhew . . . New York, Stringer & Townsend.   N

Mayhew's *Dogs: Their Management,* was published separately in 1854.

1857: The dog. By Dinks, [*pseud.*] Mayhew, and Hutchinson. Compiled, abridged, edited, and illustrated by Frank Forester. [*Pseud.* of Henry William Herbert] . . . Complete and revised edition. New York: Stringer & Townsend . . .   RT

The first part appeared first in *The Sportsman's Vade Mecum,* by "Dinks" in 1850, and the second part by Mayhew in the 1856 edition. This is the first appearance of the final part, by W. N. Hutchinson. *See: Van Winkle.*

A PEEP into the sports of youth, and the occupations and amusements of age. To which is added, The ship-wrecked sailor boy. Embellished with fifty-five copper-plates. Philadelphia: Published by Johnson & Warner . . . 1809.   AAS

Includes: *Skating, Cricket, The Sportsman, The Huntsman, The Groom, The Horseman,* etc.

PENDLETON, Mrs. A. V. The wild she deer. Words and accompaniments by Mrs. A. V. Pendleton of N. Ca., Philadelphia: Lee & Walker, 188 Chestnut St., 1854.   RT

Words and music.

[PENN, Richard.] Maxims and hints for an angler: embellished with humorous engravings, illustrative of the miseries of fishing. To which are added Maxims and hints for a chess player. Philadelphia: F. Bell, 1855.   RT

Frontispiece, 8 plates. *See also:* Jesse, Edward.

The PENNSYLVANIA gazette. Containing the freshest advices foreign and domestic. Numb. 371. From January 6. to January 15. 1735, 6. Philadelphia, 1736.   N

Poem: *Fox Hunting,* pp. 1-2. Reprinted from William Somervile's *"The Chace",* Book III. First published London, 1735.

PENNSYLVANIA. Commerce and Manufactures Committee. Memorial of sundry gun manufacturers of the Borough of Lancaster, in the State of Pennsylvania. 4th February, 1803. Referred to the Committee of Commerce and Manufactures. Washington City: Printed by William Duane & Son, 1803.   RT

Most documents of this period were burnt when Washington was destroyed by fire in 1812.

PENNSYLVANIA Province. An act for raising a fund to pay the damages, done by dogs within the city and county of Philadelphia, and the county of Bucks. Philadelphia: Printed by D. Hall, and W. Sellers, 1772.

Evans: 12504.

PENNSYLVANIA Province. In General Assembly, Saturday February 22, 1794. An act for the prevention of vice and immorality and of unlawful gaming, and to restrain disorderly sports and dissipation. [Philadelphia: Printed by T. Bradford, 1794.]
                                                                           N

Not in Evans.

PENNSYLVANIA Province. The laws of the province of Pennsylvania: now in force, collected into one volumn [sic]. Published by order of the General Assembly of the aforesaid province. Philadelphia: Printed and sold by Andrew Bradford . . . 1728.
                                                                           N

Contains: *An Act to Prevent the Killing of Deer out of Season,* August 26, 1721; *An Act to Improve the Breed of Horses and Regulate Rangers,* May 9, 1724. *An Act to Prevent Duelling and Fighting of Duels.* Evans: 3086.

The PEOPLE'S almanac [of useful and entertaining knowledge]. Vol. 1, pt. 1, 1834–[Vol. 2, pt. 4] 1842. Boston: Willard Felt & Co. and Charles Ellms, 1833–[1841].   RT

Imprint varies: 1835-1837. published by Charles Ellms, Agent; 1838, published by S. N. Dickinson; 1839-1842, printed and published by S. N. Dickinson. 1842 not numbered. RT lacks 1836 edition. Imitative of Davy Crockett almanacs. Contains short sketches and cuts of wild boar hunting, mountaineering, rhinoceros hunting, and other sporting subjects.

The PEOPLE'S magazine of useful information. Vol. 1–3. Boston: Lilly, Wait, Colman and Holden, 1833–1836.

A bi-weekly. Articles and illustrations on sport throughout: Hunting the zebra, Kentucky sports, Leopard hunting, Catching turtles on the coast of Cuba, etc. Ran from 23 March, 1833 to 1836. Title-page of volume 1 reads: *People's magazine*, dated 1834. *Union list* records 3 volumes, but does not locate volume 3. HCL has vol. 1–2.

PERRY, M[athew] C[albraith]. Narrative of the expedition of an American Squadron to the China seas and Japan, performed in the year 1852, 1853 and 1854, under the command of Commander M. C. Perry, U.S. Navy, by order of the Government of the United States. Washington, D.C.: Beverley, Tucker, 1856. 33rd Congress, Senate Document no. 79, Vol. 2.　　　　N

Contains narrative of hunting expeditions of Americans in China, p. 224 *ff.* Colored plates.

PETERS, DeWitt C[linton]. The life and adventures of Kit Carson, the nestor of the Rocky Mountains . . . With original illustrations, drawn by Lumley, engraved by N. Orr & Co. New York: W. R. C. Clark & Co. . . . 1858.　　　　N

Plates.

1859: New York, W. R. C. Clark & Meeker . . .　　　　RT

Gilt tooled cover, gilt-edges, plates.

PETERS, Robert C. The practical farrier, or Farmer's guide, in the management of cattle, horses, and sheep, under various diseases. With an explanation of the causes and symptoms attending the different disorders . . . Chester, Conn.: Published by the author. W. D. Starr, print., 1840　　　　RT

Hard-paper cover with title: *The Practical Farrier.* Pp. [1]–2, *Recommendations.*

PHILADELPHIA Glee Association. Kate Kearney, a terzetto. Fly from love's flame, a terzetto, and The boatman's glee. Arranged by request for The Philadelphia Glee Association, with an accompaniment for the piano forte by a Member. Philadelphia: Kretschmar & Nunns, no. 70 So. Third & 196 Chestnut Street [cop. 1834].　　　　RT

Words and music. A rowing song: The boatman's glee is entitled: *The waterman's boast, a glee.*

PHILADELPHIA, Wilmington and Baltimore Rail Road. A minute description of the Philadelphia Wilmington and Baltimore Rail Road, containing a brief but circumstantial notice of every object of interest on the whole route. Also, A detailed account of the various modes of duck shooting, &c. . . . Baltimore: Printed by John Murphy & Co., 1850.   Y

Paper covers.

PHILANTHROPOS, *pseud. See:* LADD, William.

PHILIPPS, Thomas. The hunter's horn. *See:* FITZSIMONS, E.

PHILLIPS, Jonas B. Light may the boat row. Duett sung with the most enthusiastic applause by Mrs. and Miss Watson . . . Written by Jonas B. Phillips, Esqre. The music arranged from a Northumbrian melody, the additions & accompaniments composed and respectfully dedicated to the New York Boat Clubs by J. Watson . . . New York: Published at Atwill's Music Saloon, 201 Broadway . . . [1836].

Words and music. Lithograph of boat race on cover. Copy in New York Historical Society.

1836: Light may the boat row . . . dedicated to the Amateur Boat Club Association by J. Watson . . . New York, Published at Atwill's Music Saloon, No. 201 Broadway . . .   RT

PHILOSOPHY in sport made science in earnest. *See:* PARIS, J. A.

PHYSICAL training in schools . . . *See:* ONTARIO. Public Instruction, Dept.

[PICTON, Thomas.] Paul Preston's Book of gymnastics: or, Sports for youth. A legacy, to promote the health and long life of his youthful friends. Boston: Munroe and Francis, 1841. RT

Frontispiece, and numerous small cuts throughout text. Includes: *Horse exercise.*

1842: Boston, Munroe and Francis.   RT

1847: Boston, Munroe and Francis.   RT

Frontispiece and numerous illustrations in text.

197

PICTON, Thomas. *Continued:*

1857: *In:* [Clarke, William.] Boys own book extended . . . New York, C. S. Francis and Co.   N

[1857]: Paul Preston's Book of gymnastics; or, Sports for youth. Profusely illustrated. Boston.

PICTORIAL primer. New York: George F. Coolidge and Brother, 1847.   CU

Frontispiece and woodcuts of various children's games. Includes cricket.

PIERPONT, James S. The one horse open sleigh. Song and chorus. Written and composed by J. Pierpont. Boston: Published by Oliver Ditson . . . 1857.   N

Words and music. No illustration on cover.

1859: Jingle bells; or, The one horse open sleigh. Song and chorus by J. Pierpont. Boston: Published by Oliver Ditson & Co. . . .   RT

Lithograph of sleigh bells on cover.

PIKE, Marshall S[pring]. Brightly, boys, brightly. A rowing quartett [sic]. Written and composed by Marshall S. Pike, Esq. of the Harmoneons and dedicated to his esteemed friend T. F. Oakes, M.D. of Boston, Mass. Boston: Published by A. & J. P. Ordway 339 Washington St. [cop. 1849].   RT

Words and music. Lithograph of boat rowing in harbor on cover.

A PLEA for the horse in a few remarks and suggestions upon his treatment and management . . . Boston, 1846.   HCL

Paper covers. Cover title: *The Horse and His Management.*

1847: Boston.   HCL

Paper covers. Cover title: *The Horse and His Management.* Woodcut on front cover.

The POCKET farrier; or, Approved receipts; collected from different authors with an intent to cure or assist any immediate accidents that may happen to a horse till further help can be had. Philadelphia: Published by Jacob Johnson . . . 1807.   N

Frontispiece lacking from RT copy. Not to be confused with Burdon's *Gentlemen's Pocket Farrier.*

The POCKET farrier, or Farmer's receipt book. *See:* The FARMER'S receipt book; and pocket farrier.

POE, Edgar Allan. *See:* The GENTLEMAN'S magazine.

POLITICAL running, or An account of a celebrated race over the Pennsylvania course, in the year 1823 . . . *See:* DUNCAN, James.

POMEROY, Samuel Wyllys. A prize essay on mules. *See:* MASON, Richard. The gentleman's new pocket companion, 1830.

POOL. By authority, Mr. Pool, the noted performer in horsemanship, lately arrived from the West India Islands, intends exhibiting—on Mr. Philpot's Hill—the following equestrian feats: mounts a single horse in full speed, fires a pistol, falls backward, with his head on the ground, hanging by his right leg, fires another pistol, under the horse's belly, etc., etc. Tickets . . . at De Witt's Coffee Houses . . . [Baltimore: Printed by William Goddard. 1785.]

Broadside. Evans: 19196.

POOL. Mr. Pool, the first American that ever exhibited the following feats of horsemanship on the continent. New York, September 21, 1786.

Broadside. In New York Historical Library.

POOR Bessy; or Kindness rewarded. An interesting story. New Haven: S. Babcock, 1835.

Orange-paper covers. Frontispiece, vignette of dog on title-page. 10.5 cm. Copy in library of Murray Horowitz, M.D., N.Y.C. Lettering on cover same as title-page.

POPPENBERG'S BAND. Snowdrift polka, as played by Poppenberg's Band. Buffalo: Published by J. Sage & Sons, 209 Main Street [cop. 1856]. RT

Music only. Lithograph of two-horse sled stuck in snowdrift.

PORTER, William T[rotter]. The big bear of Arkansas, and other tales. Philadelphia: Carey & Hart, 1845.

Copy noted in Grolier Club Exhibition, March 1971.

PORTER, William T[rotter]. A quarter race in Kentucky, and other sketches, illustrative of scenes, characters, and incidents, throughout "The Universal Yankee Nation." Edited by William T. Porter ... With illustrations by Darley. Philadelphia: Carey and Hart, 1847.   LC

On cover: *Carey & Hart's Library of Humorous American Works*. Most of the sketches previously published in: *The Spirit of the Times*. Contains: *A Shark Story*, by J. Cypress, Jr., *pseud*. of William Post Hawes.

1850: Philadelphia, A. Hart.   LC

[1854:] A quarter race in Kentucky, and other sketches, illustrative of scenes, characters, and incidents, throughout "The Universal Nation." Edited by William T. Porter, editor of "The spirit of the times," "Big bear of Arkansas, and other tales," etc. With illustrations by Darley. Philadelphia: T. B. Peterson, No. 102 Chesnut Street.   RT

Frontispiece, engraved title-page, and 6 plates. On cover: *Peterson's library of humorous American works* . . .

PORTER, William Trotter. *See also:*

AMERICAN racing calendar and trotting record.

AMERICAN Sporting Chronicle.

AMERICAN turf register and racing & trotting calendar.

AMERICAN turf register and sporting magazine.

HAWKER, Peter. Instructions to young sportsmen.

PORTER'S Spirit of the times.

SPIRIT of the times.

THORPE, Thomas Bangs. The big bear of kansas.

WALLACE, William Vincent. The angler's polka.

PORTER'S Spirit of the times. A chronicle of the turf, field sports, literature, and the stage. Vol. 1–11. New York, September 6, 1856–December 28, 1861.

Founded by William T. Porter. Vol. 1, no. 1 issued Sept. 6, 1856, running to Vol. XI, no. 17, December 28, 1861. Published weekly until Vol. XI, no. 15, Nov. 30, 1861. No. 16 was issued 2 weeks later, December 14, and the last issue on December 28, 1861. Vol. 1 has colored frontispiece of horse *Flora Temple.* Aug. 17, 1861 issue is Vol. X, no. 26, whole no. [260], misnumbered *250.* Only known complete set owned by Mr. Lindley Eberstadt. *See:* Bibliographical Society of America. *Papers.* New York, 1946, Vol. 40, pp. 164-168, and 1950, Vol. 44, pp. 372-373. *See also:* The SPIRIT of the times, and WILKES' Spirit of the times.

PORT FOLIO. By Oliver Oldschool, Esq. [*Pseud.* of Joseph Dennie.] Philadelphia: Printed by H. Maxwell, and sold by William Fry, No. 25, North Second-street, opposite Christ-Church.

N

Vol. 1-5, 1801-1805.
[Ser. 2.] Vol. 1-6, 1806-1808.
[Ser. 3.] Vol. 1-8, 1809-1812.
[Ser. 4.] Vol. 1-6, 1813-1815.
[Ser. 5.] Vol. 1-20, 1816-1825.
[Ser. 6.] Vol. 1-2, 1826-1827.
Suspended Jan.-June, 1826 and Jan.-June, 1827. Index 1816-1825 in Ser. 5, vol. 20. Although a literary and political journal, articles of slight sporting interest occasionally appeared after 1820, and a few sporting plates included as "embellishments." Ser. 5, vol. 16 (1823) has 4 plates; vol. 17 (1824) 2 plates; vol. 18 (1824) 2 plates; Ser. 6, vol. 1 (1826) 1 colored plate; vol. 2 (1826) 1 colored plate.

POWELL, Willis J. Tachyhippodamia, or, Art of quieting wild horses in a few hours, as discovered by the author in the year 1814 . . . New Orleans: Printed at the Observer office, 1838. Y

See also: RAREY, John Solomon, G. M. Bennett edition, 1857.

1844: Second edition. St. Louis: Printed by Chambers & Knapp.

RT

POWER, Thomas. Arouse ye gay comrades. A song and chorus dedicated to the Tiger Boat Club. Written by Thomas Power, Esq., the music composed by Jos. Philip Knight. Boston: Published by Parker & Ditson, 135 Washington St., 1840.

Words and music. Lithograph of eight-oar boat on cover.

POWER, Thomas. Merrily now the skaters go, a glee. The words by Thomas Power, Esqr. The music composed by Charles E. Horn. Boston: Published by C. Bradlee 107 Washington Street, 1837. RT

Words and music. RT copy lacks cover.

PRESTON, Paul, *pseud. See:* PICTON, Thomas.

PRETTY stories for pretty children, in words of one and two syllables. (Newark, N.J.) : Benjamin Olds, 1835.　　　RT

Cobb's toys. Second series, no. 11. Yellow-paper covers. Vignette of cat on cover, and of quail on title-page. Cut of boys skating. Vest-pocket size.

[PRIME, William Cowper.] Later years. By the author of "The old house by the river," and "The Owl Creek letters." New York: Harper & Brothers . . . 1854.　　　RT

[PRIME, William Cowper.] The old house by the river. By the author of The Owl Creek letters. New York: Harper & Brothers . . . 1853.　　　RT

1854: Second edition. New York, Harpers.

1859: Third edition. New York, Harpers.

[PRIME, William Cowper.] The Owl Creek letters, and other correspondence. By W. New York: Published by Baker & Scribner . . . 1848.　　　RT

Letter III: *The night hunt.*

The PRIZE for youthful obedience. Part II. Philadelphia: Published by Jacob Johnson . . . T. L. Plowman, Printer, 1803.　　　N

Contains woodcuts of game of battledoor, and shooting scene.

PROCH, Heinrich. From the Alps the horn resounding. Das Alpenhorn. Composed by Heinrich Proch. New York: Published by Firth & Hall, No 1, Franklin Square. [1832].　　　N

Words and music. Hunting scene, lithograph by Fleetwood on cover.

PROVIDENCE Bowling Club. Constitution and by-laws of the Providence Bowling Club. Providence: Printed by Knowles and Vose, 1846.　　　RT

Paper covers.

PURDY, Jr. Sporting calender! The great match race over the Pennsylvania course, in 1823. Published for the amusement of the sporting gentry. By Purdy, Jr. Clerk Jockey Club. [Philadelphia, 1823.]　　　RT

Vignette on title page, and 4 wood cuts in text. Political pamphlet relating to contest for governorship of Pennsylvania in 1823, written in reply to similar pamphlet by Jehu, the younger [James Duncan]. Bound with Duncan, James. *Political running* . . . Philadelphia, 1823. Only two copies known, RT and HTP.

PURVES, William. The Adirondac[k] Deer Hunt Galop, dedicated to that mighty hunter, John Cheeney, with the kind regards of the composer, Wm. Purves. New York: Geib & Jackson, 499 Broadway. Copyright 1853.

7 pp. folio. Noted in letter from Warder H. Cadbury.

PUTMAN, J. D. R. The rower's manual, and boat club register. Containing a short history of early boat racing—Instructions to rowers and coxswains—Training boats' crews—Diet—Manœuvres—List of boat clubs—Record of time made by winning boats . . . Written and compiled under the supervision of Stephen Roberts, Esq., President of the Empire City Regatta Club. New York [: New York Herald Book and Job Office,] 1858.   RT

[PYCRAFT, James.] The cricket field; or, The history and science of cricket . . . Boston: Mayhew & Baker, 1859.   RT

Portrait frontispiece, illustrations. First published London, 1851, preface to which is signed "J.P.", i.e., James Pycraft.

QUOIT Club carols. *See:* WASHINGTON Social Gymnasium.

RACKET Court Club. Constitution and by-Laws of the Racket Court Club; Adopted 7th April, 1845 . . . New York: George F. Nesbit . . . 1845.   RT

1846: Members of the Racket Court. New York, 1846.   RT

1853: By-laws of the Racket Court Club. New York, J. H. Burney . . .   RT

RADCLIFFE, F. P. Some love to ride. A much admired hunting song. Written by F. P. Radcliffe, Esqre. Composed & respectfully dedicated to Col. John Contee of Prince George's by C. Meineke. Baltimore: Published by G. Willig, Jr. [ca. 1830].   RT

Words and music. Fox-hunting lithograph, signed E. B., by Endicott on cover.

[ca. 1837:] Baltimore, Published by John Cole.   RT

Same lithograph as 1830 edition.

RAFINESQUE, C[onstantine] S. Ichthyologia Ohiensis, or Natural history of the fishes inhabiting the river Ohio and its tributary streams . . . Lexington, Ky.: Printed for the author, by W. G. Blunt . . . 1820.   H

Paper covers, paged as part of book. Huntington Library has also a variant. First published in *The Western review and miscellaneous* magazine, Lexington, Ky., *See:* The Western review.

RAMBLE, Robert. *See:* FROST, John.

[RANDOLPH, John.] The stud of a gentleman in the south of Virginia. 1826.   RT

Wrappers. No title page [P. 1 headed: *Stud book,* with letter to *Mr. Skinner* from John Randolph, dated *Valentine's Day, 1826,* not signed; p. 1 verso, announcement of publication of Stud book; pp. [4]-8, *The Stud;* pp. [9]-11 *Instructions for training,* by Charles Duval; pp. 11-12 a letter to J. S. Skinner, from *A Twig of the turf.*
An anonymous pamphlet, printed for John Randolph of Roanoke by John Stuart Skinner. Only two copies known, RT and JLO. *See:* Fairfax Harrison's *The Roanoke Stud,* Richmond, Va., 1930.

RAREY, J[ohn] S[olomon]. The modern art of taming wild horses. By J. S. Rarey. Columbus: Printed by The State Journal Company. 1856.   RT

Verso title-page reads: "Entered according to Act of Congress, in the year 1855." Pink-paper wrappers. 62 pp. Cover title same as title-page except for, "Printed by The Ohio State Journal Company."

1856: The modern art of taming wild horses. By J. S. Rarey. Columbus: Printed by The Ohio State Journal Company.

Olive green covers. "Ohio" appears on both title-page and cover. Noted in Catalogue no. 4., 1965, The Heritage Book Shop, Lake Zurich, Ill.

1856: The Arabian art of taming and training wild & vicious horses. By Solomon Channel. Printed for the publisher, 1856. Henry Watkins, printer. 225 and 227 Fifth Street, Cincinnati, Ohio.

Paper covers. Title from cover. A pirated edition.   RT

1856: The modern art of taming wild horses; by G. G. Black, S. T. Widner & F. Hardrick. Springfield, O.: Daily Nonpareil Print.   RT

Paper covers. A pirated edition, in which text has been slightly rewritten.

RAREY, John Solomon. *Continued:*

1856: The modern art of taming wild horses, by G. G. Black, S. T. Widmer and F. Hardrick. Lafayette, Ind.: I. H. Wright's Book & Job Print. RT

Paper covers. Text same as Black-Springfield, Ohio edition, plus one page of advertisements verso title-page. A pirated edition.

[1856:] The modern art of taming wild horses. By J. S. Rarey. Columbus: [ca. 1856]. RT

Pink-paper covers, with title on cover same as on title-page. The words, "District of Ohio" in copyright notice, verso title-page, is spelled "Didirect." A pirated edition. Iowa State College copy compared with RT copy June 20, 1941, and decision made that this was not a first edition, but a later pirated edition.

1856: Another edition of the above, but with "District" spelled correctly.

Copy owned by private collector. Seen 1955.

1856: The newly discovered process of bridling, riding and working unmanageable wild colts, kicking and runaway horses. Together with a complete farrier, and effectual remedies for all the different diseases, the horse is subject to. By J. J. Stutzman and J. W. M'Bride. [Chillicothe, Ohio:] Printed for the publisher. RT

RT copy was Rarey's own copy, and has notes by him, pencilled, apparently indicated what he considered to be pirated material. Said to have been withdrawn from the market upon representations by Rarey's attorney. Pink paper wrappers, with title only, but set differently from title page.

1856: The newly-discovered process of bridling, riding and working wild colts or horses; together with a complete farrier. By J. J. Stutzman, West Rushville, Fairfield County, Ohio. [Second edition.] Chillicothe, Ohio: Baker & Miller, Book and Job Printers. RT

Blue paper wrappers missing from RT copy. Rarey is said to have obtained an injunction against Stutzman, who published this after the Stutzman and M'Bride edition had been stopped. All copies supposed to have been destroyed by Court order—except this copy which belonged to Rarey, and which is pencil marked by him, again to show pirated material.

1856: The modern art of taming wild horses. Austin: State Times Office.

RAREY, John Solomon. *Continued:*

"Third edition, revised and corrected". Verso title-page reads: Entered according to Act of Congress in the year 1856, by J. S. Rarey, in the Clerk's Office of the District Court of the United States, for the District of Texas." Copy owned by E. W. Winkler. Noted in: *Southwestern Quarterly.* Vol. 48, Jy. 1944, p. 106. Another copy noted in *Midland Notes,* no. 72, Mansfield, Ohio, 1958.

1857: The modern art of taming wild horses. Columbus: Printed by the Ohio State Journal Company. RT

62pp., light green covers. Text same as 1856 edition, page for page, but has been reset.

1857: The modern art of taming wild horses. Columbus: Printed by the Ohio State Journal Company. RT

54pp. Blue paper covers. Text same as 1856 edition, but reset in smaller type, reducing the number of pages.

1857: *See:* NASH, Ephraim.

1857: The Arabian art of taming and training wild and vicious horses. By Brown and Miller. Noblesville [Ind.]: Printed for L. E. Rumrill, by Elder & Harkness, Indianapolis. RT

Paper covers. Title from cover. A pirated edition.

1857: The modern art of taming wild horses. By J. S. Rarey. RT

No imprint, no place of publication, no date. Paper covers. 47 pp. We assigned the date 1857(?), assuming it to be one of the earliest of the piracies.

1857: The modern art of taming wild horses. Canton [Ohio].

52 pp. printed wrappers. 6⅝ by 4⅜ inches. E. J. Wessen states, "It is quite possible that the present is the second edition." But we prefer to consider the 1857 Columbus as the second edition. Copy in Ohio Historical Society.

1857: The Arabian art of taming and training wild and vicious horses. Cincinnati: Printed and published for the author. RT

Paper covers. Title from cover. A pirated edition.

1857: The great art of taming and training wild horses, containing every instruction necessary for any person to handle young, wild, obstinate, or kicking horses, in a few hours, with perfect safety. By Gilson M. Bennett. Cobourg: Printed at the "Cobourg Sun" office, 1857. RT

RAREY, John Solomon. *Continued:*

Vignette on title-page. Paper covers. Cover title same as title-page. Although "Entered according to Act of Congress" by Gilson M. Bennett, this is mostly "Selected from the Writings of Mr. J. S. Rarey," and from J. W. Powell's *Tachyhippodamia.*

1857: The Arabian art of taming and training wild and vicious horses, under the written directions of a sheik of the Bedouin Arabs, by H. Watkin . . . Cincinnati, Henry Watkin, publisher . . . **RT**

Paper covers. Title from cover. Copyrighted by Henry Bodkin, who signed introduction.

1857: A small slip of paper, with printed notice signed by Henry Watkin, Cincinnati, Feb. 11, 1857, "This is to certify that . . . Rarey has a valid copy-right for the book entitled 'The modern art of taming wild horses,' and that the above book is an infringement of the copy-right . . . I therefore recall my advertisements of the same, and shall hereafter sell no more of said work . . ." **RT**

[1857?] Taming, or breaking the horse by new and improved method, as practiced with great success in the United States . . . Also, Rules for selecting a good horse . . . New York, Dick & Fitzgerald. **N**

1857: A new and certain way of taiming [sic!] horses or cattle, to ride or work. Together with a receipt to cure polevil and fistula without fail. By J. W. Denney, of Ganstead England, 1857. **RT**

32 pp. Pink-paper covers, lacking from RT copy, except for trace of color. Entered according to act of Congress, May 8th, 1856, by J. W. Denney. A piracy, phraseology slightly changed. Full of misspellings. No place of publication, but possibly Ohio.

1857: The Arabian art of taming and training wild and vicious horses, By L. G. Marshall. [Circleville, Ohio:] Printed for the publisher. **RT**

A 36 pp. pamphlet, pink wrappers. *The horseman's guide and farrier,* by John J. Stutzman, W. Rushville, Fairfield Co., Ohio, pp. 31–33. *The Secret of subduing wild horses and other wild animals,* pp. 34–36.

1858: The Arabian art of taming and training wild and vicious horses. By L. G. Marshall. n.p.: Calhoun, 1858.

RAREY, John Solomon. *Continued:*

A 36 p. pamphlet. Pp. 33–34: *The horseman's guide and farrier* by John J. Stutzman, West Rushville, Fairfield County, Ohio. Pp. 35–36: *The secret of subduing wild horses and other wild animals.* Copy in library of Keeneland Association, Lexington, Ky.

1858: The American art of taming horses. Originally systematized and practiced by John S. Rarey. Its history and different methods, &c. Being a complete compendium of all that is known of the system. In: New-York Tribune. Weekly. Extra edition. New York, August, 1858.   RT

One leaf, printed both sides, reprinting entire Rarey pamphlet, with illustrations. Also excerpts from *The London Athenaeum, The Household Words,* July 10, 1858.

1858: The Arabian art of taming and training wild and vicious horses. Published by Eastman & Quick. Valparaiso, Ind.: "Democrat" Power Press Print, 1858.   RT

Paper covers. Cover title same as title-page. A pirated edition.

1858: Taming, or breaking the horse on Rarey's system and practice . . . New York: Wilson & Co., [ca. 1858.]

Pictorial wrappers. Wrapper imprint: Published at the Brother Johnathan Office. Noted in *Midland Notes,* no. 89, item 219, 1963.

1858: The modern art of taming horses. Jacksonville, O. T.: Wm. J. Beggs & Co.

Only recorded copy in Library of Congress.

1858: Mr. Rarey's system of horse taming. In: *Oregon Farmer,* October, 1858.

1858: The modern art of taming horses. Portland, Ore.

Only recorded copy in Yale University Library. *See: The Call Number.* Library of the University of Oregon. Vol. 22, no. 1., p. 10. Eugene, Oregon, 1960.

1858: The modern art of taming wild horses. By J. S. Rarey. Columbus: Printed by Follett, Foster & Company.

Blue-paper covers. 59 pp. Copy in library of Keeneland Association, Lexington, Ky.

1858: Secret of horse taming. *In:* Cincinnati Daily Chronicle. Cincinnati, August 3, 1858.   RT

RAREY, John Solomon. *Continued:*

An "elaborate and reliable account of Mr. Rarey's mode of Treating and Curing Vicious Horses." A freely rendered piracy.

1858: *See:* BENTWRIGHT, Jeremiah.

[1858:] Taming, or Breaking the horse by a new and improved method, as practiced with great success in the United States . . . Also, The complete farrier, or horse doctor . . . By John C. Knowlson . . . New York, Dick & Fitzgerald.   N

Cover title: *The Complete Horse Tamer and Farrier.*

1858: The Arabian art of taming and training wild and vicious horses. By L. Rupert. Providence, A. C. Greene & Brothers. HCL

A pirated edition.

1859: The art of taming horses: the Rarey system fully explained. By an experienced horseman. [Abram Bradley.] A new edition, revised, with important emendations, notes, plates and diagrams. Buffalo, N.Y., Clapp, Matthews & Co.'s Steam Printing House . . .   RT

1859: *See:* HERBERT, Henry William. Hints to horse-keepers.

See: Henderson, Robert W. *John Solomon Rarey the great American horse tamer.* In: *Bookmen's holiday. Notes and studies written and gathered in tribute to Harry Miller Lydenberg.* New York: The New York Public Library, 1943.

RAREY, John Solomon. Wild horses. I wish to announce . . . I have a system of taming wild horses . . . J. S. Rarey, Groveport, O. Groveport, O. [1855].   RT

Broadside.

The REAL advantages which ministers and people may enjoy. *See:* WELLES, Noah.

REDHEAD, H. W. The horseman; with practical rules to buyers, breeders, breakers, smiths, &c. To which is prefixed An account of all the breeds of horses in the world. With numerous illustrations. H. W. Redhead, Veterinarian. Cleveland, Ohio: Cowles, Pinkerton & Co., Printers, Leader Job Office, 1855.   RT

Paper wrappers. Lettering on cover same as on title-page, but vignettes differ.

REED, R. Rhodes. Harry the hunter. Written by R. Rhodes Reed, the music composed & dedicated to Miss Emily Blanche Dixon, by Carlo Minasi. [Philadelphia: Lee & Walker, ca. 1855]. RT

Words and music. Hunting lithography by T. Sinclair's Lith., Philadelphia on cover.

REEVS, J. H. The farmer's practical horse farriery. *See:* NASH, Ephraim.

REFF, Henrich. Das durch viele Curen bestätigte, und sicher befundene Pferdearzney-Büchlein; welches viele Mittel wider die jetzt unter den Pferden, wie auch unter dem Rindvieh, herrschende und bösartige Krankheiten enthält. Von langer Erfahrung und zulänglicher Kenntniss der Pferdearzney-Kunst hergeleitet. Von Henrich Reff. Zum erstenmal herausgegeben. Ephrata: Gedruckt bey Baumann und Cleim, 1804. RT

Paper covers.

The REFORMED rake . . . [Verso] A dialogue between one of the greatest sportsmen and dead fox. Boston: Sold by N. Coverly . . . [1810.] RT

One of a number of ballad sheets issued by Nathaniel Coverly and his son between 1800 and 1814.

REID, Mayne. The boy hunters; or, Adventures in search of a white buffalo . . . With illustrations, by William Harvey. Boston: Ticknor and Fields, 1856. RT

First published London, 1852.

1857: Boston, Ticknor and Fields. N

REID, Mayne. The hunter's feast; or, Conversations around the camp-fire . . . With eight original designs, engraved by N. Orr. New York: De Witt & Davenport . . . [1856]. LC

First published London, 1854.

REID, Mayne. The plant hunters; or, Adventures among the Himalaya Mountains. With illustrations. Boston: Ticknor and Fields, 1858. RT

First published London, 1858.

RICHARDS, A. Keene. The Arab horses, Mokhladi, Massoud, and Sacklowie; imported by A. K. Richards, Georgetown, Kentucky. Lexington: Kentucky Statesman Print, 1857.   N

Contains three photographs, inserted at front of pamphlet.

RICHARDS, John. A discourse on gambling; delivered in the Congregational Meeting-House at Dartmouth College, November 7th, 1852 . . . Hanover, N.H.: D. Kimball & Sons . . . 1852.   CU

On paper cover: *Rev. Dr. Richards' Discourse on Gambling.*

RICHARDSON, H. D. Dogs: their origin and varieties, directions as to their general management, and simple instructions as to their treatment under disease. By H. D. Richardson, . . . With numerous illustrations on wood. New York: D. Appleton & Company, 200 Broadway. Philadelphia: Geo. S. Appleton, 148 Chesnut Street, 1847.   RT

Frontispiece and illustrations throughout text. First published Dublin, 1847?

1857: Dogs: their origin and varieties, directions as to their management, and simple instructions as to their treatment under disease. By H. D. Richardson . . . With numerous illustrations on wood. New York: C. M. Saxton and Company, 1857.   LC

RICHARDSON, H. D. Horses: their varieties, breeding, and management in health and disease. New York: C. M. Saxton, 1852.   LC

Illustrated. *Saxton's Rural Handbooks.* First published Dublin, 1848.

1855: New York, C. M. Saxton.   B

RICHARDSON, Josiah, compiler. The New-England farrier, and family physician; containing, firstly, Paul Jewett's Farriery, in four parts, wherein most of the diseases which horses, neat cattle, sheep and swine are liable to, are treated of, in 41 pages. Secondly, A collection of brutal receipts . . . Thirdly A very valuable collection of receipts for human diseases: 90 pages. Fourthly, Receipts by a very learned, skilful and pious English author . . . Fifthly An extraordinary English author, of great experience and information on neat cattle, sheep . . . Sixthly, A number of valuable receipts from Capt. Joseph Smith . . . Last

RICHARDSON, Josiah. *Continued:*

of all, Doct. J. Williams' Family physician . . . Compiled by Josiah Richardson. Exeter: Published by Josiah Richardson, 1828. RT

Bound in contemporary leather. 468 plus 24 pp. Dr. John Williams's *Last legacy and useful family guide* occupies the additional 24 pp. *See:* JEWETT, Paul.

RICKETSON, Shadrach. Means of preserving health, and preventing diseases: founded principally on an attention to air and climate, drink, food, sleep, exercise . . . New York: Printed by Collins, Perkins, and Co. . . . 1806. RT

RIMBAULT, S[tephen] F[rancis]. At morning dawn the hunters rise. A favorite hunting song. Composed by S. F. Rimbault. Sung by Mrs. Burke. Philadelphia: Published and sold by G. Willig [ca. 1830.] RT

Words and music. Fox-hunting song.

ROBINSON, J[ohn] H[ovey]. Nick Whiffles. A drama, in three acts. Dramatized by Dr. J. H. Robinson, from his stories of "Nick Whiffles" and "Buck Bison." With casts, costumes, and all the stage business. Boston: William V. Spencer, 128 Washington Street, corner of Water. [1858]. RT

At head of title: *Spencer's Boston Theatre.—CLXXVIII.* Paper covers. Front cover lacking from RT copy. Characters are hunters, trappers, guide, etc. Scene: Open country—Prairie at sunrise.

ROBINSON, John Hovey. Silver-Knife; or, The hunters of the Rocky Mountains. An autobiography. Boston: William V. Spencer, 1854. RT

Paper cover, fiction. RT copy bound in cloth.

ROHLWES, Johann Nicolaus. Allgemeines Vieharzneibuch, oder unterricht, wie der Landmann seine Pferde, sein Rindvieh, seine Schafe, Schweine und Hunde aufziehen, warten und süttern, und ihre Krankheiten erkennen und heilen soll; nebst einem Anhange. Schellsburg, (Pennsylvanien): Gedruckt und zu haben bey Friedrich Goeb, 1823. RT

Boards. First American edition.

ROHLWES, Johann Nicolaus. Vollständiges Gäuls-Doctor-Buch, oder Grundlicher Unterricht wie der Bauer under jeder Pferde-Besitzer alle Krankheiten seiner Pferde erkennen und auf die leichteste Art heilen kann . . . Nebst einer Abhandlung von den Krankheiten der Hunde. Reading, Pa. Gedrucht und herausgegeben von Heinrich B. Sage, 1817.   RT

ROMANS, Bernard. A concise natural history of East and West Florida. Containing an account of the natural products of all the southern part of British America . . . By Captain Bernard Romans. Illustrated with twelve copper plates . . . Vol. I. New York: Printed for the author, 1775.   N

Evans: 14440. On p. 76, an account of a Choctaw ball game.

1776: [Second edition.] New York printed, Sold by R. Aitken.

Evans: 15069.   N

ROMER, Jonathan. *See:* MAYO, William Starbuck.

ROSS, H. P. Away, away, with hearts so gay! Quartette for male voices. Poetry by H. P. Ross, music by W. F. Sherwin. Albany: Published by J. H. Hidley, 519 Broadway. Boston: Oliver Ditson & Co. . . . 1859.   RT

Words and music. At head of title: *To the Hiawatha Boat Club, of Albany, N. Y.* Lithograph of boat race on Hudson River by Greene & Walker, Boston.

ROSSINI, Gioachino Antonio. What wild sounds the hunters attending. The celebrated Chorus of Hunters, in the much-admired opera of *Cinderella*. The music composed by Rossini. New York: Bourne, 359 Broadway [ca. 1827–1832].   RT

Words and music. Chamois hunting.

[ROWORTH, C.] The art of defence on foot, with the broad sword and sabre: adapted also for the spadroon, or cut and thrust sword. Improved, and augmented with the ten lessons of Mr. John Taylor, late broadsword master to the Light Horse Volunteers of London and Westminster. Illustrated with plates by R. K. Porter, Esq. New-York: Published by H. Durell. Johnstone & Van Norden printers, 1824.   RT

First published London, 1798. Folded frontispiece, and 13 plates, mostly folded. Plate XI is mis-numbered IX.

The ROYAL American magazine; or, Universal repository of instruction and amusement. For April, 1774. America: Boston: Printed by and for I. Thomas, 1774.　　　　AAS

Contains *The Hill Tops: a New Hunting Song.* Illustration of deer hunt. Engraved by J. C[allender]. Evans: 13590. *See* p. xxvi.

The ROYAL Pennsylvania gazette. Philadelphia: Published by James Robertson, in Front-Street . . . No. VI. Friday, March 20, 1778, p. 2, col. 2.　　　　N

An advertisement reads: *Any Person acquainted with the making of CRICKETT BATS or BALLS, may have good encouragement. Enquire of the Printer.* This was during the British occupation.

RULES and regulations for the sword exercise of the cavalry.
　　　　　　　　　　　　　　　　See: HEWES, Robert.

RUPERT, L. The Arabian art of taming and training wild and vicious horses. *See:* RAREY, John Solomon. The modern art of taming wild horses.

RUPP, I[srael] Daniel. The farmer's complete farrier, comprising a historical description of all the varieties of that noble and useful animal, the horse, giving instructions in all things that relate to him; his rearing, feeding, training, fattening and treatment . . . Accompanied with the Annals of the turf, American stud book, Rules for training, racing. &c. Lancaster, Pa.: Published by Gilbert Hills . . . 1842.　　　　RT

Folding frontispiece and plates.

1844: Lancaster, Pa., Published by Isaac L. Eshleman.　　　　LC

1847: Lancaster, Pa., Isaac L. Eshleman.　　　　RT

Does not contain: *Annals of the Turf, American Stud Book* . . .

[RUSH, Benjamin.] Sermons to gentlemen upon temperance and exercise . . . Philadelphia: Printed by John Dunlap . . . 1772.
　　　　　　　　　　　　　　　　　　　　　　LC

Evans: 12547. Mentions golf and tennis.

RUSH, Jacob. Charges, and extracts of charges, on moral and religious subjects; delivered at sundry times, by the Honorable Jacob Rush . . . To which Is annexed, The act of the Legisla-

RUSH, Jacob. *Continued:*

ture of the State of Pennsylvania, respecting vice and immorality. Philadelphia—Printed: New-York; Re-printed by Geo: Forman . . . for Jonathan Weeden, May, 1804.   RT

Contains addresses to Grand Juries on gaming and duelling. Mentions cockfighting.

1815: Lenox, (Mass.) Published and sold by John G. Stanley. A. Stoddard, printer, Hudson.   N

RUSH, John. The hand-book of veterinary homœopathy: or, The homœopathic treatment of the horse, the ox, the sheep, the dog and the swine. By John Rush, Veterinary Surgeon. From the London edition. With numerous additions translated from the 7th German Edition of Dr. F. E. Gunther's Homœopathic veterinary, by Jacobs F. Sheek, M.D. Philadelphia: Published by Rademacher & Sheek . . . New York: William Radde . . . St. Louis: J. G. Wesselhœft . . . New Orleans: D. R. Luyties, M.D., 1854.   RT

RUSSELL, Henry. The fisher boy merrily lives. A song, sung with great applause by Mrs. Seguin. The music composed and dedicated as a mark of respect to Edward Bertie Ranger, Esquire. By Henry Russell. Boston: Published by Oakes & Swan, 8½ Tremont Row [cop. 1840].   RT

Words and music. Lithograph on cover of boy with fishing nets and oars, E. W. Bouvé's Lithographic Press. R. Cooke, *del.*

RUXTON, George F[rederic Augustus]. Adventures in Mexico and the Rocky Mountains. New York: Harper & Brothers . . . 1848.   N

First published London, 1847.

RUXTON, George Frederic [Augustus]. Life in the Far West. New York: Harper & Brothers . . . 1849.   RT

1855: New York: Harper & Brothers.

1859: New York: Harper & Brothers.   N

S., M. Hark! hark! the soft bugle. Composed and inscribed to his

RUXTON, George Frederic. *Continued:*

friend J. H. Hewitt, by M. S. Balto.: Published by Geo. Willig, Jr. [1831.] RT

Words and music. Unsigned lithograph of huntsman on horseback on cover.

[1837:] Hark! hark! the soft bugle. Composed and inscribed to his friend J. H. Hewitt, by M. S. Baltimore, Published by G. Willig, Jr. RT

Words and music. Lithograph of huntsman on horseback by [Moses] Swett, similar to, but not identical with, 1831 edition. At head of title: *Second Edition.*

SABINE, Lorenzo. Notes on duels and duelling, alphabetically arranged, with a preliminary historical essay. Boston: Crosby, Nichols & Company, 1855. RT

Appendix Nos. I–XVII.

1856: [Second edition.] Boston, Crosby, Nichols and Company.

Appendix Nos. I–XX. RT

1859: Third edition. Boston, Crosby, Nichols & Company. RT

Appendix Nos. I–XX.

The SAGACITY of dogs. Boston: Marsh & Capen, 362 Washington St. Press of Putnam & Hunt, 1828. N

A juvenile, wrappers with border and vignette. Vignette repeated on title page. Frontispiece.

The SAGACITY and intelligence of the horse. New York: Kiggins & Kellog, 88 John Street [ca. 1848]. RT

A juvenile, wrappers, with title within border. At head of wrapper: *Third series.—No. 7.* Vignettes on wrapper and title-page; 5 full page illustrations. One of Redfield's Toy Books.

St. MARGUERITTE, T. de. A Treatise on the art of fencing, taken from the best authorities, for the use of the officers of the United States. Dedicated, by T. de St. Margueritte, to the officers of Virginia. Winchester, (Va.): Printed by Isaac Collett, 1808.

SALZMANN, C[hristian] G[otthilf]. Gymnastics for youth: or, A practical guide to healthful and amusing exercises . . . Freely translated from the German . . . Illustrated with copper plates. Philadelphia: Printed by William Duane . . . 1802. RT

Ten plates including folding frontispiece. First English translation published London, 1800, plates by William Blake. Plates in this edition are American reproductions.

1803: Philadelphia, Printed for P. Byrne . . . AAS

Plates same as 1802 edition.

SAMPSON, William. The trial of Lieutenant Renshaw, of the U.S. Navy. Indicted for challenging Joseph Strong, Esq. attorney at law, to fight a duel. With the speeches of the learned counsel, Colden, Hoffman and Emmett. Taken in short-hand by William Sampson, Esq. With an Appendix, containing the proceedings of the Naval Court of Enquiry, held by order of the Secretary of the Navy. New-York: Published by Frank, White and Co. No. 132 Water-Street, 1809.

SANFORD, R. B. Just twenty years ago. Song composed by R. B. Sanford. New York: Published by Gould & Berry, 297 Broadway. Boston: Oliver Ditson . . . 1852. RT

Words and music. Lithograph on cover showing childhood games: sleighing, hoops, etc. "Wicket ground" mentioned in text.

SANGSTER, Charles. The St. Lawrence and the Saguenay, and other poems. Kingston: C. W., John Creighton and John Duff. New York: Miller, Orton & Mulligan, 1856. RT

Contains: *Canadian sleigh song*.

[SAUNDERS, Frederick] Salad for the solitary. By an epicure. New York: Lamport, Blakeman & Law, No. 8 Park Place, 1853. RT

Frontispiece, engraved extra title-page, vignette title-page, and small engravings throughout text. *Pastimes and sports*. [An essay], pp. 132-153.

1853: Third thousand. Identical with first edition, except for "Third thousand" added to title-page. N

1853: Fifth thousand. Identical with first edition, except for "Fifth thousand" added to title-page. N

SCHILLER, [Johann Christoph Friedrich von]. To the chase! Glee for four voices as sung by the Tremont Vocalists. Words from the German of Schiller. Music by B. F. Baker. Author of the celebrated glees, "Blow On" and Death of Osceola. Boston: Published by Henry Tolman, 153 Washington St. Opposite the Old South . . . 1847.   RT

Words and music. Deer hunting.

[SCHNEYDER, John.] Nützliches und bewährt befundnes Rossarznen-Büchlein, welches viele auserlesene Mittel wieder die Meinsten innerlichen Krankheiten und auesserliche Zufälle der Pferde enthält . . . Ephrata: Zum zten mal gedruckt bey Johann Baumann, 1805.   AAS

Foreword signed: John Schneyder. A piracy of KURZ *gefasztes Ross-Arzney Buchlein*. Ephrata, 1802.

The SCHOOL Boy's friend; a manual of scientific and useful recreations, exercises and pursuits, for the leisure hours of youth. By the author of The young man's own book. Philadelphia: Key and Biddle, 23 Minor Street, 1835.   RT

Vignette on title-page, frontispiece, illustrations. "With upwards of 100 Engravings on wood, by Atherton, Mason and Bowen." Boards illustrated with wood cuts. Contains: *Active sports and exercises*.

SCHREINER, William H. Schreiner's Sporting manual. A complete treatise on fishing, fowling and hunting, as applicable to this country, with full instructions for the management of the dog. Illustrated with numerous engravings. In two parts. Philadelphia: [Stereotyped by S. D. Wyeth,] 1841.   RT

Frontispiece, and cuts in text.

SCHUYLKILL Fishing Company. Charter, by-laws, rules and regulations of the Schuylkill Fishing Company. Philadelphia, 1851.

Copy owned by Mr. Lindley Eberstadt.

SCHUYLKILL Fishing Company. *See* MILNOR, William, Jr.

The SCHUYLKILL Navy. Constitution of the Schuylkill Navy, & by-laws of the Naval Board, of Philadelphia. Organized, Oct. 19th, 1858. Philadelphia, 1859.

A rowing club. Folding plate, signal flags in color. Noted in Goodspeed's Catalogue 514, no. 326.

The SCIENCE of swimming, as taught and practiced in civilized and savage nations, with particular instructions to learners: also showing its importance in the preservation of health and life. Illustrated with engravings. By an experienced swimmer . . . New York: Fowler and Wells, publishers, 308 Broadway . . . [cop. 1849].   RT

Paper covers with title and vignette within borders.

SCOTT, Sir Walter. Huntsman rest! Thy chace is done. From The Lady of the Lake. Composed by J. Mazzinghi. New York: John Paff [ca. 1811].

Noted in: Dichter, Harry. Handbook of American sheet music. Philadelphia, 1947.

SCRIBBLINGS, and sketches, diplomatic, piscatory and oceanic.
                    See: WATMOUGH, Edward Coxe.

[SECCOMBE, Joseph.] Business and diversion inoffensive to God, and necessary for the comfort and support of human society. A discourse utter'd in part at Ammauskeeg-Falls in the fishing season. 1739 . . . [By Fluviatulis Piscator, *pseud.*] Boston: Printed for S. Kneeland and T. Green . . . 1743.   N

A sermon approving angling. Evans: 5285. *See: Gee.*

SEDGWICK, A. Buckley's celebrated sleighing song. Sung by them with immense applause. [Written and] Composed by A. Sedgwick. New York: Published by Horace Waters, 333 Broadway . . . 1853.   RT

Words and music. Lithograph on cover by Hays, of couple in two-horse sleigh.

SEGA, James. An essay on the practice of duelling, as it exists in modern society. Occasioned by the late lamentable occurrence near Philadelphia. Translated from the Italian, by the author. Philadelphia, 1830.   RT

SEGA, James. What is true civilization, or the means to suppress the practice of duelling, to prevent, or to punish, crimes, and to abolish the punishment of death. By James Sega, L.L.D. From the University of Pavia . . . Boston: William Smith—printer, 1830.   RT

SETTIN' on a rail; or, Racoon hunt. A celebrated comic extravaganza as sung at the theatres. New York: Published by Jas. L. Hewitt & Co., 239 Broadway [ca. 1836]. RT

Words and music. Lithograph on cover of a black with banjo, seizing a racoon.

1836: Sitting on a rail; or, The racoon hunt. A celebrated comic extravaganza, as sung by Mr. Leicester. With an accompaniment for the piano forte. New York: Published by Firth & Hall, no. 1 Franklin Square, 1836. RT

Words and music. Lithograph on cover same subject as above, but by different artist.

The SHAD fishers. *See:* CANNING, Josiah Dean.

SHERWIN, W. F. Away, away, with hearts so gay! *See:* ROSS, H. P.

SHIELD, [William]. Old Towler. A favorite hunting song. Composed by Mr. Shield. Sung by Mr. Williamson at the Boston Theatre. Boston: Published by E. W. Jackson, no. 44 Market St. [1822]. RT

Words and music. Lithograph of dog hunting deer at head of page.

SHORTFIELD, Luke. *See:* JONES, John Beauchamp.

SHUFELT, Peter. The beautiful chesnut-brown horse, Young Richmond, will stand for covering, the ensuing season, at the stable of Peter Shufelt . . . Printed at Waterford, Halfmoon-Point [N.Y.] April 12, 1797. RT

Broadside. Cut of horse held by groom.

SICHER und bewährt befundenes Gäuls-Doktor Büchlein. Enthaltend die aller auseresenste Mittel für Pferde, nebst einen Anhang für das Rindvieh, Schasse und der Gleichen. Ephrata: Zum 4tenmal Gedruckt bey Johannes Baumann, 1809. AAS

SIMMONS, John. The American pocket farrier; comprehending a description of the various diseases incident to horses, and prescriptions for their cure . . . Carefully selected from the most approved authors . . . Philadelphia: The compiler, 1825. LC

1834: . . . Embellished with five appropriate copperplate engravings. Second edition. Philadelphia, For sale by the compiler . . . RT

SIMMS, Jeptha R[oot]. Trappers of New York, or A biography of Nicholas Stoner & Nathaniel Foster; together with anecdotes of other celebrated hunters, and some account of Sir William Johnson, and his style of living. By Jeptha R. Simms, author of The history of Schorie County, and Border wars of New York . . . Albany: Printed by J. Munsell, 1850. Y

Portrait frontispiece and three plates. A reprint of the 1850 edition, limited to fifty copies, with index and extra plates, was published in 1871.

1851: Second edition. Albany, Joel Munsell, 58 State Street. N

Portrait frontispiece, and 3 plates.

1857: Albany, Printed by J. Munsell. N

Portrait, frontispiece, and 3 plates. Identical with 1851 edition.

[SIMMS, William Gilmore.] The code of honor: or, The thirty-nine articles; with an Appendix, showing the whole manner in which the duel is to be conducted; with amusing anecdotes, illustrative of duelling; to which is prefixed a dissertation on the origin and progress of the duello. By a Southron . . . Baltimore: William Taylor & Co., Jarvis' Building, 1847. RT

Brown-paper covers. Title on cover omits "To which is prefixed . . ."

SITTING on a rail; or, The racoon hunt. See: SETTIN' on a rail.

SKINNER, J[ohn] S[tuart]. The dog and the sportsman. Embracing the uses, breeding, training, diseases, etc. etc., of dogs, and an Account of the different kinds of game, with their habits . . . With illustrations. Philadelphia: Lea & Blanchard, 1845. RT

Extra engraved title-page. Gilt tooling on spine, blind tooling, panel design on covers. Dark Green.

1845: Philadelphia: Lea & Blanchard. RT

Same edition as above. Light green covers. Blind tooling the same, but with additional tooling on spine and on covers.

SKINNER, John Stuart. See also:

AMERICAN farmer.

AMERICAN turf register.

BADCOCK, John. The veterinary surgeon, 1848.

CLATER, Francis. Every man his own farrier.

GENERAL stud book.

MASON, Richard. The gentleman's new pocket companion, 1848.

RANDOLPH, John. Mr. Randolph's printed book.

YOUATT, William. The horse.

SKITT, *pseud. See:* TALIAFERRO, Harden E.

SLEDGE quadrilles. Boston: Published by Henry Prentiss, 33 Court St., 1842.   RT

Music only. Lithograph of horse-drawn sleigh on cover, by Thayer & Co., Boston.

SLOAN, W. B. The complete farrier or horse doctor: also The complete cattle doctor; containing full and complete directions for choosing, breeding, rearing, and general management, together with accurate descriptions, causes, peculiar symptoms, and the most approved method of curing all diseases to which horse and cattle are subject. Chicago: Published by W. B. Sloan . . . Second edition. 1848.

Copy in Chicago Historical Society. No copy of first edition located.

1849: Third edition, enlarged and improved. Chicago: Published by W. B. Sloan . . .

Copy noted in Catalogue no. 17, March 1965, Robert G. Hayman, Carey, Ohio. Note on verso title-page: Jewett, Thomas & Co. Stereotypers and printers, Buffalo, N.Y.

1851: The complete farrier, or horse doctor: also The complete cattle doctor; containing full and complete directions for choosing, breeding, rearing, and general management; together with accurate descriptions, causes, peculiar symptoms, and the most approved method of curing all diseases to which horses and cattle are subject. Fourth edition, enlarged and improved. Chicago: Published by W. B. Sloan. No. 40 Lake Street.   RT

Frontispiece. Cover title: *Sloan's complete farrier,* [cut of horse] *and cattle doctor. Price 50 cents* . . . Back cover blank. Printed in Buffalo, N.Y.

1851: Edition identical with above except for covers. Front

cover: *Sloan's complete farrier and cattle doctor.* [No cut]. *A new edition—revised and improved.* Price fifty cents . . . Back cover: *Sloan's complete farrier* [Cut of horse as above] *and cattle doctor.* RT

The cut of the horse used on the covers of the Sloan *Complete farriers* is the same as used on the wrappers of some editions of Knowlson's *Complete farrier,* published by U. P. James of Cincinnati. Printed in Buffalo, N.Y.

SMITH, Gideon B., editor. *See:* AMERICAN turf register and sporting magazine.

SMITH, Horatio. Festivals, games and amusements . . . New York: J. & J. Harper, 1831. RT

Frontispiece and two plates. Printed tan cloth.

1831: Festivals, games, and amusements. Ancient and modern . . . With additions, by Samuel Woodworth, Esq. of New York. New York: Printed and published by J. & J. Harper . . . 1831. RT

Frontispiece and 2 plates. *Harper's Family Library, No. 25.* First published London, 1831.

1832: New York, Printed and published by J. & J. Harper. N

1833: Festivals, games and amusements . . . New York: Harper & Brothers.

1833: New York, Printed and published by J. & J. Harper. LC

1834: Festivals, games and amusements . . . New York: Harper and Brothers.

Title page dated 1833, but front cover dated 1834.

1836: Festivals, games, and amusements. Ancient and modern. With additions by Samuel Woodworth, Esq. of New-York. New York, Published by Harper & Brothers, no. 82 Cliff-Street.

Frontispiece and two plates. Harper's Family Library. No. XXV. Title page dated 1836, but front cover dated 1837. RT

1836: New York, Published by Harper & Brothers. RT

SMITH, Horatio. *Continued:*

A variant of the above 1836 edition, with p.1. preceding frontispiece: p.[11]-4. *Valuable Works published by Harper & Brothers.*

1836: New York, Printed and published by J. & J. Harper.

1841: New York, Harper and Brothers.

1842: New York, Printed and published by J. & J. Harper. HPL

1844: New York, Harper & Brothers.   RT

1858: New York, Harper and Brothers.   DCL

SMITH, Jerome V[an] C[rowinshield]. Natural history of the fishes of Massachusetts, embracing a practical essay on angling. Boston: Allen and Ticknor, 1833.   RT

Part Second has separate title: *On Trout, Interspersed with Remarks on the Theory and Practice of Angling.* Wood engravings throughout text. Vignettes on both title-pages. Author's preface states: To David Eckley, Esq., of Boston, the author is particularly indebted . . . All that is interesting to the practical angler in the second part of this volume, originated with that gentleman.

1843: Second edition. Boston, William D. Ticknor. *See: Gee.*
                                                                RT

S[MITH], J[ohn]. The husbandman's magazene. Being a treatise of horses, mares, colts . . . With directions for their breeding . . . With cutts. By J.S. Boston in New England: Reprinted by John Allen, for Nicholas Boone, 1718.   N

How to Know the Age of a Horse by His Teeth, p. 43.

SOCIAL amusements; or, Holidays at Aunt Adela's cottage. Translated, with some alterations, from the French, "Les jeudis dans le chateau de ma tante." Boston: William Crosby and Company, 1839.   RT

Yellow boards, with title on cover, vignettes front and back covers. 7 pl, vignettes throughout. Childrens' games, including shuttlecock, hoops, etc.

1849: Social sports; or, Holiday amusements. Boston: W. J. Reynolds and Company.   RT

Text as in 1839 edition except for different title-page with vignette. 7 pl. and vignettes.

The SOLITARY hunter . . . *See:* PALLISER, John, *pseud.*

SOMERVILE, William. The chace . . .
See: PENNSYLVANIA gazette.

SOUTH Carolina Jockey Club. Rules of the South Carolina Jocky [*sic*] Club, established February 1824. Revised in 1836. Charleston: Printed by A. E. Miller, No. 4 Broad-Street, 1836.

Yellow paper covers. Title from cover.   N

SOUTH Carolina Jockey Club. *See also:* IRVING, John B.

The SOUTHERN sportsman. Devoted to the sports of the turf and the field, the agricultural interests of the South, literature and stage . . . T. B. Thorpe and R. L. Brenham, editors. Vol. 1, Nos. 1–12, March 18, 1843–June 5, 1843. New Orleans, La., 1843. B

Newspaper format. Boston Public Library has only complete set.

[SOUTHEY, Robert.] Letters from England: by Don Manuel Alvarez Espriella. Translated from the Spanish. In two volumes. Second American edition . . . Vol. I [–II]. New-York: Published by David Longworth, at the Shakespeare Gallery, 1808. D. & G. Bruce, print.   RT

RT copy bound in 1 vol. First American edition was published in Boston, 1806, but without the American editor's notes. Internal evidence is almost conclusive that the American editor was John Howard Payne's friend, and first producer, William Dunlap. RT copy has autograph of Payne, with marginal notes, probably by him. One of editor's notes denies a statement by Southey on American boxing.

SOUTHGATE, F[red]. Wild wood mazurka. By F. Southgate. Baltimore: Published by Henry McCaffrey. John F. Ellis, Washington [1855].   RT

Music only. Lithograph on cover by A. Hoen & Co., Baltimore, of Woodland scene, with deer.

SOUTHRON, A., [*pseud.*]. *See:* SIMMS, William Gilmore.

SPAFFORD, Horatio Gates. Some cursory observations on the ordinary construction of wheel-carriages: with an attempt to point out their defects, and to show how they may be improved . . . With appropriate engravings. By Horatio Gates Spafford,

SPAFFORD, Horatio Gates. *Continued:*

A.M. . . . Albany: Printed and published by E. & E. Hosford, 1815. RT

One engraved plate.

SPARKS, Jared. The library of American biography. Conducted by Jared Sparks. Second series. Vol. XIII. Boston: Charles C. Little and James Brown, 1847. RT

Vol. XIII: *Lives of Daniel Boone* [By John M. Peck] *and Benjamin Lincoln* [by Francis Bowen.].

The SPIRIT of the times. A chronicle of the turf, agriculture, field sports, literature and the stage. Edited by William T. Porter. New York, December, 1831–June 22, 1861. (Vol. 31, no. 20.) N

1831, December 10, vol. 1, no. 1, published by William T. Porter and James Howe under the title *Spirit of the Times & Life in New York.*

1832, March 3, vol. 1, no. 12, published by William T. Porter & Co.

1832, November 17, vol. 1, no. 49, published by James D Armstrong.

1832, December 1, vol. 1, no. 51, n.s. Sold to Hunt & Adams, former proprietors of *New-York Traveller,* and title changed to *The Traveller: Spirit of the Times and Life in New-York.* William T. Porter resumed management of the sporting department. This was also vol. 1, no. 40, of *The Traveller.*

1832, February 2. Absorbed *Porter's Family Journal,* and title changed to *The Traveller, Family Journal and Spirit of the Times and Life in New York.*

1833, March 16. Hunt and Adams sell to Charles J. B. Fisher.

1833, June 22. Firm becomes Fisher and Inman.

The American Antiquarian Society has almost a complete file from December 10, 1831. No perfect set known. Available on film in Library of Congress, New York Public Library, and a few other large libraries. Not to be confused with *Porter's Spirit of the Times,* or *Wilkes' Spirit of the Times,* which are separate and distinct publications. *See:* Carvel Collins. *"The Spirit of the times,"* in: Bibliographical Society of America. *Papers.* New York, 1946, pp. 164-168; Carvel Collins, An extra issue of *The Spirit of the Times,* in: Bibliographical Society of America. *Papers.* New York, 1954, p. 198; Norris Yates, *The Spirit of the Times:* its early history . . . in: Bibliographical Society of America. *Papers.* New York. 1954, pp. 117-148.

[SPOFFORTH, Reginald.] Hark the Goddess Diana. A favorite duett. Sung by Messrs. Hodgkinson & Williamson at the Anacreontic Society. New York: Printed & Sold at J. Hewitt's

Musical Repository, no. 131 William Street. Sold also by B. Carr, Philadelphia & J. Carr, Baltimore, [ca. 1798].

Two leaves. Words and music. Fox hunting.   RT

1809: Hark the Goddess Diana. A favorite duett. Philadelphia: Printed for G. Willig & sold at his Musical Magazine, no. 12 South 4th street, [ca. 1809].   N

1810: Hark the Goddess Diana. Philadelphia: Published by G. E. Blake, no. 1 South 3d. Street, [ca. 1810].   RT

Covers lacking from RT copy.

SPORTING CALENDER! The great match over the Pennsylvania course, in 1823. *See:* PURDY, Jr.

SPORTS for all seasons. New-York: T. W. Strong, 98 Nassau-st. [ca. 1840].   RT

Title from colored front cover, with illustration and border. 12 pp. with woodcut on each page. Trap-ball and cricket, p. 8. Publisher's advertisement on back cover.

[ca. 1850:] Sports for all seasons. Published by Fisher and Brother, publishers, 8 S. 6th Street, Philadelphia and 71 Court Street, Boston, 74 Chatham Street, N.Y., 64 Baltimore Street, Baltimore.

SPORTS and amusements, for the juvenile philosopher. A present for the young. Part first. Middletown: Published by E. Hunt, 1835.   RT

Frontispiece, and illustrations throughout text.

1836: Second edition.   RT

Except for title page, appears to be from same plates as 1835 edition.

SPORTS of childhood. Northampton: Published by E. Turner [ca. 1840].   RT

4⅞ inches by 3 inches. Pictorial paper covers lacking from RT copy. Vignette on title-page, small cuts throughout text. Games include quoits, football, fives, trap-ball, cricket, etc. Different from following item.

227

The SPORTS of childhood; or, Pastimes of youth. New Haven: Published by S. Babcock [ca. 1839].   RT

2¾ inches by 1¾ inches. Paper covers, with border round title. Vignette on title-page, illustrated. Games are: blowing bubbles, cricket, walking on stilts and archery.

SPORTS of the turf. *See:* WORSHAM, John.

SPORTS of the turf and pit. *See:* BATES, Richard.

SPORTS of youth; a book of plays. New Haven: S. Babcock, Church Street, 1838.   RT

Paper covers. Vignette on title-page of squirrel. Front cover same as title-page. 7.5cm. x 4.8cm. Includes, *"Playing ball,"* which appears to be base-ball.

The SPORTSMAN'S companion; or, An essay on shooting: illustriously shewing in what manner to fire at birds of game, in various directions and situations—and Directions to gentlemen for the treatment and breaking their own pointers and spaniels . . . By a gentleman . . . New York: Printed by Robertsons, Mills and Hicks, 1783.   Y

Not in Evans. *See* p. xxvii.

1791: Second edition. Burlington, Printed by Isaac Neale.   RT

Evans: 23785.

[1792:] Third edition. Philadelphia, Printed for the purchasers.
                    LC

Evans: 24809. Although written by an English army officer, this is the first book to actually describe hunting in America as a sport, and therefore is of great importance. It contains a reference to hunting the now extinct heath hen, on Long Island. Only 2 copies known of first edition, Y and Maclay. 5 copies of the second edition are knowwn. *See: Gee.*

The SPORTSMAN'S dictionary; or Cyclopedia, n.p., 1833.

Two numbers only issued: Vol. 1, no. 1. February 1833; Vol. 1, no. 2. March 1833. No title-page. Dictionary runs through A–B. Wood engravings in text. Only known copy formerly owned by Mr. E. R. Gee.

The SPORTSMAN'S portfolio of American field sports. Boston: M. M. Ballou, corner of Tremont and Bromfield Streets, 1855.
                    RT

Paper covers. Front cover has additional wording and emblematic border: *Twenty-four illustrations. Price, 25 cents. Finely illustrated.* There are 20 illustrations as listed in the Index, vignette on title-page, and plates on p. 44 and back cover. Originally issued in: *Gleason's Pictorial,* Boston, 1853–1854. *See:* VAN WINKLE. Hunting . . .

SPRAGUE, William B. A sermon addressed to the Second Presbyterian congregation in Albany, March 4, 1838, the Sabbath after intelligence was received that the Hon. Jonathan Cilley, Member of Congress from Maine, had been shot in a duel with the Hon. William J. Graves, Member from Kentucky . . . Published by request of many who heard it. Albany: Printed by Joel Munsell, 1838.   RT

Paper wrappers. Cover title: *Doctor Sprague's sermon, occasioned by the late tragical deed at Washington.*

SPRING, Rev. Samuel. The sixth commandment friendly to virtue, honor and politeness. A discourse in consequence of the late duel, addressed to the North Congregational Society of Newburyport: August 5, 1804. Newburyport, Mass.: From the press of E. W. Allen . . . 1804.   RT

RT copy lacks paper covers.

SPRINGER, John S. Forest life and forest trees: comprising winter camp-life among the loggers, and wild-wood adventure . . . New York: Harper & Brothers . . . 1851.   RT

Frontispiece, 8 plates, and woodcuts throughout text.

1856: New York, Harper & Brothers.   N

Frontispiece, 8 plates, and woodcuts throughout text.

SPRINGFIELD, Rollo. The horse and his rider; or, Sketches and anecdotes of the noble quadruped, and of equestrian nations. New York: Wiley & Putnam . . . 1847.   RT

Six plates.

[SQUIER, Ephraim George.] Waikna; or, Adventures on the Mosquito shore. By Samuel A. Baird. [*Pseud.* of Ephraim George Squier.] With sixty illustrations. New York: Harper & Brothers, 329 & 331 Pearl Street, 1855.   RT

SQUIER, Ephraim George. *Continued:*

Extra engraved title-page. Later editions issued under title: *Adventures on the Mosquito shore,* which is in Jamaica.

[STEDMAN, Charles Ellery.] Mr. Hardy Lee, his yacht. Being XXIV sketches on stone, by Chinks. Boston: Published by A. Williams & Co., 100 Washington Street, 1857.   RT

Title from cover, with rope border and vignette. 5949. "Chinks," who drew the sketches published under the title "Mr. Hardy Lee, His Yacht," etc. was Dr. Charles Ellery Stedman, a physician for many years in Dorchester. This book, and a few other drawings, were the only ones published, as Dr. Stedman was not fully satisfied with them . . . A.S. From note in Notes and Queries column of the *Boston Transcript,* "a good many years ago". G. T. Goodspeed, Dec. 26, 1940.

[STEPHEN, Sir George.] The adventures of a gentleman in search of a horse. By Caveat Emptor, gent., One etc. Philadelphia: Carey, Lea & Blanchard, 1836.   RT

Label on spine. Small wood engravings throughout text. First published London, 1835.

1838: *In:* The rural library, a publication of standard works . . . Vol. I. Conducted by S. Fleet. At the Agricultural Warehouse and Seed Store . . . New York.   RT

Reprint of 2 ed., London, 1836, with woodcuts in text.

1857: Philadelphia, John W. Moore . . .   N

Vignette on title-page. Published in a variety of colored cloth bindings, with variant tooling.

STEPHENS, Thomas. A new system of broad and small sword exercise, comprising the broad sword exercise for cavalry and the small sword cut and thrust practice for infantry. To which are added, instructions in horsemanship. Illustrated by forty-five handsome and effective engravings. Prepared and arranged by Thomas Stephens, professor of broad and small sword exercise. Philadelphia: I. R. & A. H. Diller, republishers, 1843.   RT

Illustrations in text.

STERRET, James. The patent horse-breaker, and economical farrier; with lessons for breeding . . . Compiled . . . By James Sterret, (who has been afflicted with the loss of his eyesight since the 16th of August, 1846,) and published by him for his own pecuniary benefit . . . Harrisonburg, Va.: Wartmann & Stevens . . . 1854.   RT

Paper covers.

STEVENSON, Sir J[ohn] A[ndrew], composer. *See:* ATKINSON, Joseph. See our bark.

STEVENSON, Sir J[ohn] A[ndrew]. See our oars with feather'd spray. The celebrated boat glee sung with unbounded applause at "The Glee." Composed by Sir J. A. Stevenson. New York: Published by Hewitt, 137 Broadway [ca. 1830].   RT

Words and music. A rowing song. RT copy lacks cover.

STEWART, Adam. Knickerbocker Saloon quick step. Composed and respectfully dedicated to the proprietors of the Knickerbocker Saloon. By Adam Stewart. [Boston:] Published by Martin & Beals, 184 Washington St. . . . [cop. 1845].   RT

Music only. Lithograph on cover of bowling alley, by W. Sharp & Co., Lith.

STEWART, John. Stable economy: a treatise on the management of horses, in relation to stabling, grooming, feeding, watering, and working . . . From the third English edition, with notes and additions, adapting it to American food and climate, by A. B. Allen . . . New York: D. Appleton & Co. . . . 1845.   RT

Small cuts throughout text. First published Edinburgh and London, 1838.

1846: New York, D. Appleton & Co. . . .   RT

1853: New York, D. Appleton & Company.   N

1856: The stable book; being a treatise on the management of horses . . . New York, C. M. Saxton & Co. . . .   RT

Frontispiece.

1859: New York, A. O. Moore.   LC

[STEWART, Sir William Drummond.] Altowan; or, Incidents of life and adventure in the Rocky Mountains. By An amateur traveller. Edited by J. Watson Webb. In two volumes. Vol.

I [–II]. New York: Harper & Brothers, publishers, 82 Cliff Street, 1846.   RT

Attributed to Sir William Drummond Stewart. Binder's title: *Life and adventure in the Rocky Mountains.* Gilt buffalo hunt on covers.

STITH, William. The sinfulness and pernicious nature of gaming. A sermon preached before the General Assembly at Williamsburg, March 1, 1752. . . . Williamsburg: Printed by William Hunter, 1752.

Evans: 6939.

STORIES about dogs. Concord, N.H.: Rufus Merrill, 1850.

Paper covers. Vignette of dog on t.-p. 11 cm. Copy in the library of Murray Horowitz, M.D., N.Y.C.

STORIES of hunters and hunting. New York: Leavitt and Allen, 21 & 23 Mercer Street [ca. 1850].   RT

Frontispiece, vignette on title-page and 7 plates all colored. Bound with this is: 1. *Stories of squirrels, marmots, and other animals.* 2. *Fables for children.* 3. *Scenes in Europe.* 4. *Scenes in Africa.* 5. *Stories of the Arctic Regions.* All have separate title pages, separate pagination and colored plates. Binder's title: *The Child's present* (on spine), *Child's keepsake* (on cover).

STORIES of hunters and travelers. Philadelphia: James L. Gihon, 1857.   Y

STORY of the old man and his dog Trim: together with The affectionate dog, a tale of truth. Watertown: Published by Knowlton & Rice, 1830.   RT

Paper covers. Vignette title page, small woodcuts on covers and throughout text. Different from: *William Middleton and his dog Trim,* Cincinnati, [ca. 1845.]

STOUCHTOWN Society for Pursuing and Detecting Horse Thieves and House Breakers. Rules regulating the Stouchtown Society for pursuing and detecting horse-theives [sic] and housebreakers, adopted at a full meeting of the members, the 29th day of December, 1821, on the report of a committee, appointed for that purpose. Lebanon [Pa.]: J. Stoever, printer [1822]. RT

Broadside 36 cm. x 45 cm.

STREET, Alfred B[illings]. The burning of Schenectady, and other poems. Albany: Weare C. Little. New York, D. Appleton and Co.—Boston: Little and Brown. Philadelphia, Carey and Hart, 1842.　　　　　　　　　　　　　　　　RT

Contains poems: *Angling, Deer shooting, Spearing.* Section *Poems,* with half-title, separately paged [1–36]. An edition, probably the first, Albany: Printed by C. Van Benthuysen and Co., 1842, contains the first section only, not the *Poems.*

STREET, Alfred B[illings]. The poems of Alfred B. Street. Complete edition. New York: Published by Clark & Austin . . . 1845.　　　　　　　　　　　　　　　　　　　　　RT

Added engraved title-page dated 1846. Engraved frontispiece. Contains: *Forest Sports, The Lost Hunter, The Hunter's Flight, Angling, Deer Shooting,* and other hunting poems.

STRONG, J. D. A plea against dueling. A discourse delivered in the First Presbyterian Church, at Oakland, California, Sunday, September 25th, 1859. By Rev. J. D. Strong. Published by request. San Francisco: Towne & Bacon . . . 1859.　　RT

Paper covers. Cover title identical with title-page.

STUTZMAN, J. J. The newly-discovered process of bridling . . . wild colts . . . *See:* RAREY, John Solomon.

STUTZMAN, J. J. and M'Bride, J. W. The newly discovered process of bridling . . . wild colts . . . *See:* RAREY, John Solomon.

SUE, Eugene. The Godolphin Arabian; or, The history of a thoroughbred. New York: E. Winchester . . . 1845.　　RT

First published in *La Presse,* "a popular Paris journal," ca. 1838, running through 12 numbers. A request for information appeared in *The Sporting Magazine,* London, in December, 1838, and the editor responded with a synopsis of the Sue article in the issue of Feb., 1839, pp. 307–312. This synopsis was reprinted in *The American Turf Register,* Feb., 1839, Vol. 10, pp. 25–30. The translation was originally made for *The Sunday Times,* London, and first reprinted as a separate in London, 1845. This translation sometimes *erroneously* attributed to H. W. Herbert. Illustrated paper covers, frontispiece, wood engravings throughout text. Illustrations in New York edition are copies of those in London edition. The London edition has 2 plates and 5 small cuts in text: the New York edition has one plate and 3 small cuts. The frontispiece of the London edition is omitted, and the plate is the frontispiece in the New York edition. The illustrations in the London edition are signed: *T. Onwhyn;* those in the New York edition are not signed. Both editions in RT.

[1850:] The Godolphin Arabian; or, The history of a thorough-bred. By Eugene Sue, author of "The Wandering Jew," "Latreaumont," "The Temptation," etc. etc. Philadelphia: J. & J. L. Gihon, 98 Chesnut St. For sale by all booksellers and periodical agents throughout the United States.   RT

Vignette on title page as in New York 1845 edition, and text and illustrations in text seem to be identical with this edition, except for different title page, and absence of the frontispiece as in the 1845 edition.

1857: The King of the winds [The Godolphin Arabian], Translated expressly for *Porter's Spirit of the times* [by Henry William Herbert], in: *Porter's Spirit of the times.* New York, April 25, 1857 (Vol. 2, no. 8. Whole no. 34.)—May 30, 1857. (Vol. 2, no. 13. Whole no. 39.)   N

This translation (but not the London and New York 1845 editions) was made by H. W. Herbert, who added a new chapter (Ch. 11).

1861: Godolphin Arabian, or The King of the winds. [Translated by Henry William Herbert.] In: *Wilkes' Spirit of the Times.* New York, April 20, 1861 (Vol. 4, no. 7. Whole no. 85.) —June 15, 1861 (Vol. 4, no. 15. Whole no. 93.)

This is the same translation and extra chapter by H. W. Herbert as in the 1857 *Porter's Spirit. See:* Bibliographical Society of America. *Papers.* New York, 1946. Vol. 40, pp. 162–164.

SURE methods of improving health, and prolonging life; or, A treatise on the art of living long and comfortably, by regulating the diet and regimen . . . To which is added, The art of training for health, rules for reducing corpulence, and maxims of health . . . Illustrated by cases. By a physician. First American edition, with additions. Philadelphia: Carey, Lea & Carey—Chesnut Street . . . 1828.   RT

Of exercise, Section II, pp. 113–164.

SURTEES, R[obert] S[mith]. The horseman's manual: being a treatise on soundness, the law of warranty, and generally on the laws relating to horses . . . New York: W. R. H. Treadway, 1832.   N

Boards, paper label. First published London, 1831.

[SURTEES, Robert Smith.] Jorrocks's jaunts and jollities; or, The hunting, shooting, racing, driving . . . exploits of that renowned sporting citizen, Mr. John Jorrocks . . . In two volumes. Philadelphia: E. L. Carey and A. Hart, 1838.   HTP

Boards, paper labels. First appeared in *New Sporting Magazine,* London, between 1832 and 1834. First edition in book form, London, 1838.

[SURTEES, Robert Smith.] Mr. Sponge's sporting tour. Edited by Frank Forester. [*Pseud.* of Henry William Herbert.] . . . With illustrations by John Leech. New York: Stringer & Townsend . . . 1856.   RT

Colored plates. First published London, 1853.

1859: New York, W. A. Townsend & Co.

Also remainder of this edition, with uncolored frontispiece only.

SWELL life at sea; or, Fun, frigates and yachting. A collection of nautical yarns. From the log-book of a youngster of the mess. New York: Stringer & Townsend, 222, Broadway, 1854.

Frontispiece and extra engraved title-page. Six "articles . . . selected . . . from the writings of some of the best authors of the age."

SWIFT, Jonathan. The journal of a gaming lady of quality, in a letter to a friend. A tale. By Messieurs Swift, and Pope. New York: Printed and sold by J. Parker, and W. Weyman . . . 1758.

Evans: 8265.

SWIFT, Owen. Boxing without a master; or, Scientific art and practice of attack and self defence . . . New York: O. A. Roorbach . . . [ca. 1852.]   N

Paper covers, small cuts throughout text. First published London, 1848.

[ca. 1853:] New York, R. M. DeWitt.   HCL

Cover title: *Art of Self Defence* . . .

[ca. 1854:] Boston, W. Berry & Co.   HCL

1856: New York, Akarman.   HCL

SYKES, Jo. Jo Sykes at Sharon Springs. New York: Published by Sherman & Co. . . .   Y

Wood engraving of hunter on paper cover.

[TALIAFERRO, H. E.] Fisher's river (North Carolina). Scenes and characters. By "Skitt" [*Pseud.*], who was raised thar. Illustrated by John M'Lenan. New York: Harper & Brother . . . 1859.   RT

Frontispiece and 12 plates.

TALLY ho, a favorite hunting song as sung by Mrs. Burke. New York: Published by J. A. & W. Geib, 23 Maiden Lane [1819].

Sheet music and words, fox hunting. Not same as WILLSON, Joseph.

TAPLIN, William. The American farrier; or, New York horse doctor: being a further improvement upon Adancourt's "Taplin improved" . . . *See:* BRACKEN, Henry. Farriery improved . . .

TAPLIN, William. A compendium of practical and experimental farriery, originally suggested by reason and confirmed by practice. Equally adapted for the convenience of the gentleman, the farmer, the groom, the smith . . . Wilmington: Printed by Bonsal & Niles . . . 1797.   RT

Folding frontispiece. First published Brentford, 1796. Evans: 32906.

TAPLIN, William. The gentleman's stable directory: or, Modern system of farriery . . . Also Particular directions for buying, selling, feeding, bleeding, purging, and getting into condition for the chase . . . With a successful method of treating the canine species, in that destructive disease called the distemper. Two volumes in one. Twelfth edition. Philadelphia: Printed by T. Dobson . . . 1794.

Second title: The gentleman's stable directory: or, Modern system of farriery. Volume the second. Containing experimental remarks upon breeding, breaking, shoeing, stabling, exercise, and rowelling. To which are added particular instructions for the general management of hunters and road horses; with concluding observations upon the present state of the turf. Philadelphia: Printed by T. Dobson . . . 1794.   RT

See also: Bracken, Henry; Mills, John. First published London, 1788. Evans: 27771.

1812: New edition. Philadelphia, Published by James Webster. Two volumes in one.   RT

TAUTPHOEUS, Baroness. Quits: a novel. In two volumes. Philadelphia: J. B. Lippincott & Co., 1858. 2 vols. in 1. N

Chapter XI describes a game of battledore and shuttlecock.

TAYLOR, Jane. "Sporting on the village green." Written by Jane Taylor, composed by Stephen Glover. Philadelphia: Lee & Walker, 188 Chestnut St. [ca. 1850]. RT

Words and music. At head of cover: *The Young Vocalist*. Lithograph on cover of childhood games: hoops, skipping, etc.

TAYLOR, John. The art of defence on foot . . .
See: ROWORTH, C.

TAYLOR, Joseph. Curious antiquities: or, The etymology of many remarkable old sayings, proverbs, and singular customs; explained by Joseph Taylor. New York: Published by Samuel Wood & Sons, No. 261, Pearl-Street; and Samuel S. Wood & Co. . . . Baltimore, 1820. RT

Frontispiece. Contains: *Origin and antiquity of cock-fighting, The origin of duelling, The antiquity of boxing and wrestling.*

TAYLOR, Joseph. The general character of the dog: illustrated by a variety of original and interesting anecdotes . . . Philadelphia: Published by Benjamin Johnson . . . 1807. RT

Frontispiece. First published London, 1804.

1836: The general character of the dog: illustrated by a variety of original and interesting anecdotes of that beautiful and useful animal, in prose and verse. New-York, Mahlon Day, No. 374 Pearl Street. RT

Published anonymously. Preceded by four plates, with two cuts of dogs on each.

[TAYLOR, Joseph.] Wonders of the dog; displayed by numerous entertaining and instructive anecdotes, in prose and verse. With illustrative engravings. Philadelphia: Willis P. Hazard, 178 Chestnut Street, 1851. RT

Boards. Frontispiece and 3 plates.

TAYLOR, Joseph. The wonders of the horse, recorded in anecdotes, and interspersed with poetry. Selected by Joseph Taylor . . . New York: Published by George G. Sickels . . . 1828.

TAYLOR, Joseph. *Continued:*

Four wood engravings, marbled paper covers. First published London, 1808.

1836: New York, Mahlon Day. RT

TELLER, Thomas. The mischievous boy: a tale of tricks and troubles. New Haven: Published by S. Babcock [1845]. RT

Paper covers. Cover title: *The mischievous boy; a tale of tricks and troubles.* Edited by Thomas Teller. Embellished with new and beautiful engravings . . . *Teller's tales.* New series. Number five. Numerous engravings of children's games: fishing, gymnastics, archery, baseball, etc.

TEN minutes advice to every gentleman going to purchase a horse out of a dealer, jockey, or groom's stables. In which are laid down established rules for discovering the perfections and blemishes of that noble animal. Philadelphia: Printed by Joseph Crukshank, for W. Aikman, bookseller in Annapolis, 1775.

Second title on E2: [Burdon, William]. The gentleman's pocket farrier; shewing how to use your horse on a journey: and what remedies are proper for common accidents that may befal him on the road . . . Philadelphia: Printed by Joseph Crukshank, for W. Aikman, bookseller in Annapolis, 1775. RT

1787: Philadelphia, Printed and sold by Joseph Crukshank . . .

Also reprinted in many farriers. AAS

THOMAS, Uncle. *See:* CHRISTMAS blossoms.

THOMPSON, D[aniel] P[ierce]. Gant Gurley; or, The trappers of Umbagog. A tale of border life. Boston: John P. Jewett & Co., 1857. Y

THOMPSON, J. Modern practice of farriery; or, Complete horse-doctor . . . Likewise the most certain rules for chusing horses. With easy directions for riding . . . New York: Printed for Berry, Rogers and Berry [1793]. RT

Engraved frontispiece. Not in Evans.

1807: Philadelphia, Printed by Joseph Crukshank. RT

THOMPSON, P., editor. *See:* WASHINGTON Social Gymnasium.

[THOMPSON, William Tappan.] Chronicles of Pineville: embracing sketches of Georgia, scenes, incidents, and characters. By the author of "Major Jones' courtship." With twelve original engravings by Darley. Philadelphia: Carey and Hart, 1845. LC

Added engraved title-page. Of the eight sketches in this volume, three are humorous sporting anecdotes.

1853: Philadelphia, Getz, Buck & Co. N

THOMSON, Edward. Address, delivered before the Trustees and patrons of Norwalk Seminary July 12th 1836. By Edward Thomson, M.D. Published by the Trustees. Norwalk [Ohio] S. & C. A. Preston, printers [1836]. RT

Stiff paper covers. A discourse on the benefits of exercise, advocating swimming, pedestrianism, gymnastics, fencing and riding.

THOREAU, Henry David. Walden; or, Life in the woods. Boston: Ticknor & Fields, 1854. N

THOREAU, Henry David. A week on the Concord and Merrimack Rivers. Boston & Cambridge: James Munroe & Co. . . . 1849. N

[THORPE, Thomas Bangs.] The big bear of Arkansas, and other sketches, illustrative of characters and incidents in the South and Southwest. Edited by William T. Porter, With illustrations by Darley . . . Philadelphia: T. B. Peterson & Bros. [1843.] Y

Collection of sketches of sport by popular writers of the time.

1845: Philadelphia, Carey & Hart. LC

Added engraved title-page.

1847: Philadelphia, Carey & Hart.

Illustrated.

1855: Philadelphia, H. S. Getz. LC

[1858:] Philadelphia, T. B. Peterson & Brothers. LC

See: Wright.

239

THORPE, Thomas Bangs. *Continued:*

THORPE, [Thomas Bangs.] Colonel Thorpe's Scenes in Arkansaw. Containing the whole of the Quarter race in Kentucky; and Bob Herring, the Arkansas bear hunter . . . To which is added Drama in Pokerville; A night in the swamp, and other stories. By J. M. Field, Esq., of the St. Louis *Reveille.* With sixteen illustrations, from original designs by Darley. Philadelphia: T. B. Peterson and Brothers . . . [cop. 1858.]   N

2 vols. in 1, with separate title-pages and pagination. *First title:* Porter, William T., editor. A quarter race in Kentucky and other sketches, illustrative of scenes, characters, and incidents, throughout "The Universal Yankee Nation" . . . With illustrations by Darley. Philadelphia: T. B. Peterson and Brothers . . . *Second title:* Field, J[oseph] M. The drama in Pokerville; The bench and bar of Tareytown, and other stories. By "Everpoint," (J. M. Field, Esq., of the St. Louis *Reveille.*) With eight illustrations . . . By F. O. C. Darley. Philadelphia: T. B. Peterson. . . . [cop. 1850].

THORPE, T[homas] B[angs]. The hive of "The bee-hunter." A repository of sketches, including peculiar American character, scenery and rural sports. Illustrated by sketches from nature . . . New York: D. Appleton & Co., 1854.   RT

Frontispiece, 8 plates, and illustrations throughout text. Issued in blue and brown cloth.

THORPE, T[homas] B[angs]. The mysteries of the Backwoods; or, Sketches of the Southwest: including character, scenery, and rural sports. With illustrations by Felix O. C. Darley. Philadelphia: Carey and Hart, 1846.   RT

Frontispiece, 5 plates. The plates were repeated in his: *The hive of "The bee-hunter."*

THORPE, Thomas Bangs. *See also:* The SOUTHERN sportsman.

THRILLING stories of the forest and frontier. By an Old Hunter. Philadelphia: H. C. Peck & Theo. Bliss, 1853.   RT

Frontispiece, 34 plates, and cuts throughout text. Contains extracts from R. G. Gordon-Cumming's *Five Years of a Hunter's Life.*

1859: Philadelphia, H. C. Peck & Theo. Bliss.   RT

TIMBS, John. Knowledge for the people: or, The plain why and because. Familiarizing subjects of useful curiosity and amusing research . . . Domestic series. Hartford: S. Andrus and Son, 1844.   RT

Section *Sports and pastimes* includes hunting, horse-racing, tennis, etc.

TIMONY, Patrick, *pseud. See:* EGAN, Pierce.

TODD, John. Long Lake. Edited by J. Brace, Jr. Pittsfield, Mass.: E. P. Little, 1845.   N

Chapter on deer hunting.

TOME, Philip. Pioneer life; or, Thirty years a hunter. Being scenes and adventures in the life of Philip Tome . . . Buffalo: Published for the author, 1854.   AAS

See: Van Winkle. Hunting . . .

TOWAR, Alex[ander]. Der Amerikanische Pferdearzt, enthaltend eine Anweisung zur Erziehung und Haltung der Pferde, so wie auch eine Beschreibung aller der Krankheiten, welchen sie unterworfen sind, und den bewährtesten und besten Arzeneymitteln dagegen. Nebst einem Anhang, worin alle vorkommenden Krankheiten des Kindviehs, der Schaafe und der Schweine beschrieben, und die nöthigen Heilmittel, ihnen zu helfen, angezeigt sind. Aus den besten Amerikanischen und Englischen Schriftstellern zusammen getragen und übersetzt. Philadelphia: Herausgegeben von Alex. Towar, Nre. 19 St. James Strasse; für Hogan und Thompson . . . 1832.   RT

Frontispiece.

TOWNSEND John K. Narrative of a journey across the rocky mountains to the Columbia River . . . Philadelphia: Henry Perkins . . . 1839.   N

Reprinted as: *Sporting Excursion in the Rocky Mountains, etc.* London: Henry Colburn, 1840. 2 vols.

[1843:] Philadelphia, Published at the office of the Saturday Museum.   AAS

TRALL, R[ussell] T[hacher]. The illustrated family gymnasium; containing the most improved methods of applying gymnastic, calisthenic, kinesipathic, and vocal exercises to the development of the bodily organs, the invigoration of their functions, the preservation of health, and the cure of diseases and deformities. With numerous illustrations. New York: Fowler and Wells, publishers, No. 308 Broadway, 1857.   RT

Frontispiece and 6 plates, and illustrations in text.

TRICKS and traps of New York City. *See:* HERBERT, Henry William.

[TRIPP, Alonzo.] The fisher boy. By Willie Triton [*pseud*]. Boston: Whittemore . . . 1857.   HCL

First edition of a scarce New England fishing novel.

TRITON, Willie, *pseud. See:* TRIPP, Alonzo.

TUFFNELL, B. F. The gentleman's pocket farrier.
                                              See: BURDON, William.

The TURF horse. Columbus, by Oscar. Danville, Ky.: J. W. Dismukes. [ca. 1845.]

Broadside. Contains an account of the horse by Josiah Dunn, with pedigree of Columbus and performance of his colts. *See: Van Winkle. Hunting* . . .

TURNER'S comic almanac. With lots of comic engravings, for 1838. Philadelphia: Turner & Fisher . . . [1837].   RT

Sporting jokes and caricatures. RT has 1849, same publisher; 1845, Boston, Published by James Fisher; 1847, Philadelphia, Turner & Fisher; 1849, Boston, Published by James Fisher; 1850, New York, Published by Fisher & Brothers.

TURNER, J. W. Rippling wave waltz. Composed by J. W. Turner. Boston: Published by Oliver Ditson & Co. . . . 1856. RT

Music only. At head of title: *To the Union Boat Club of Boston.* Lithograph on cover.

UNCLE John. *See:* NOYCE, Elisha.

UNITED Bowmen of Philadelphia. *See:* The ARCHER'S Manual.

UNION Race Course [Long Island]. Rules and regulations to be observed on the Union Race Course from and after October 1831. [New York?: 1831.]

Four leaves, pp. [1]-8. Two copies known. One owned by Lynn Eberstadt, the other by a private collector.

United States. Circuit Court, (Third Circuit). The opinion of the Circuit Court of New Jersey, on the rights of fishery in the river Delaware; delivered by Justice Baldwin. Philadelphia: Printed by Thomas Kite, 64 Walnut Street, 1831.

Concerns provisions of two laws of New Jersey, 26 November 1808 and 28 November 1822, prohibiting the use of gilling nets in the river Delaware. Copy in New York Historical Society.

UNITED STATES. House of Representatives. Report of the Committee of Claims, to whom was referred, on the 10th of February last, The petition of Amey Dardin. 18th March, 1800. Committed to a committee of the whole House to-morrow. [Washington:] Published by order of the House of Representatives. [1800]. RT

Concerns a claim for a horse named Romulus, which General Greene requisitioned during the Revolution, and which was appraised at "seven hundred and fifty pounds hard money."

1803: United States. Committee of Claims. Petition of Amey Dardin. 3d February, 1803. Referred to the Committee of Claims. Washington City: Printed by William Duane & Son, 1803. RT

The UNITED States sporting magazine, and Annals of the American and English turf . . . A work entirely dedicated to sporting subjects and fancy pursuits . . . Edited by C. R. Colden . . . New York: Printed and published by Scott & Co. . . . 1835-1836. Y

Vol. 1: November, 1835-April, 1836.
Vol. 2: May, 1836-August, 1836.
Issued monthly in paper covers. A successor to: *New York Sporting Magazine*. Plates in black and white only. *See: Gee*.

The UNIVERSAL songster; a collection of the most fashionable, popular, sentimental, comic, patriotic and naval songs. Together

UNIVERSAL songster. *Continued:*

with *Catches, glees, &c.* New-York: Printed by T. H. Turney, 1832.   RT

Words only. Contains: *The Mail Coach, Tally ho, The hunter's horn* [by Thomas Philipps], *The Mail Coach Adventure.*

UNIVERSITY Boat Club. The constitution of the University Barge Club. Philadelphia: Inquirer Printing Office, 1856.   RT

Brown-paper covers. Six pp. Title on cover only. Membership limited to twenty-five.

VAN DYK, Harry Stoe. Merrily, merrily sounds the horn. The German minstrel. Written by Harry Stoe Van Dyk, composed by John Barnett. New York: Published at Hewitt's Music Store, 137 Broadway. Sold at the Music saloon, 36 Cornhill, Boston. [ca. 1830.]   RT

Words and music. Cover lacking from RT copy.

[VAN RANST, C. W.] An authentic history of the celebrated horse *American Eclipse,* containing an account of his pedigree and performances . . . Embellished with a correct likeness of this famous horse, engraved on wood, in the best style, By Dr. A. Anderson. New-York: Printed by E. Conrad . . . 1823.   N

Paper covers.

VARIOUS methods of catching. Philadelphia: J. Johnson [ca. 1790].   LC

A small, child's book, illustrated with wood engravings. Among the subjects are: *Angling, Spearing of Eel, Catching a Wolf, Catching a Horse.*

[1805:] Various modes of catching. Philadelphia, Published by J. Johnson.   N

VEREINIGTE Gesellschaft von Bernville und der Taunschips Penn, Bern, Heidelberg, Tulpehoccon und Jefferson in Berks Caunty, um Pferde-Diebe und Haus-Erbrecher zu verfolgen. Grundregeln der . . . Reading: Gedrucht bey Ritter und Comp., 1852.   RT

Small pamphlet of 16 pages, title on p. [1] as cover. p. [16] blank. Vignette on title-page.

VERMONT. Acts passed at the Legislature of the State of Vermont, at their October session, 1829. Published by authority. Woodstock: Printed by D. Watson, 1829.   RT

Paper wrappers. Title from cover.
Ch. 15: *An act, to preserve fish in . . . the town of Starksborough.*
Ch. 16: *An act, to preserve fish in . . . Ludlow and Plymouth.*
Ch. 17: *An act, to repeal an act, entitled "An act, to preserve fish in Woodford pond."*
Ch. 18: *An act, repealing an act, entitled "An act, to preserve the fish in . . . Bennington . . ."*

VIEL, Edmond. Chanson Styrienne: Le hardi chasseur de Chamois. The hunters song. Paroles d'Edmond Viel. Musique par Gustave Blessner. Philadelphia: George Willig, 171 Chestnut St. [cop. 1842].   RT

Words (English and French) and music. At head of cover: À Madame C. B. Lord. Cover lacking from RT copy.

The VILLAGE green; or, Sports of youth. New Haven: Published by S. Babcock, 1840.   RT

Vest-pocket size "Toy book". Paper covers. A poem describing various games, including baseball, battledore and shuttlecock, etc.. with cuts of games.

VIRGINIA and Maryland Farmer. The domestic animal's friend, or, the complete Virginia and Maryland farrier, being a copious selection from the best treatises on farriery now extant in the United States, in five parts. I. Advise to purchasers of horses . . . Winchester, Va.: Printed and published by J. Foster, 1816.

436 pp. Noted in Catalogue no. 2, 1964, Edward C. Fales, Salisbury, N.H.

VIRGINIUS. Political truth; or, an examination of a case, right against law, told in plain English, concerning the laws of Virginia against gaming: with sundry general observations, shewing things as they are, and man as he is. By Virginius. Richmond: Printed for the author [ca. 1805].   LC

Paper wrappers.

WALKER, Donald. British manly exercises: in which rowing and sailing are now first described; and riding and driving are for the first time given in a work of this kind; as well as . . . walking,

WALKER, Donald. *Continued:*

running . . . skating . . . wrestling, boxing, training &c., &c., &c. Philadelphia: Thomas Wardle . . . 1836. RT

Added engraved title-page, and frontispiece included in fifty engravings, reproductions of those in edition of London, 1834. Engravings grouped together between *Contents* and text.

1837: Philadelphia.

1856. Walker's manly exercises; containing rowing, sailing, riding, driving, racing, hunting, shooting, and other manly sports. The whole carefully revised or written, by "Craven." From the ninth London edition. Philadelphia: Published by John W. Moore, No. 195 Chesnut Street. RT

Added engraved title-page, 44 plates, and woodcuts in text.

WALLACE, W[illia]m Vincent. The angler's polka. Composed by Wm. Vincent Wallace. New York: Published by Wm. Hall & Son . . . [1854]. RT

Sheet music, 9 pp. Fly-fishing lithograph by Sarony & Co. on cover. At head: *To His Friend Wm. T. Porter, Esq.* Text descriptive of music throughout composition: . . . *some cast the fly . . . a big fish takes hold . . .*

[1854:] New York, Published by Wm. Hall & Son. RT

Same as above. Part of descriptive text omitted.

WALLACE, W[illia]m Vincent. Winter polka, or, Recollections of a merry sleigh ride. Composed and dedicated to Maurice Strakosch by Wm. Vincent Wallace. New York: Published by William Hall & Son, 239 Broadway . . . 1853. RT

Music only. Lithograph of sleighing scenes on cover.

WALLIS, William. The Western gentleman's farrier; containing remedies for the different diseases to which horses are incident in the Western and South Western States . . . To which is added an Appendix; containing receipts for the cure of many diseases to which horses . . . are liable . . . Dayton-Ohio: Printed and Published by E. Lindsley . . . 1832. RT

1838: The Western gentleman's farrier, containing remedies for the different diseases to which horses are incident in the Western and South Western States. By William Wallace . . . To which is

added an Appendix, containing receipts for the cure of many
diseases to which horses . . . are liable . . . Troy, O., Printed
and published by John T. Tullis.   RT

A piracy of the 1832 edition, but contains extra, a full page letter of recommendation signed by six well-known pioneer stage-horse proprietors.

[WALN, Robert.] The hermit in Philadelphia. Second series.
Containing some account of . . . dandies and ruffians . . . dandy
slang . . . lotteries and quacks; billiards and pharo; gambling
and sporting . . . theatricals and horse racing . . . By Peter
Atall, Esq. [*Pseud.* of Robert Waln.] Philadelphia: Published
for the author by J. Maxwell and Moses Thomas . . . 1821.   RT

The first series: *The Hermit in America on a Visit to Philadelphia*, Philadelphia, 1819, is non-sporting.

WALTON, Izaak. The complete angler, by Izaak Walton and
Charles Cotton. Vol. I [–II]. London: Charles Tilt, 86 Fleet-
Street; J. Menzies, Edinburgh; T. Wardle, Philadelphia, 1837.
                                                   N

Extra colored title-pages, frontispieces. Since this was printed in England,
it should not, perhaps be regarded as a first American edition, although
the American publisher appears on the title-page. Small, leather bound,
gilt tooling.

WALTON, Isaac. The complete angler; or, The contemplative
man's recreation, and instructions how to angle for a trout or
grayling in a clear stream, by Charles Cotton . . . A notice
of Cotton and his writings, by the American editor [George
Washington Bethune] . . . Part I [–II]. New York and London:
Wiley & Putnam, 161 Broadway, 1847.   RT

Large paper edition. Two parts, with separate title-pages, bound in one
volume. First American edition. 2 portraits, 2 plates and many illustrations in text. The Philadelphia 1844 edition listed by Peter Oliver is probably of much later date. Contains: *Trout fishing on Long Island*, by
H. W. Herbert. This edition not listed in Oliver. Also occurs in 2 volumes bound, and in wrappers. 29cm x 18cm.

1847: New York and London, Wiley and Putnam.   RT

An edition from same plates as above, but 19.7cm x 13cm. Cloth, gilt top,
rules blind stamped.

WALTON, Isaac. *Continued:*

1847: New York and London, Wiley and Putnam.   RT

Apparently a gift issue, 19.2cm x 12.7cm. Gilt edges, rules and tooling stamped in gold.

1848: New York, John Wiley.   AAS

1852: New York, John Wiley.   N

1859: New York, John Wiley.   VW

See: Van Winkle.

WARE, Henry, Jr. The law of honor. A discourse, occasioned by the recent duel in Washington; delivered March 4, 1838, in the Chapel of Harvard University . . . Cambridge: Folsom, Wells, and Thurston . . . 1838.   RT

Paper covers.

WARE, James. The pocket farrier: or, Gentleman's guide in the management of horses under various diseases . . . Directions for judging of the horse's age, and useful observations on the breeding, raising, and training of colts. Hints to purchasers, and general directions for using a horse on a journey . . . By James Ware, Amherst County, Virginia . . . [Richmond, Va.:] T. W. White, printer, 1828.   RT

Frontispiece.

WARREN, John C. The importance of physical education. Boston, 1831.

WASHINGTON Jockey Club. Rules of the Washington Jockey-Club. George-Town: Printed by William A. Rind, 1803.

Marbled paper covers.   HTP

WASHINGTON Social Gymnasium. Quoit Club carols, or Noctes gymnasii. Published by order of the Washington Social Gymnasium . . . Washington, 1839.   RT

Yellow paper wrappers, lettering identical with title-page. Edited by P. Thomson.

The WATERMAN'S boast. *See:* PHILADELPHIA Glee Association.

WATKIN, Henry. The Arabian art of taming and training wild and vicious horses . . . *See:* RAREY, John Solomon.

WATKINS, J. S. The Persian and Arabian farrier . . .
See: FANCHER, O. H. P.

[WATMOUGH, Edward Coxe.] Scribblings and sketches, diplomatic, piscatory, and oceanic. By a fisher in small streams. Philadelphia: Printed for the publisher, 1844.   RT

1844: Second edition, with additions. Philadelphia, C. Sherman.
RT

Cushing lists under William Linn Brown, and states: Wrongly attributed to Edmund C. Watmough. Sabin lists under William Linn Brown, but later corrects to Edward Coxe Watmough. A copy in the Fearing Collection at Harvard University is signed: Edmd. C. Watmough. Titcomb's *New England Families* refers in text, familiarly, as Edmund, but lists in index under Edward C. "Edward Coxe Watmough A.B., 1839; A.M., 1842 d. July 14, 1848 Phila. Pa." (From *"General Alumni Catalogue* of the University of Pennsylvania 1922" p. 21.)

WATSON, Henry C[lay]. Thrilling adventures of hunters, in the old world and the new. Boston: Kelley & Bro., 1853.   LC

Illustrations and colored plates.

1855: Boston, Kelley & Bro.   N

WAYNE, Henry C[onstantine]. The sword exercise, arranged for military instruction . . . Published by authority of the War Department. Washington: Printed by Gideon and Co., 1850.   RT

Two volumes in one. 23 plates (22 folded). Each volume has special title page dated 1849; *Fencing with the Small Sword,* and *Exercise with the Broadsword.*

WEBBE, Samuel. Huntsman's call. A great favorite hunting glee. Composed by Samuel Webbe. Philadelphia: Published and sold by Geo. Willig, 171 Chestnut St., [ca. 1840].   RT

Words and music. Fox hunting. RT copy lacks covers.

WEBBER, C[harles] W[ilkins]. The hunter-naturalist. Romance of sporting; or, Wild scenes and wild hunters. Philadelphia: J. W. Bradley [1851].   N

WEBBER, Charles Wilkins. *Continued:*

Frontispiece and 9 chromo-lithographs. Vignette title-page, 2 full page wood engravings, and numerous small wood engravings throughout text. Chapters 20 through 24 are Adirondack stories, and are an abridged version of a series of letters that first appeared in the *New York Courier and Enquirer,* and reprinted in *The Spirit of the Times,* all in vol. 18, 1848, as follows:

Courier:		*Spirit:*	
	July 21		July 29, p. 272
	August 7		August 12, p. 295
	August 9 and 11		August 19, pp. 307–8
	August 18		August 26, p. 321
	August 24		September 2, pp. 328–9
	September 4		September 16, p. 352
	September 8 and 23		September 30. pp. 376–7
	October 3		October 21, p. 416

Most of the letters are entitled: *Letters from the sporting grounds.* Three letters of October 3 in the *Courier* were not reprinted in the *Spirit.* They are critical of the landlords of Lake Pleasant. Webber complains that local guides saved the best fishing for a few favored gentleman sportsmen, and duped the rest of the tourists. Abridged English editions of *The hunter naturalist* were published in England under the title *The romance of forest and prairie life* by Charles H. Clarke, London, [ca. 1855], and Henry Vizetelly, London, [ca. 1853]. Both were anonymous.

1852: Wild scenes and wild hunters of the world. Philadelphia, J. W. Bradley. RT

1852: The hunter-naturalist . . . Philadelphia, Lippincott, Grambo & Co. RT

1852: Romance of natural history; or, Wild scenes and wild hunters. Philadelphia, Lippincott, Grambo & Co. RT

1854: The hunter-naturalist . . . Philadelphia, Lippincott, Grambo & Co. N

Binder's title: *Wild Scenes and Wild Hunters.*

1856: The hunter-naturalist . . . Philadelphia, J. B. Lippincott & Co. RT

Added colored engraved title-page, with imprint: Lippincott, Grambo, and Co. Colored frontispiece differs from 1852.

1858: Wild scenes in the forest and prairie; or, The romance of natural history. By W. C. [*sic*] Webber. London; Edinburgh; and New York: T. Nelson and Sons. RT

Added engraved title-page. Frontispiece and 4 plates.

1859: The hunter-naturalist . . . Philadelphia, J. B. Lippincott & Co.   N

Added engraved title-page with imprint: Lippincott, Grambo & Co.

WEBBER, C[harles] W[ilkins]. The hunter-naturalist. Wild scenes and song-birds. Illustrated with twenty-five colored lithographs, drawn by Mrs. C. W. Webber and Alfred J. Miller. New York: George P. Putnam & Co. . . . 1854.   Y

This work is different from the author's *Hunter-Naturalist. Wild Scenes and Wild Hunters.*

WEBBER, Charles W[ilkins]. Old Hicks the guide; or, Adventures in the Camanche Country in search of a gold mine. New York: Harper & Brothers . . . 1848.   RT

Chapter XVIII: *The games* [Indian].

WEBER, Carl Maria Friedrich Ernst von. The hunter's chorus (English and French) from Weber's Celebrated opera Der Freyschutz. [New York:] Published by E. S. Mesier, 28 Wall St., [ca. 1827].   RT

Begins: What equals on earth the delight of the huntsman? Words and music. Stag hunting. Blue paper. Covers lacking.

[ca. 1827]: Philadelphia: Published and sold by G. E. Blake, no. 13 South 5th Street.   RT

Covers lacking.

[ca. 1830:] Weber's Hunting chorus, from the opera of Der Frieschutz, arranged for the piano forte, by M. H. Parnell. Composer and Director of Music to Boston Theatre. Boston: Published by C. Bradlee, no. 164 Washington Street [ca. 1827–1834].   RT

Words and music. RT copy lacks covers. Begins: We roam thro' the forest and over the mountain.

[ca. 1840:] The hunters chorus from the favorite opera Der Freyschutz by C. M. Von Weber, with variations arranged for two performers on the piano forte by G. F. Harris. Baltimore: Published and sold by Geo. Willig, Jr. [ca. 1844].   RT

Music only

WEBBER, Charles Wilkins. *Continued:*

[ca. 1840:] The huntsman's chorus and waltz, in Der Freyschutz. Arranged for the pianoforte. Boston: Published by Thomas Spear, no. 21 School Street. RT

Music only. Lithograph of three operatic hunters by Senefelder Lith. Co.

WEBER, Carl Maria Friedrich Ernst von. Lutzow's wild hunt. A glee for four voices as sung by the Messrs. Herrmann & Co. Composed by C. M. von Weber. Boston: Published by C. Bradlee, Washington St., [ca. 1836]. RT

Words and music. Cover lacking. Major Lutzow commanded a free Corps in the years 1813 and 1814 in the German war against France. This Corps chiefly consisted of students, and from their wearing a black uniform they were commonly called *The Black Hunters.* Begins: From yonder dark forest what horsemen advance.

WEEMS, M[ason] L[ocke]. God's revenge against duelling, or The duellist's looking glass; exhibiting that gentlemanly mode of turning the corner, in features altogether novel, and admirably calculated to entertain and instruct the American youth. By M. L. Weems, author of the Lives of Washington, Marion, Drunkard's Looking Glass &c. . . . Georgetown, D.C.: Published by Elijah Weems, for the author. Gideon, print. Washington, 1820. N

On verso of title-page is D.C. copyright to M. L. Weems, dated 1819, 'forty-fourth year.'

1821: God's revenge against duelling, or The duellist's looking glass; exhibiting that gentlemanly mode of turning the corner, in features altogether novel, and admirably calculated to entertain and instruct the American youth. Second edition . . . Revised and greatly improved . . . Philadelphia, printed for M. L. Weems. J. Bioren, printer. RT

Frontispiece and 2 plates. Plates numbered 14 and 16. Text differs from first edition; on verso title-page is Pennsylvania copyright dated 1816.

1821: God's revenge against duelling, or The duellist's looking glass; exhibiting that gentlemanly code of turning the corner, in features altogether novel, and admirably calculated to entertain and instruct the American youth. Second edition . . . Revised and greatly improved . . . Philadelphia, Printed for M. L. Weems. J. Bioren, printer. N

Frontispiece and 2 plates. Title plates and plates identical with 1821 edition, including date. Cover imprint: *God's revenge against duelling; or, The duellists looking glass; exhibiting that gentlemanly mode of turning the corner . . . Third edition.* Probably only nominally a third edition.

[1827:] God's revenge against duelling, or The duellist's looking glass; exhibiting that gentlemanly code of turning the corner, in features altogether novel, and admirably calculated to entertain and instruct the American youth. Third edition—Revised and greatly improved . . . Philadelphia, Published by Joseph Allen. Sold by John Grigg, North Fourth Street.

Frontispiece, plate. Frontispiece folded, identical with that in 1821 edition. Copyright to Joseph Allen dated 1827, on verso of title-page. Text same as 1821 edition.

WEEMS, Mason Locke. God's revenge against gambling exemplified in the miserable lives and untimely deaths of a number of persons of both sexes . . . Philadelphia, 1810.

No copy of this edition *extant,* but Sabin dates as probably 1810.

1812: Second Edition. Philadelphia, Printed for the author. AAS

1816: Third Edition. Philadelphia, Printed for the author.   N

1818: Fourth Edition. Philadelphia, Printed for the author.

1822: Fourth Edition. Philadelphia, Printed for the author.   RT
Frontispiece.

1824: Anecdotes of gamblers, extracted from a work on gambling, by M. L. Weems, formerly rector of Mount Vernon Parish. Philadelphia, To be had of Benjamin & Thomas Kite, No. 20, North Third Street.   RT
Extracts from: *God's revenge against gambling.*

[WELLES, Noah.] The real advantages which ministers and people may enjoy especially in the Colonies, by conforming to the Church of England; faithfully considered, and impartially represented, in a letter to a young gentleman. Printed in the year 1762.   RT

A satire opposing the establishment in America of the Episcopal Church. Contains a long reference and quotation from the *King's Book of Sports. See:* Henderson, Robert W. *The King's Book of Sports in England and America.* New York Public Library. *Bulletin.* New York, November 1948.

The WESTERN agriculturist and practical farmer's guide. Prepared under the superintendence of the Hamilton County Agricultural Society. Cincinnati: Published by Robinson and Fairbank, 1830. RT

Engraved frontispiece and plates. Contains: *Blooded Horses in the West,* by Daniel Gano. A basic source on the history of the Kentucky thoroughbred.

1832: The farmer's guide and Western agriculturist. By several eminent practical farmers of the West, and published under the patronage of the Hamilton County Agricultural Society. Cincinnati: Published by Buckley, Deforest and Co., 1832. RT

Illustrations, plates.

The WESTERN review and miscellaneous magazine, a monthly publication devoted to literature and science. Lexington, Ky.: Published by William Gibbes Hunt, August 1819–July 1821.

"Paramount in importance are the contributions of Constantine S. Rafinesque, who, if not the actual editor of the first three volumes, was by far the heaviest contributor. His articles run the gamut from verses in original French . . . to his monumental work *Ichthyologia Ohiensis,* which appears here for the first time, under the titles *Description of the Ohio River,* and *Natural history of fishes in the Western Waters.* As a matter of fact, R. E. Call is authority for the statement that the quarto sheets which made up the book were struck off from the same type. Only the supplementary material does not appear in the *Western review."*—Ernest J. Wessen in: *Midland Notes,* June, 1948.

WESTERN side-saddle scenes and young lady's equestrian manual . . . *See:* The YOUNG lady's equestrian manual.

WHIP, The. May 1 (?) 1839. New York: C. R. Colden.

Only one issue. Editor died day after publication of first issue.

WHITE, Edward L. The hunted deer. Duet & chorus, sung at a concert given by the New Bedford Philharmonic Society. Written by a lady of Fairhaven. Music composed & respectfully dedicated to the Ladies of New Bedford by Edward L. White. Boston: Pub. by C. Bradlee, 1836. RT

Words and music. Lithograph of dogs pursuing deer on cover.

WHITE, James. A complete system of farriery, and veterinary medicine. Containing a compendium of the veterinary art . . .

and the principles and practice of shoeing . . . First American edition, newly arranged from the 10th London edition. Pittsburgh: Published by R. Patterson and Lambdin . . . 1818.   RT

18 plates at end. First published London, 1804.

1832: Second American edition, newly arranged from the tenth London edition. Pittsburgh: Published by Henry Holdship & Son . . . 1832.   RT

18 plates at end, except that plate 5 is used as frontispiece.

The WHITE palfrey. By the author of "Thomas Mansfield," "The waning moon," &c. Boston: Cottons and Barnard, 184 Washington St., 1829.   RT

Pink stiff paper covers. Cover title same as title-page, including vignette, but with border additional. Back cover border with floral emblem. Juvenile horse story.

The WHOLE art of boxing: replete with instruction in the manly art of self-defence. To which is added, The art of swimming, and bather's companion, with full directions for learners. Philadelphia: Published by Fisher & Brother, no. 8 South Sixth Street Philadelphia; 64 Baltimore Street, Baltimore; 74 Chatham Street, New York; 71 Court Street, Boston, [ca. 1850].   RT

Frontispiece. Bound with, and paged in, pp. [65-128]: The AMATEUR, or guide to the stage. Containing lessons for theatrical novices . . . Philadelphia: Fisher & Brother . . . ca. 1850.

WIESENTHAL, T. V. Cheer up! pull away. A boat-song, from Forrest's travels, composed & dedicated to William B. Finch, Esqr. of the United States Navy, by T. V. Wiesenthal. Philadelphia: Published by J. G. Klemm, Music Seller, no. 3 South 3d. Street [ca. 1823–1825].   RT

Words and music. No illustration on cover.

WILD western scenes. *See:* JONES, John Beauchamp.

WILKES' Spirit of the times. A chronicle of the turf, field sports, literature and the stage. New York, September 10, 1859–December 13, 1902.   N

Founded by George Wilkes. Title changed July 4, 1868 to *Spirit of the Times. See:* Bibliographical Society of America. *Papers.* New York, 1946.

WILKES' Spirit of the times. *Continued:*

Vol. 40, pp. 164-168. *See also: The* SPIRIT *of the times* . . . and: PORTER'S *Spirit of the times.* Three separate publications, not to be confused with one another. Absorbed the *New York Sportsman,* May 7, 1892. Absorbed by *The Horseman,* which continued as *The Horseman and Spirit of the Times.*

WILLIAM Middleton and his dog Trim. Cincinnati: Truman & Spofford [ca. 1845]. RT

Truman's entertaining and instructive toy books. Title from cover. Paper covers with border and vignette of children's games. Back cover, cut of boy on dog. 5 full page cuts. Different from: *Story of the old man and his dog Trim, Watertown, 1830.*

WILLIAMS, Charles. Facts not fables. New-York: Published by J. P. Peaselee, 49 Cedar-Street, 1835. CU

Woodcut illustrations. *The chamois-hunter,* p. 88.

WILLIAMS, John M. Extracts from a charge delivered to the Grand Jury at Northampton at the March term of the C. C. Pleas, A.D. 1838. By John M. Williams, an Associate Justice of said Court. Northampton, [Mass.]: Published by J. H. Butler, 1838. RT

Blue-paper wrappers. Cover title: Judge Williams' charge to the Grand Jury, at Northampton, on duelling.

WILLIAMS, S. D. Horsemanship. Training of the colt; training of the vicious horse. The American trotter, how to train and drive him. The saddlehorse, shoeing. A chapter of prescriptions for diseased horses, with rules for trotting, racing, etc. Adrian [Mich.:] [ca. 1858.]

Author mentions Rarey as a contemporary.

WILLIAMS, R. F. The hunters horn is sounding. The poetry by R. F. Williams. Music composed and arranged for the piano-forte by S[ydney] Nelson. New York: Published by Dubois & Bacon, 167 Broadway [ca. 1830]. RT

Words and music. Deer hunting song. RT copy lacks cover.

WILLIS, J. H. Hark, brothers hark! A regatta song & chorus. Written by J. H. Willis. Music composed & dedicated to the boat clubs of the United States by John H. Hewitt. Philadelphia: John F. Nunns, no. 70 South Third Street, [cop. 1837]. RT

Words and music. Rowing song.

WILLIS, Nathaniel P. Al' Abri, or The tent pitched. New York: Samuel Colman, 1839.

Chapter on trout fishing in the Susquehannah Valley.

WILLIS, N[athaniel] P[arker]. The legendary, consisting of original pieces, principally illustrative of American history, scenery, and manners. Edited by N. P. Willis. Vol. I [–II]. Boston: Samuel G. Goodrich, 141 Washington Street, 1828.   N

Angling by I. M'Lennan, vol. I, pp. 208–212.

WILLIS, N[athaniel] P[arker]. Letters from under a bridge. The Mirror library. [No. 7.] New York: Morris, Willis & Co., publishers, no. 4 Ann-Street, 1844.   N

Originally published London, 1840. Paper covers.

WILLSON, Joseph. Tally ho. A favorite hunting song. Compos'd by Joseph Willson Esq.: Organist of Trinity. Published by J. &. M. Paff Maiden Lane. [ca. 1803].   RT

Sheet music. Words and music. Fox hunting. No covers.

WILMOT, Anna, editor. *See:* The AMERICAN keepsake.

[WILSON, Alexander.] The foresters: a poem, descriptive of a pedestrian journey to the Falls of Niagara, in the autumn of 1804. By the author of American ornithology. Newton, (Penn.): Published by S. Siegfried & J. Wilson . . . 1818.   RT

1838: The foresters: a poem, descriptive of a journey to the Falls of Niagara, in the Autumn of 1804. By Alexander Wilson, author of American ornithology. West Chester, Pa.: Printed by Joseph Painter, 1838.   RT

WILSON, John. The recreations of Christopher North. Complete in one volume. Philadelphia: Carey & Hart, 126 Chestnut Street, 1848.   RT

Added title-page: The modern British essayists. Vol. IV. Philadelphia: Carey and Hart, 1848. Portrait frontispiece. Contains: Christopher in His Sporting Jacket.

WILSON, John Lyde. The code of honor; or, Rules for the government of principals and seconds in duelling. Charleston [S.C.]: Printed by T. J. Eccles, 1838.   HCL

Paper covers. A reprint was published in Kennesaw, Ga., 1959.

1845: Charleston [S.C.], Printed by S. S. Miller. N

1858: Charleston, S.C., Printed by James Phynney. N

WILSON, Yorick. The gentleman's veterinary monitor, and stable guide; a concise treatise on the various diseases of horses, their symptoms, and most humane methods of cure. Calculated to enable persons to form an accurate judgement of the diseases of their own horses, and apply proper remedies, without the assistance of a farrier . . . Philadelphia: Published by Johnson and Warner . . . 1810 . . . RT

Boards. First published London, 1809.

1811: The gentleman's modern system of farriery, or stable directory. A concise treatise on the various diseases of horses, their symptoms, and most human methods of cure . . . without the assistance of a farrier. Trenton: Published by James Oram, 1811.

Contemporary half calf.

[WINNER, Septimus]. Our Jenny. A story for young people. By "Alice Hawthorne." Philadelphia: Ch. H. Davis, 1854.

Contains: *The squirrel hunters,* with illustration.

WINTER, George Simon. George Simon Winters wohlerfahrner Pferde-Arzt, welcher gründlich lehrt wie Man die Complexion der Pferde, ihre Natur und alter Erkennen, alle innerlichen und äusserlichen Krankheiten heilen, so wie auch wie Man dieselben vor bevorstehenden Uebeln verwahren könne, nebst einigen höchst seltenen, für junge Fohlen vielfach bewährt gesundenen Arzenei-Mitteln. Durchgesehen, verbessert, mit neuen Zusätzen und erleichternten Küpfern versehen von Valentin Trichter. Philadelphia: Herausgegeben von Edmund N. Schelly, 1840. RT

Plates numbered: A, B, 1-16, Seite 450, 20-32, 34-36, 38-41. First published Nurnberg, 1678.

1841: [Easton?] Northampton County: Herausgegeben von Kleckner, Nolf und Williams. N

Plates identical with 1840 edition.

258

WINTER. [Woodcut] Old age—the winter of life. New-York: Published by Samuel Wood & Sons, No. 261, Pearl-street, and Samual S. Wood & Co. No. 212, Market-st. Baltimore, 1818. RT

Wrappers. "Toy" juvenile, 6 small woodcuts, including vignette on title-page. Includes: *Skating*.

WOHL-EINGERICHTETES Vieh-Arzney-Buch, worin enthalten die Wartung und Pflege, sowol als die Krankheiten und Heilungsmittel. I. Der Pferde . . . Philadelphia: Gedruckt und zu finden bey Henrich Miller . . . 1771. RT

Evans: 12292.

WONDERS of the dog. *See:* TAYLOR, Joseph.

The WOODBURN Stud Farm, property of R. Aitcheson Alexander, near Spring Station P.O., Woodford County, Kentucky . . . Lexington: Kentucky Statesman Print., 1857. Y

Paper covers. Cover title same as title-page. The first Woodburn stud catalog.

WOODMAN, H. F. Row thy boat lightly. Words by Miss H. F. Woodman. The music composed & respectfully inscribed to Mrs. R. S. Jameson (of Hartford) by I[saac] B[aker] Woodbury. Boston: Published by Prentiss & Clark, Washington St., [cop. 1847]. RT

Words and music. Cover lacking from RT copy.

WOODWORTH, S[amuel]. The hunters of Kentucky. Written by S. Woodworth, as sung in character by Mr. Petrie with unbounded applause at Chatham Garden Theatre, the symphonies & accompaniments by William Blondell. Philadelphia: Published and sold by Geo. Willig 171 Chesnut st. [ca. 1820]. RT

Words and music. Cuts of two figures with rifles and hunting horns engraved in text. *See: Dictionary of American Biography.*

1832: Hunters of Kentucky, Or . . . Half horse and half alligator. Sold, wholesale and retail, by L. Deming, No. 62, Hanover Street, Boston, and at Middlebury, Vt. [ca. 1832–1836]. RT

WORSHAM, John. Sports of the turf. [Cuts of two horses.] A grand match race between [blank] by Sir Archy, the property of James J. Harrison, Esq. and Optimus, by Potomac, the property of Abner Robinson, Esq. for the sum of fiive thousand dollars . . . The subscriber, who is the proprietor of the course . . . John Worsham. Pescud, printer. March 18, 1815.   RT

Broadside.

The WREATH: or, Verses on various subjects . . . See: LITTLE-FORD, Mrs.

[YALE University.] The foot ball controversy between the classes of '55 and '56. New Haven: For sale at E. Richardson's, News Office and Book Store, New Haven Hotel Block, 1852.

Wrappers. Noted in American Autograph Shop. *American Clipper,* January 1941.

The earliest PRINTED reference to football in America is in:

Moreri, Louis. The great historical, geographical and poetical dictionary. London 1694. Under the heading: New-York.

The earliest reference in MANUSCRIPT, but not printed till later is in: Dunton, John. Letters written from New England, A.D. 1686. Boston, 1867.

Both references are to the game *played by Indians,* and there is no certainty as to how they played.

Moreri is in the Racquet & Tennis Club.
Photostats of Dunton are laid in Moreri.

[YALE UNIVERSITY]. Regattas on Lake Winnipissiogee! See: BAKER, N. B.

YOUATT, William. The dog. Edited, with additions, by E. J. Lewis. New York: Published by Leavitt & Allen [1846].

Illustrations. First published London, 1845.

1847: Philadelphia, Lea & Blanchard.   N

1848: Philadelphia, Lea & Blanchard.   N

1850: Philadelphia, Lea & Blanchard.   RT

Extra engraved title-page dated 1848.

[185–?] Philadelphia, J. B. Lippincott & Co.   N

YOUATT, William. *Continued:*

1853: Philadelphia, Blanchard and Lea.   RT

Extra engraved title-page dated 1852.

1857: Philadelphia, Blanchard & Lea.   HPL

YOUATT, William. The horse . . . A new edition . . . Together with a general history of the horse; a dissertation on the American trotting horse, how trained and jockeyed . . . and an Essay on the ass and mule by J. S. Skinner . . . Philadelphia: Lea & Blanchard, 1843.   RT

Frontispiece, illustrations. First published anonymously, London, 1831, as: *The Horse; with a Treatise on Draught . . .*

[1843:] New York: Leavitt & Allen, 379 Broadway   RT

[1843:] New York: Leavitt & Allen Bros., no. 8 Howard St.   RT

No frontispiece.

1844: Philadelphia, Lea and Blanchard.   RT

[1845:] Philadelphia, Porter & Coates.   RT

1847: Philadelphia, Lea and Blanchard.   DCL

1848: Philadelphia, Lea & Blanchard.   Y

1849: Philadelphia: Lea & Blanchard.   RT

1850: Philadelphia, Lea & Blanchard.   AAS

1851: Youatt on the structure and the diseases of the horse with their remedies. Also, Practical rules to buyers, breeders, breakers . . . Brought down . . . by W. C. Spooner . . . To which is prefixed, an Account of the breeds in the United States, compiled by Henry S. Randall. With numerous illustrations. Auburn, Derby and Miller.   RT

At the head of title: Seventh thousand.

1851: The horse . . . By J. S. Skinner. Philadelphia, Blanchard & Lea.   CU

261

YOUATT, William. *Continued:*

1852: Youatt on the structure . . . By W. C. Spooner. Eighth thousand. New York, C. M. Saxton. RT

1853: The horse . . . By J. S. Skinner. Philadelphia, Blanchard & Lea. AAS

1853: The history, treatment, and diseases of the horse. Hartford, Published by A. Andrus & Son. RT

Published anonymously, but based on Youatt.

1854: The horse . . . By J. S. Skinner. Philadelphia, Blanchard & Lea. JLO

1855: Youatt on the structure . . . By W. C. Spooner. Twenty-third thousand. New York and Auburn, Miller, Orton & Mulligan. JLO

1856: Youatt on the structure . . . By W. C. Spooner. Twenty-eighth thousand. New York and Auburn, Miller, Orton and Mulligan. JLO

1856: Youatt on the Structure . . . By W. C. Spooner. Thirty-second thousand. New York: C. M. Sexton; Miller, Orton & Mulligan. RT

1856: The horse . . . By J. S. Skinner. Philadelphia, Blanchard & Lea. N

1859: The horse . . . By J. S. Skinner. London, New York, Routledge, Warner & Routledge. LC

1859: Youatt on the structure . . . By W. C. Spooner. New York, C. M. Saxton. JLO

The YOUNG girl's book of healthful amusements and exercises. *See:* The GIRL'S book of healthful amusements and exercises . . .

The YOUNG lady's book: a manual of elegant recreations, exercises and pursuits. Boston: A. Bowen and Carter & Hendee; Philadelphia: Carey & Lea [1830]. LC

Preface signed: *Abel Bowen.* Over 700 engravings (including small initial letters) by Abel Bowen, Alexander Anderson, and others, after cuts by Thompson, S. Williams, Bonner, and others. Includes archery and riding.

1833: Third edition. Boston, Published by Lilly, Wait, Colman and Holden, and Abel Bowen. N

YOUNG lady's book. *Continued:*

1837: Sixth edition. Boston, Published by C. A. Wells.   RT

Frontispiece and added gilt title-page.

1857: Manual of the arts, for young people; or, A present for all seasons. Boston: James French and Company, 1857.   RT

Frontispiece and added gilt title-page. Text, except for introduction, same as *The Young Lady's Book.*

The YOUNG lady's equestrian manual. Philadelphia: Haswell, Barrington, and Haswell . . . 1839.   RT

Frontispiece, illustrations.

1844: Western side-saddle scenes and young lady's equestrian manual. Edited by a Citizen. Rochester, Published by Fisher & Co., 1844.   JLO

Paper cover. Frontispiece, illustrations.

1854: The lady's equestrian manual, in which the principles and practice of horsemanship for ladies are thoroughly explained, to enable every lady to ride with comfort and elegance. With fifty illustrations. Philadelphia, Willis P. Hazard.   RT

Cover title: *The Young Lady's Equestrian Manual.* Text based largely on the chapter on riding, with the engravings, in: *The young lady's book: a manual of elegant recreations.* Boston. . . . Philadelphia, [1830].

YOUTHFUL amusements. A new edition. Philadelphia: Published by Johnson & Warner, No. 147 Market Street, 1810.   RT

Stiff paper covers. Describes thirty games, illustrated in text, including skating, quoits, and trap ball. Is not the same as: *Youthful recreations.*

YOUTHFUL recreations. *See:* YOUTHFUL sports.

YOUTHFUL sports. Philadelphia: Published by Jacob Johnson, 1802.

Marbled wrappers. Plates illustrate 23 sports, including archery, cricket and skating.

[ca. 1810]: Youthful recreations. Philadelphia: Published by J. Johnson. No. 147 Market-Street.   RT

Stiff paper-gilt wrappers. Vignette on title page of boy pushing another in wheelbarrow. 15 full page illustrations of games, including trap ball, football, etc. Vest pocket size.

YOUTHFUL sports. *Continued:*

[ca. 1825:] Youthful sports. [Verse:] *When chilly Winter's reign is o'er* . . . Stereotyped by James Conner, [sic] New-York. New-York: Printed & sold by Mahlon Day at the New Juvenile Book-Store, No. 376, Pearl Street.   N

Paper covers. Vignette on title-page of boy pushing another in wheelbarrow, and caption: *Don't fall off!* Cover title: *Juvenile pastimes in verse.* [Vignette: Moonlight scene. Verse:] *Come boys and girls, Come out to play* . . . Contains trap ball, football etc. Each page to a game, with cut, verse and text.

[ca. 1830:] Youthful sports. [Verse:] *When chilly Winter's reign is o'er* . . . Stereotyped by James Connor, New-York. New York: Printed & sold by Mahlon Day at the New Juvenile Book-Store, no. 376 Pearl-Street.   RT

Cover identical with title-page. Verso of title-page, verse: *Do you want a little Book.* 16 pp. Small cut on each page. Smaller than 1810 edition. Contains football, &c.

1847: Youthful sports . . . New York: S. M. Crane, 374 Pearl-St. Egbert, Hovey & King, printers.   RT

Wheelbarrow cut and verse on title-page. Verso title-page blank. Blue-paper covers, with cut of boy spinning top. Vest-pocket size.

ZELLER, Johann A. Durch viele Curen bestaetigtes Ross-Arzney-Buchlein. Harrisburg, 1806.

Noted in: Cowen, David L. *America's pre-pharmacopoeial literature.* Madison, Wis., 1961.

ZUEND, Joh[ann] Joseph. Handbuch der Pferde-und Vieh-arzney-Kunde, in besonderer Beziehung auf innerliche Krankheiten, Heilmittellehre, Wundarzney, Geburtshülfe u.s.w., für den Landmann und Pferdebesitzer. Herausgegeben von Joh. Joseph Zünd, Thierarzt. Erste Auflage. Philadelphia: Gedruckt für den Verfasser von Heinrich Horn . . . 1832.   RT

Folding frontispiece, wood engraving.

1834: Handbuch der Pferde-und Vieharzney-Kunde in beson-derer Beziehung auf innerliche Krankheiten, Heilmittellehre, Dundarzney . . . für Landmann und Pferdehelftzer. Herausge-geben von Johann Joseph Zünd . . . Erste Auflage. Philadelphia, Gedruckt für den Verfasser . . . bey Augustus Gräter.   JLO

Folding frontispiece, wood engraving.

INDEX OF SUBJECTS

INDEX OF SUBJECTS

Books are listed in chronological order within each subject. Hyphenated dates, such as 1809–1835, indicate two or more editions, the two dates given are for the first and last. It does not follow that because a book is listed under a subject, that the whole book is devoted to that subject: the entry may indicate a chapter, or reference to the subject only.

Almanacs.
1794: Beers's *Almanac.*
1798: *The Annual visitor.*
1831–1839: *The American comic almanac.*
1835–1855: Crockett, David. *Davy Crockett's almanac.*
1836: Crockett, David. *Crockett's Yaller flower almanac.*
1838–1840: *The People's almanac.*
1838–1850: Turner's *Comic almanac.*
1846: *Farmer's and farrier's almanac.*
1848–1851: Brown, John J. *The angler's almanac.*
1849: *Great western almanac.*

Anecdotes, facetiae, etc.
> 1822: Egan, Pierce.
> 1829: *The Humorist.*
> 1831–1839: *The American comic almanac.*
> 1835: Blewitt, Jonathan.
> 1835: Crockett, David. *Davy Crockett's almanac.*
> 1835–1859: Longstreet, Augustus Baldwin.
> 1836: Crockett, David. *Crockett's Yaller flower almanac.*
> 1837: Carey, David.
> 1837: Egan, Pierce.
> 1838–1844: *The Old American comic almanac.*
> 1843–1858: Thorpe, Thomas Bangs. *The hive of "The Bee-Hunter."*
> 1845–1853: Thompson, William Tappan.
> 1846: Thorpe, Thomas Bangs. *The mysteries of the backwoods.*
> 1847–1858: Porter, William Trotter. *A quarter race.*
> 1859: Taliafero, H. E.

Angling. *See* Fishing.

Arabian horse. *See:* Horse, Arabian.

Archery.
> 1802–1830: *Youthful sports.*
> 1820: *Children's amusements.* (*See* p. xviii.)
> 1830: *The Archer's manual.* (*See* p. xix.)
> 1830–1857: *The Young lady's book.*
> 1831–1858: Smith, Horatio.
> 1837: Comstock, John Lee.
> 1839: *The Sports of childhood.*
> 1845: Hoyle, Edmond.
> 1847–1852: *The Boy's treasury of sports.*

Archery: Songs.
> 1836: Brown, Bartholomew.

Associations, Horse racing. *See:* Racing: Associations and clubs.

Ball games. *See also* names of games: Baseball, Cricket, etc.
> 1785: Friends, Society of.
> 1820: *Children's amusements.*
> 1823: *The New York primer.*
> 1830: *Children at play.*
> 1833: Olney, Jesse.

Ball games. *Continued:*

    1841: *Boy's own book of amusements and instruction.*
    1843: *The Choice medley.*
    1847: Paris, J. A.
    1859: *Games and sports.*
   Ball games, Indian.
    1775–1776: Romans, Bernard.
    1854: Eastman, Mary Henderson.
Baseball.
    1762–1787: *A Little pretty book.*
    1820: *Children's amusements.*
    1823: *The New York primer.*
    1828: Mitford, Mary Russell.
    1829–1859: Clarke, William.
    1834: Carver, Robin. (*See* p. xxi.)
    1835–1839: *The Boy's book of sports.*
    1835–1845: *Boy's and girl's book of sports.*
    1837: *Female Robinson Crusoe.*
    1838: *Sports of youth.*
    1840: *The Village green.*
    1845: Teller, Thomas.
    1848–1854: Noyce, Elisha.
    1849: *Juvenile pastimes.*
    1858: Eagle Ball Club.
    1858: Knickerbocker Base-Ball Club.
    1858: Newburgh Base Ball Club.
    1858–1860: *A Manual of cricket and base ball.*
    1859: *Amherst express.*
Bass fishing. *See also:* Fishing.
    1831: Cincinnati Angling Club.
    1858: Herbert, Henry William. *Fishing with a hook and line.*
Bat ball.
    1854: Noyce, Elisha.
Battledore.
    1803: *The Prize for youthful obedience.*
    1804: *Father's gift.*
    1821: Adelaide.
    1835–1836: *Sports and amusements.*

Battledore. *Continued:*

    1840: *The Village green.*
    1858: Tautphoeus, Baroness.
Bear. *See also:* Big game hunting, Hunting.
    1839–1840: *The Corsair.*
    1841–1857: Jones, John Beauchamp.
    1843: Hoffman, Charles Fenno.
    1843–1858: Thorpe, Thomas Bangs. *The big bear of Arkansaw.*
    1845: Porter, William Trotter.
    1845–1852: Goodrich, Samuel Griswold.
    1846: Flagg, John W.
    1846–1859: Elliott, William.
    1847–1848: Porter, William Trotter. *A quarter race.*
    1850: Cooke, Philip St. George.
    1850–1857: Simms, Jeptha Root.
    1852: Beardsley, Levi.
    1853: Prime, William Cowper. *The old house by the river.*
    1854: Robinson, John Hovey.
    1854: Thorpe, Thomas Bangs. *The hive of "The Bee-Hunter."*
    1856: Palliser, John.
    1857–1859: Hammond, Samuel H.
    1858: Reid, Mayne.
    1858: Thorpe, Thomas Bangs. *Scenes in Arkansaw.*
Beaver. *See also:* Hunting, Trapping.
    1831–1847: Pattie, James Ohio.
    1848: Ruxton, George Frederic Augustus.
    1850: Cooke, Philip St. George.
    1850–1857: Simms, Jeptha Root.
    1858–1859: Peters, DeWitt Clinton.
Big game hunting. *See also:* Bear, Elephant, Lion, etc.
    1844–1856: Hawks, Francis Lister.
    1850–1859: Gordon-Cumming, Roualeyn George.
    1851–1857: Frost, John.
    1853: Kennedy, J. Pendleton.
    1853–1859: Campbell, Walter.
    1853–1859: *Thrilling stories.*
    1854–1857: Dielitz, Theodore.

Big game hunting. *Continued:*

    1856–1859: Gerald, Cecile Jules Basile.

    1858: Drayson, Alfred Wilks.

    1858: Reid, Mayne.

Birds. *See also:* Game birds, Wild fowl, and names of birds, Grouse, Woodcock, etc.

    1831–1835: Audubon, John James.

    1844–1859: Audubon, John James.

    1847: Audubon magazine.

Boar, Wild.

    1833–1842: *The People's magazine.*

Boone, Daniel.

    1784–1824: Filson, John.

    1794: Beers's *Almanac.*

    1813: Bryan, Daniel.

    1833–1858: Flint, Timothy.

    1836: *Family magazine.*

    1841–1857: Jones, John Beauchamp.

    1843: *The Book of a thousand songs.*

    1844–1856: Hawks, Francis Lister.

    1847: Sparks, Jared.

    1853–1858: Frost, John.

    1854–1859: Bogart, William Henry.

    1857: *Incidents and sketches.*

    1859: Hartley, Cecil B.

Bowling.

    1796: New Jersey.

    1845: Hoyle, Edmond.

    1846: Providence Bowling Club.

    1847: *Boy's own book of fun.*

  Bowling: Songs.

    1845: Stewart, Adam.

Boxing.

    1808: Southey, Robert.

    1819: Moore, Thomas.

    1820: Taylor, Joseph.

    1822: Egan, Pierce.

    1828: Dagley, Richard.

    1829: *The Complete art of boxing.*

Boxing. *Continued:*

    1832: Barrington, George.
    1833–1834: *New-York sporting magazine.*
    1835: New Jersey.
    1835: O'Rourke, Samuel.
    1835–1859: Longstreet, Augustus Baldwin.
    1836–1856: Walker, Donald.
    1843: Maeder, James G.
    1847: *Boy's own book of fun.*
    1849: Egan, Pierce.
    1850: *The Whole art of boxing.*
    1852–1856: Swift, Owen.
    1854: *Life and battles of Yankee Sullivan.*
    1855: *Life of William Poole.*
    1859: Dowling, Frank Lewis.
    1859: Matsell, George W.
Buffalo. *See also:* Hunting.
    1839–1843: Townsend, John K.
    1841–1847: Jones, John Beauchamp.
    1844–1856: Hawks, Francis Lister.
    1845–1852: Goodrich, Samuel Griswold.
    1846: Stewart, Sir William Drummond.
    1848: Ruxton, George Frederick Augustus.
    1850–1859: Cooke, Philip St. George.
    1851–1858: Webber, Charles Wilkins.
    1854: Eastman, Mary Henderson.
    1854: Thorpe, Thomas Bangs.
    1856: Palliser, John.
    1856–1857: Reid, Mayne.
    1857: *Incidents and sketches.*
    1858–1859: Peters, DeWitt Clinton.
    1859: Johnes, Merideth.
Buffalo: Songs.
    1848: Murray, Sir Charles Augustus.

Calisthenics. *See:* Physical education.
Canoeing.
    1836: Gilman, Chandler Robins.
    1841–1853: Lanman, Charles. *Essays for summer hours.*
    1847: Lanman, Charles. *A summer in the wilderness.*

Canoeing. *Continued:*

1848–1856: Lanman, Charles. *A tour of the river Saguenay.*

1856: Lanman, Charles. *Adventures in the wilds.*

Carriages.

1807: *Book of trades.*

1815: Spafford, Horatio Gates.

Cavalry drills.

1798–1818: Hoyt, Epaphrates.

1799: Davie, William Richard.

1802–1813: Hewes, Robert. *Rules and regulations.*

1804: Hewes, Robert. *An elucidation of regulations.*

1812: Craig, Robert H.

1822: Darrow, Pierce.

1844–1847: Hershberger, H. R.

Chamois.

1835: Williams, Charles.

Chamois: Songs.

1827: Rossini, Gioacchino Antonio.

1846: Neukomm, S.

Children's games. *See:* Games, Children's.

Clubs, Horse racing. *See:* Racing: Associations and clubs

Coaching. *See also:* Carriages.

Coaching: Songs.

1832: *The Universal songster.*

Cock fighting.

1796: New Jersey.

1803: Murray, John.

1820: Taylor, Joseph.

1830: Hoyle, Edmond.

1833–1834: *New-York sporting magazine.*

1835–1836: *The United States sporting magazine.*

1843–1847: Green, Jonathan H. *An exposure of the arts.*

1851–1859: Dixon, Edmond Saul.

1856: *The Baked head.*

1859: Cooper, J. W.

Cricket.

1762–1787: *A Little pretty book.*

1778: *The Royal Pennsylvania gazette.*

1809: *A Peep into the sports of youth.*

Cricket. *Continued:*

1811–1842: Kingston Academy.
1814: Hoyle, Edmond.
1827: Mant, Alicia Catherine.
1828: Dagley, Richard.
1833: *Book of the atmosphere.*
1835: *The Little keepsake.*
1839: *The Sports of childhood.*
1840–1850: *Sports for all seasons.*
1843: Maeder, James J.
1844: *The Cricketer's handbook.*
1847: Peterson, Alexander D.
1847: *Pictorial primer.*
1848–1854: Noyce, Elisha.
1854: Graham, Archibald, H.
1854: Noyce, Elisha.
1858–1860: *A manual of cricket and base ball.*
1859: Irving, John B.
1859: Pycraft, James.

Deer. *See also:* Hunting.
1776: New Jersey.
1830: Miller, James William.
1833–1847: Maxwell, William Hamilton.
1841–1857: Jones, John Beauchamp.
1842: Street, Alfred Billings.
1843: Hoffman, Charles Fenno.
1845: Street, Alfred Billings.
1845: Todd, John.
1846–1859: Elliott, William.
1847: Lover, Samuel.
1849: Herbert, Henry William. *The deerstalkers.*
1850: Headley, Joel Tyler.
1850–1857: Simms, Jeptha Root.
1852: Beardsley, Levi.
1852: Huntington, Jedidiah Vincent.
1854: Egghard, Jules.
1854: Tome, Philip.
1855: *The Sportsman's portfolio.*

Deer. *Continued:*

    1856: Burnham, George P.
    1856: Palliser, John.
    1857: Fuller, R. M.
    1857–1859: Hammond, Samuel H.
    1858: Reid, Mayne.
  Deer: Songs.
    1774: *The Royal American magazine.*
    1818–1821: Harrington.
    1820: Fitzsimmons, E.
    1820: Philipps, Thomas.
    1822: Shield, William.
    1823: Farren, P.
    1830: Lee, Alexander.
    1830: Van Dyke, Harry Stoe.
    1830: Williams, R. F.
    1833: Hewitt, John H.
    1834: Iucho, Wilhelm.
    1836: White, Edward L.
    1847: Schiller, Johann Christoph Friedrich von.
    1850: Huenten, Franz.
    1852: Munck, Johann.
    1854: Marshall, Leonard.
    1854: Pendleton, Mrs. A. V.
    1855: Reed, R. Rhodes.
Dictionaries.
    1833: *The Sportsman's dictionary.* (*See* p. xxviii.)
    1859: Matsell, George W.
Dog.
    1783–1792: The Sportsman's companion.
    1794–1812: Taplin, William.
    1796: Mills, John.
    1799: *A Method of raising.*
    1807–1836: Taylor, Joseph.
    1809: *The Mother's gift.*
    1809–1821: *The Council of dogs.*
    1817: Rohlwes, Johann Nicolaus.
    1818: *My dog and my gun.*
    1828: *The Sagacity of dogs.*

Dog. *Continued:*

1830: Goodrich, Samuel Griswold. *Peter Parley's story.*
1830: *Story of the old man and his dog Trim.*
1834: Goodrich, Samuel Griswold. *The every day book.*
1835: *Poor Bessy.*
1836: Lamb, J.
1837: Marryat, Frederick.
1841: *The Canine race.*
1843: Bailey, F. W. N.
1843: Bingley, Thomas.
1843: Hoffman, Charles Fenno.
1843: *A History of my father's dog Towzer.*
1845: *William Middleton and his dog Trim.*
1846–1857: Youatt, William.
1847–1857: Richardson, H. D.
1848: *The Dog as an example of fidelity.*
1850: *Stories about dogs.*
1850–1857: Peel, Jonathan.
1851: Taylor, Joseph.
1853: *Anecdotes of the dog.*
1854: Mayhew, Edward.
1854: Rush, John.
1856: Butler, Francis. *Dogo-graphy.*
1857: Butler, Francis.
1859: Brown, John.
Dog: Breeding.
1845: Skinner, John Stuart.
1857: Butler, Francis. *Breeding, training, management.*
Dog: Hunting.
1822: Shield, William.
1827–1828: *The American shooter's manual.*
1841: Schreiner, William H.
1845: Skinner, John Stuart.
1846: Mills, John.
1856: Herbert, Henry William. *Complete manual.*
1856: Hooper, Johnson Jones.
Dog: Songs.
1822: Shields, William.
1843: Bailey, F. W. N.
1853: Foster, Stephen Collins.

Dog. *Continued:*

    Dog: Taxation.

        1807: Fleming, Joseph H.

Duck. *See also:* Wild fowl.

        1850: Philadelphia, Wilmington and Baltimore Rail Road.

Duelling. *See also:* Fencing.

        1728: Colman, Benjamin.

        1752: Stith, William.

        1804: Coleman, William.

        1804: Hopkins, Joseph R.

        1804: Ladd, William.

        1804–1815: Rush, Jacob.

        1804: Spring, Rev. Samuel.

        1805: Dwight, Timothy.

        1807–1828: Beecher, Lyman.

        1809: Sampson, William.

        1811–1822: Beasley, Frederick.

        1820: Jewett, Stephen.

        1820: Taylor, Joseph.

        1820–1827: Weems, Mason Locke.

        1821: Bates, Elisha.

        1828: Colton, Walter.

        1830: Newton, Augustus.

        1830: Sega, James. *An essay.*

        1830: Sega, James. *What is true civilization.*

        1838: Barrett, Samuel.

        1838: Niles, M. A. H.

        1838: Sprague, William B.

        1838: Ware, Henry, Jr.

        1838: Williams, John M.

        1838–1858: Wilson, John Lyde.

        1843: *The Book of a thousand songs.*

        1844: Patton, Rev. W. W.

        1845: *Great Duellist.*

        1845–1853: Thompson, William Tappan.

        1847: Simms, William Gilmore.

        1855–1859: Sabine, Lorenzo.

        1859: Berriman, Matthew W.

        1859: Strong, J. D.

Education, Physical. *See:* Physical education.

Elephant. *See also:* Big game.
    1850–1859: Gordon-Cumming, Roualeyn George.
Elk.
    1850–1859: Cook, Philip St. George.
    1853: Kennedy, J. Pendleton.
    1856: Palliser, John.
Elk hound.
    1835: Crockett, David. *Davy Crockett's almanac.*
Exercise. *See also:* Gymnastics, Physical education.
    1745–1804: Armstrong, John.
    1806: Ricketson, Shadrach.
    1813: Cheyne, George.
    1828: *Sure methods of improving health.*
    1830–1833: *The Journal of health.*
    1835: *The School boy's friend.*
    1836: Thomson, Edward.
    1836–1856: Walker, Donald.
    1837: Comstock, John Lee.

Farriers. *See also:* Horse; Diseases.
    1711–1727: *The Husbandman's guide.*
    1724: Gibson, William.
    1734–1843: Burdon, William.
    1764–1840: Markham, J.
    1775–1787: Bartlet, J.
    1787–1799: Erra Pater. *Book of knowledge.*
    1793–1807: Thompson, J.
    1794: Erra Pater. *The fortune teller.*
    1794–1812: Taplin, William. *The gentleman's stable directory.*
    1794–1826: Bracken, Henry.
    1795–1834: Jewett, Paul.
    1796: Mills, John.
    1797: Taplin, William. *Compendium of practical . . .*
    1798: *A Concise system of farriery.*
    1803: Franklin, Augustus.
    1807: Johnson, Jacob.
    1807: *The Pocket farrier.*
    1809–1810: *The Complete farrier.*
    1810–1811: Wilson, Yorick.

Farriers. *Continued:*

    1811–1858: Mason, Richard.
    1816: *Virginia and Maryland farmer.*
    1818: *The Domestic animal's friend.*
    1818: *Farrier's magazine.*
    1818–1826: Carver, William.
    1818–1832: White, James.
    1819: Burris, William.
    1825–1834: Simmons, John.
    1828: Richardson, Josiah.
    1828: Ware, James.
    1829–1835: Hughs, Willis.
    1830: Miller, David.
    1830–1858: Badcock, John. *The veterinary surgeon.*
    1831: Barnum, H. L. *Farmer's farrier.*
    1831–1840: *Farmer's receipt book.*
    1832–1838: Wallis, William.
    1832–1856: Barnum, H. L. *The American farrier.*
    1840: Moore, B. W.
    1840: Peters, Robert C.
    1841: Lamb, Cornelius.
    1842–1847: Rupp, Israel Daniel.
    1844: Girardey, G.
    1845: Cheek, Henry.
    1845: Clater, Francis.
    1845: *The New American pocket farrier.*
    1845–1858: Knowlson, John C.
    1846: *Farmer's and farrier's almanac.*
    1848–1851: Sloan, W. B.
    1852–1860: Fancher, O. H. P.
    1853: Marshall, Josiah T.
    1856: Brandon, A. C.
    1857: *Every man his own farrier.*
    1857–1859: Nash, Ephraim.
    1858: Bentwright, Jeremiah.
Fencing. *See also:* Duelling.
    1734: Blackwell, Edward.
    1808: St. Margueritte, T. de.
    1812: Craig, Robert H.

Fencing. *Continued:*

> 1821: Darrow, Pierce. *The artillerist.*
> 1822: Darrow, Pierce. *Cavalry tactics.*
> 1823: D'Eon, Frederik.
> 1824: Roworth, C.
> 1836: Thomson, Edward.
> 1850: Wayne, Henry Constantine.
> 1859: Berriman, Matthew W.

Fish culture.

> 1854: Fry, William Henry.
> 1857: Garlick, Theodatus.
> 1857: Marsh, George P.
> 1857: Massachusetts. *Report of Commissioners.*
> 1857: New Hampshire.

Fishing. *See also:* Bass, Trout, Salmon, etc.

> 1707: Beverley, Robert (1855).
> 1739: Seccombe, Joseph, (1743).
> 1762–1787: *A Little pretty book.*
> 1789: Fitch, Elijah.
> 1790–1805: *Various methods of catching.*
> 1800: Low, Samuel Parker.
> 1804: *Father's gift.*
> 1813: Fisher, James.
> 1814: Mitchell, Samuel L.
> 1819: *Family receipt book.*
> 1819–1821: *The Western review.*
> 1820: Irving, Washington.
> 1820: Rafinesque, Constantine S.
> 1825: *Innocent poetry.*
> 1828: Dagley, Richard.
> 1828: Willis, Nathaniel Parker.
> 1830: Miller, James William.
> 1830: Milnor, William, Jr.
> 1831: Cincinnati Angling Club.
> 1831: United States. Circuit Court.
> 1833: Jesse, Eward.
> 1834: Goodrich, Samuel Griswold.
> 1835: *Morning walk.*
> 1836: Ball, T.

Fishing. *Continued:*

1837–1859: Walton, Isaac.
1840: Hawes, William Post.
1841: Schreiner, William H.
1841–1853: Lanman, Charles. *Essays for summer hours.*
1842: Street, Alfred Billings.
1844: *The Little fisherman.*
1844: Watmough, Edward Coxe.
1845: Hunt, James Henry Leigh.
1845: Street, Alfred Billings.
1845–1850: Bethune, George Washington.
1845–1857: Brown, John J. *The American Angler's guide.*
1846: Mills, John.
1847: Lanman, Charles. *A summer in the wilderness.*
1847–1857: Walton, Isaac.
1847–1848: Porter, William Trotter. *A quarter race.*
1848–1851: Brown, John J. *The angler's almanac.*
1848–1856: Lanman, Charles. *A tour of the river Saguenay.*
1849: Herbert, Henry William. *Fish and fishing.*
1850: Cooper, Susan Fenimore.
1850: Herbert, Henry William. *Supplement . . . Fish and fishing.*
1850: Irving, John B.
1850: Lippincott, Sara Jane (Clarke).
1850–1855: Frost, John.
1851: *Christmas blossoms.*
1852: Huntington, Jedidiah Vincent.
1854: Canning, Josiah Dean.
1854: Prime, William Cowper. *Later years.*
1855: Abbott, Jacob.
1855: Beecher, Henry Ward.
1855: Beverley, Robert (**1707**).
1855: Penn, Richard.
1855: Squier, Ephraim George.
1856: Burnham, George P.
1856: Herbert, Henry William. *Complete manual.*
1856: Lanman, Charles. *Adventures in the wilds.*
1857: Flagg, Wilson.

Fishing. *Continued:*

    1857: Tripp, Alonzo.
    1857–1859: Hammond, Samuel H.
    1858: Herbert, Henry William. *Fishing with hook and line.*
    1858: North Woods Walton Club.
    1859: Blakey, Robert.
    1859: Cozzens, Frederick Swartwout.
Fishing, Fly.
    1832: Davy, Sir Humphrey.
    1833–1843: Smith, Jerome Van Crowinshield.
    1841: Schreiner, William H.
    1847–1852: *The Boy's treasury of sports.*
    1857: Nettle, Richard.
    1859: Blakey, Robert.
Fishing: Songs.
    1826: *The Memorial.*
    1854: Wallace, William Vincent.
    1856: Jenks, Joseph. (Henry Wadsworth Longfellow.)
    1835: Bailey, Johanna.
    1836: Ball, T.
    1840: A., S. A.
    1840: Russell, Henry.
    1854: Crosby, L. V. H.
    1856: Burnham, George P.
Fives.
    1811–1842: Kingston Academy.
    1820: *Children's amusements.* (*See* p. xviii.)
Fly fishing. *See:* Fishing, Fly.
Football.
    1702: Boston, Massachusetts. *Several rules.*
    1786: Boston. *The by-laws.*
    1802–1830: *Youthful sports.*
    1811–1842: Kingston Academy.
    1829–1839: Clarke, William.
    1840: *Sports of childhood.*
    1847: Miller, Thomas.
    1848–1858: *Boy's own book of sports.* Noyce, Elisha.
    1852: Yale University.

Fowling. *See:* Wild fowl.

Fox hunting.

    1736: *The Pennsylvania gazette.*

    1808: Breck, Charles.

    1810: *The Reformed rake.*

    1822: Egan, Pierce.

    1830: *The Casket.*

    1830: Milnor, William, Jr.

    1836: Apperley, Charles James.

    1838: Surtees, Robert Smith. *Jorrock's jaunts and jollities.*

    1847: Miller, Thomas.

    1849: *Great Western almanac.*

    1851–1858: Webber, Charles Wilkins.

    1852: Beardsley, Levi.

    1852: Herbert, Henry William. *The Quorndon hounds.*

    1856–1859: Surtees, Robert Smith. *Mr. Sponge's sporting tour.*

    1857: Herbert, Henry William. *Sporting scenes.*

Fox hunting: Songs.

    1798: Hook, James. *Bright Phoebus.*

    1803: Wilson, Joseph.

    1819: *Tally ho!*

    1821–1825: Hook, James. *Diana.*

    1830: Radcliffe, F. P.

    1830: Rimbault, Stephen Francis.

    1830–1842: Hyatt, George W.

    1832: Imlah, John.

    1835: Moxley, Alfred.

    1835–1859: Longstreet, Augustus Baldwin.

    1840: Webbe, Samuel.

    1854: H., W.

Gambling.

    1720: *Letter to a friend.*

    1758: Swift, Jonathan.

    1775: *Letter to a gentleman.*

    1785: Friends, Society of.

    1786: Connecticut. Statutes.

    1792–1856: Moore, Edward.

    1796: New Jersey.

Gambling. *Continued:*

1804–1815: Rush, Jacob.
1805: Virginius.
1810–1824: Weems, Mason Locke.
1812: Hyde, Eli.
1821: Waln, Robert.
1828: Dagley, Richard.
1835: Caldwell, Charles.
1840: Methodist Episcopal Church.
1843–1847: Green, Jonathan. *An exposure of the arts.*
1844–1853: Beecher, Henry Ward.
1845: Green, Jonathan H. *The gambler's mirror.*
1848: Green, Jonathan H. *The secret band of brothers.*
1849: Green, Jonathan H. *Gambling in its infancy.*
1850: Green, Jonathan H. *An exposition of games and tricks.*
1850: Green, Jonathan H. *Gambler's tricks with cards exposed.*
1851: Green, Jonathan H. *A report on gambling.*
1852: Richards, John.
1857–1858: Herbert, Henry William.
1857–1858. *Tricks and traps of New York City.*
1858: Green, Jonathan H. *The reformed gambler.*
1859: Matsell, George W.

Game animals. *See also:* Hunting, and names of animals: Bear, Hare, Otter, etc.
1789: Fitch, Elijah.
1815: Clinton, DeWitt.
1845–1855: Audubon, John James. *The viviparous quadrupeds.*
1849: Herbert, Henry William. *Field sports.*
1853: Herbert, Henry William. *American game.*

Game birds. *See also:* Hunting, and names of birds: Grouse, Partridge, Quail, Woodcock, etc.
1783–1792: *The sportsman's companion.*
1789: Fitch, Elijah.
1815: Clinton, DeWitt.
1819–1820: Johnson, Charles Britten.
1827–1828: *The American shooter's manual.*

Game birds. *Continued:*

   1830–1834: *The Cabinet of natural history and American rural sports.*
   1831–1835: Audubon, John James. *Ornithological biography.*
   1835: *Essays on various subjects.*
   1836: *Family magazine.*
   1838: Surtees, Robert Smith.
   1839–1840: *The Corsair.*
   1840–1859: Audubon, John James. *Birds of America.*
   1842: Hawes, William Post.
   1843: Greene, Nathaniel.
   1845: Herbert, Henry William. *The Warwick woodlands.*
   1845: Skinner, John Stuart.
   1846: Herbert, Henry William. *My shooting box.*
   1846: Mills, John.
   1846–1853: Hawker, Peter.
   1849: Herbert, Henry Williams. *Field sports.*
   1851–1857: Lewis, Elisha Jarett.
   1853: Herbert, Henry William. *American game.*
   1853: Krider, John.
   1855: *The Sportsman's portfolio of American field sports.*
   1856: Herbert, Henry William. *Complete manual.*
   1856: Perry, Mathew Calbraith.
   1857: Herbert, Henry William. *Sporting scenes.*
Game birds: Songs.
   1854: Marshall, Leonard.
Games.
   1831–1858: Smith, Horatio.
   1833: Norris, Charles & Co.
Games, Children's.
   1790–1805: *Various methods of catching.*
   1802–1847: *Youthful sports.*
   1810: *Youthful amusements.*
   1811–1842: Kingston Academy.
   1815–1832: *Juvenile pastimes.*
   1820: *Children's amusements.* (*See* p. xviii.)
   1821: Adelaide.
   1829–1859: Clarke, William.

Games. *Continued:*

    1830: *Children at play.*
    1830–1847: *Juvenile pastimes, in verse.*
    1833: *Book of the atmosphere.*
    1833–1837: Child, L. Maria.
    1834: Carver, Robin. (*See* p. xxi.)
    1835: *Juvenile sports.*
    1835: *The School boy's friend.*
    1835–1836: *Sports and amusements.*
    1835–1839: *The Boy's book of sports.*
    1835–1845: *Boy's and girl's book of sports.*
    1839: *The Sports of childhood; or, Pastimes of youth.*
    1839–1849: *Social amusements.*
    1840: *Sports of childhood.*
    1840: *The Village green.*
    1840–1850: *Sports for all seasons.*
    1841: *Boy's own book of amusement and instruction.*
    1845: *The Child's pictorial mentor.*
    1845: Teller, Thomas.
    1847: *Boy's own book of fun.*
    1847: Miller, Thomas.
    1847: *Pictorial primer.*
    1847–1852: *The Boy's treasury of sports.*
    1848–1858: *Boy's own book of sports.*
    1849: *Juvenile pastimes.*
    1849: *Social sports.*
    1850: Taylor, Jane.
    1854: Noyce, Elisha.
    1856–1857: *Little Charley's games and sports.*
    1858: *Every boy's book.*
    1859: *Games and sports.*
Games, Indian.
    1837: *Female Robinson Crusoe.*
    1843: *The Choice medley.*
    1848: Webber, Charles Wilkins.
    1854: Eastman, Mary Henderson.
    1855: Beverley, Robert (**1707**).
Games, Olympic. *See:* Olympic games.

Golf.
  1772: Rush, Benjamin.
  1814: Hoyle, Edmond.
  1829–1839: Clarke, William.
  1847–1852: *The Boy's treasury of sports.*
Grouse. *See also:* Game birds.
  1835: *Essays on various subjects.*
  1847: Lanman, Charles. *A summer in the wilderness.*
  1855: *The Sportsman's portfolio.*
Guns. *See:* Rifles, shotguns, etc.
Gunsmithing.
  1836–1841: Hazen, Edward.
Gymnastics. *See also:* Exercise, Physical education.
  1802–1803: Salzmann, Christian Gotthilf.
  1825: Classical and Scientific Seminary.
  1828: Jahn, Friedrich Ludwig.
  1830: *Elements of gymnastics.*
  1841–1857: Picton, Thomas.
  1845: Teller, Thomas.
  1851: Alfonce, J. E. d'.
  1852: Ontario. Public Instruction.
  1853: Ling, P. H.
  1855: Chiosso, James.
  1855: *The Illustrated manners book.*
  1857: Trall, Russell Thacher.
  1859: Grau, Charles William.

Hare.
  1802: Hare.
  1815: Benham, Asahel.
Hawking.
  1831–1858: Smith, Horatio.
Heath hen.
  1783–1792: *The Sportsman's companion.*
Hockey.
  1811–1842: Kingston Academy.
  1847–1852: *The Boy's treasury of sports.*
Horse. *See also:* Cavalry drills, Farriers, Racing, Riding, Trotting.

Horse. *Continued:*

288

Horse. *Continued:*

1852–1855: Richardson, H. D.
1854: Sterret, James.
1857: The Woodburn stud farm.
1859: Herbert, Henry William. *Hints to horse-keepers.*
Horse: Care, stable management.
1794–1826: Bracken, Henry.
1798: *The Annual visitor.*
1799: Parkinson, Richard.
1830: Lawrence, John.
1831: Badcock, John. *The groom's oracle.*
1844–1847: Mills, James.
1845: Bindley, Charles.
1845–1859: Stewart, John.
1846–1847: *A Plea for the horse.*
1847–1848: Cole, S. W.
1852–1855: Richardson, H. D.
1853: Hare.
Horse: Diseases. *See also:* Farriers.
1770–1791: Deigendesch, Johann.
1771: *Wohl-Eingerichtetes Vieh-Arzny-Buch.*
1790–1805: *Kurtzgefasstes Arzney-Büchlein.*
1791: Clark, James.
1794: *Neuer erfanger, Amerikanischer, Haus-und Stallarzt.*
1802: *Kurz gefasstes Ross-Arznen Buchlein.*
1804: Reff, Henrich.
1805: Schneyder, John.
1806: Zeller, Johann A.
1809: Freitag, Eberhard.
1809: *Sicher und bewährt . . .*
1817: Carver, James.
1817: Rohlwes, Johann Nicolaus.
1818: Hohman, John George. *Die Land-und Haus-Apotheke.*
1820–1856: Hohman, John George. *Die lange verborgene Freund.*
1827–1843: Ballmer, Daniel.
1831: Aikin, Jesse.

Horse. *Continued:*

1832: Towar, Alexander.
1840: Fiehrer, Joseph.
1840–1841: Winter, George Simon.
1842: Leib, Isaac.
1846–1849: *The Horse: its habits.*
1847–1848: Allen, Richard Lamb.
1847–1848: Cole, S. W.
1850: Dadd, George H. *The advocate of veterinary reform.*
1851–1859: *The American veterinary journal.*
1854: Rush, John.
1854–1857: Dadd, George H. *The modern horse doctor.*
1855–1856: Dadd, George H. *The horse owner's guide.*
1856: Guenther, Friedrich August.
1857: Dadd, George H. *Anatomy and physiology.*
1857–1858: Koogle, J. D.
Horse: Foot.
1832: Haslam, John.
1847–1856: Miles, William.
Horse: Shoeing.
1817: Carver, James.
1818–1832: White, James.
1821: Goodwin, Joseph.
1832: Haslam, John.
1856: Miles, William.
Horse: Stud books.
1811–1858: Mason, Richard.
1826: Jeffreys, George Washington.
1826: Randolph, John.
1833: Edgar, Patrick Nisbett.
1834: *General stud book.*
1842–1847: Rupp, Israel Daniel.
Horse: Training.
1794–1826: Bracken, Henry.
1838: Powell, Willis J.
1846: Offutt, Denton. *Method of gentling horses.*
1848–1854: Offutt, Denton. *A new and complete system.*
1850–1856: Baucher, Francois.

Horse. *Continued:*

    1854: Sterret, James.
    1856: Brandon, A. C.
    1856–1859: Rarey, John Solomon. (*See* p. xxv.)
    1857–1859: Nash, Ephraim.
    1858: Bentwright, Jeremiah.
    1858: Booth, Dr. G.
    1858: Williams, S. D.
    1859: Hamilton, R. P.
    1859: Herbert, Henry William. *Hints to horse-keepers.*
Horse, Arabian.
    1857: Richards, A. Keene.
Horse, Morgan.
    1857–1859: Linsley, Daniel Chipman.
Horse, Wild.
    1857: *Incidents and sketches.*
Horse racing. *See:* Racing.
Horse thieves: Preventive associations.
    1822: Stouchtown Society.
    1852: Vereinigten Gesellschaft von Bernville.
    1853: Lebanon County Horse Company.
    1855: Good Intent Horse Company.
    1859: Farmer's Association of Christiana Hundred.
Hunting. *See also:* Big game, Game animals, Game birds, Songs,
  Trapping, and names of animals: Bear, Fox, Lion, etc.
    1786: Boone, Daniel.
    1801–1805: Port folio.
    1815: *Eine Kurtzgefasste neue Sammlung.*
    1818: *My dog and my gun.*
    1820: Littleford, Mrs.
    1825: *Innocent poetry.*
    1826: Flint, Micah P.
    1826: *The Memorial.*
    1827: Depping, J. B.
    1831–1847: Pattie, James Otis.
    1831–1861: *The Spirit of the times.*
    1833: Crockett, David. *Life and adventures.*
    1833–1841: *The People's almanac.*
    1833–1847: Crockett, David. *Sketches and eccentricities.*

Hunting. *Continued:*

1833–1847: Maxwell, William Hamilton.
1834: *The People's magazine.*
1834–1848: Crockett, David. *A narrative of the life.*
1835–1848: Crockett, David. *An account of Col. Crockett's tour.*
1835–1855: Crockett, David. *Davy Crockett's Almanac.*
1836: Crockett, David. *Crockett's Yaller flower almanac.*
1836: *Family magazine.*
1836–1848: Crockett, David. *Col. Crockett's exploits.*
1837–1840: *Gentleman's magazine.*
1839: Krummacher, Friedrich Adolf.
1839–1843: Townsend, John K.
1841: Schreiner, William H.
1844: Timbs, John.
1845: Street, Alfred Billings.
1845–1853: Thompson, William Tappan.
1845: Todd, John.
1846: Napier, Edward D. E. E.
1846: Stewart, William Drummond.
1846: Thorpe, Thomas Bangs. *The mysteries of the backwoods.*
1846–1853: Hawker, Peter.
1846–1859: Elliott, William.
1847–1859: Coyner, David H.
1848: Massachusetts Hunting Club.
1848: Prime, William Cowper. *The Owl Creek letters.*
1848: Ruxton, George F. A. *Adventures in Mexico.*
1848–1853: Bennett, Emerson.
1848–1856: Lanman, Charles. *A tour of the river Saguenay.*
1849: Jones, John Beauchamp.
1849: Mayo: William Starbuck.
1849–1856: Lanman, Charles. *Letters from the Alleghany.*
1849–1859: Ruxton, George F. A. *Life in the far West.*
1850: Cooper, Susan Fenimore.
1850: Grandfather Merryman, *pseud.*
1850: Greenwood, Grace.
1850: Lippincott, Sara Jane (Clarke).

1850: *Stories of hunters and hunting.*
1851–1858: Webber, Charles Wilkins.
1852: Crockett, David. *Pictorial life and adventures.*
1852–1859: *Adventures of hunters and travellers.*
1853: Herbert, Henry William. *American game.*
1853: Kennedy, John Pendleton.
1853–1858: Frost, John.
1853: Hammett, Samuel Adams.
1853–1855: Watson, Henry Clay.
1854: Dielitz, Theodore.
1854: *New York monthly.*
1854: Tome, Philip.
1854: Webber, Charles Wilkins.
1854–1857: Herne, Peregrine.
1854–1859: Gerstaecker, Friedrich Wilhelm Christian.
1854–1859: Hammond, Samuel H.
1855: Beverley, Robert (1707).
1856: Herbert, Henry William. *Complete manual.*
1856: Lanman, Charles. *Adventures in the wilds.*
1856: Reid, Mayne.
1857: *Stories of hunters and travellers.*
1858: Gray, John W.
1858: Robinson, John Hovey.
1858–1859: Peters, DeWitt Clinton.
1859: Blakey, Robert.
1859: Browning, Meshach.
1859: Crockett, David. *Life of Col. David Crockett.*
1859: Hartley, Cecil B.
1859: Taliafero, H. E.
1859: *Wilkes' Spirit of the times.*
Hunting: Songs.
1811: Scott, Sir Walter.
1820–1832: Woodworth, Samuel.
1830: Hart, Joseph.
1831–1837: S., M.
1832: Proch, Heinrich.
1834: Moschelles, I.
1836: Weber, Carl Maria Friedrich Ernst von.

Hunting. *Continued:*

    1837: Hodson, G. A.
    1839: Linley, George.
    1841–1850: Morris, George P.
    1842: Viel, Edmond.

Indian ball games. *See:* Ball games, Indian.
Indian games. *See:* Games, Indian.

Jockey clubs. *See:* Racing: Associations and clubs.

Kangaroo.
    1858: Bowman, Anne.

Lacrosse.
    1775–1776: Romans, Bernard.
Law.
    Law: Coaching.
    1832: New York City.
    Law: Deer.
    1726: Pennsylvania Province.
    Law: Dogs.
    1772: Pennsylvania Province.
    Law: Duelling.
    1726: Pennsylvania Province.
    Law: Fishing.
    1641: Massachusetts Bay Colony.
    1734: New York City.
    1763: Massachusetts Bay Province.
    1829: Vermont.
    Law: Gambling.
    1794: Pennsylvania Province.
    Law: Horse.
    1763: Massachusetts Bay Colony.
    Law: Horse breeding.
    1726: Pennsylvania Province.
    Law: Horse racing.
    1677: Massachusetts Bay Colony.
    1847: Oliphant, George Henry Hewitt.

Law. *Continued:*

Law: Horse thieves.
1700: Massachusetts Bay Colony.
Law: Salmon.
1763: Massachusetts Bay Province.
Law: Wild fowl.
1641: Massachusetts Bay Colony.
Lion. *See also:* Big game.
1850–1859: Gordon-Cumming, Roualeyn George.
1851–1857: Frost, John.
1859: Johnes, Merideth.

Moose. *See also:* Big game.
1814: *The Hunters.*
1849–1853: Headley, Joel Tyler.
1855: *The Sportsman's portfolio.*
Morgan horse. *See:* Horse, Morgan.
Mountaineering.
1818: *The Mountaineer.*
1821: Howard, William.
1843: Hoffman, Charles Fenno.
1856: Ball, Benjamin Lincoln.
Mountaineering: Songs.
1844: Morris, George P.

Olympic games.
1831–1858: Smith, Horatio.
Otter.
1833–1847: Maxwell, William Hamilton.
1835: Davis, J.
1835: *Essays on various subjects.*
1850–1857: Simms, Jeptha Root.
1853: Kennedy, J. Pendleton.
Outdoor life.
1818–1838: Wilson, Alexander.
1830–1833: *The Journal of health.*
1836: Gilman, Chandler Robins.
1841–1853: Lanman, Charles. *Essays for summer hours.*
1848: Prime, William Cowper. *The Owl Creek letters.*

Outdoor life. *Continued:*

  1849: Thoreau, Henry David. *A week in the Concord.*
  1849–1853: Headley, Joel Tyler. *The Adirondack.*
  1850: Headley, Joel Tyler. *Letters.*
  1851–1856: Springer, John S.
  1854: Prime, William Cowper. *Later years.*
  1854: Thoreau, Henry David. *Walden.*
  1855: Hammond, Samuel H.
  1856: Sangster, Charles.

Panther.
  1854: Robinson, John Hovey.
Partridge. *See also:* Game birds.
  1845: *The Child's pictorial mentor.*
  1853: Krider, John.
Pedestrianism. *See:* Walking.
Periodicals.
  1736: *Pennsylvania gazette.*
  1774: *The Royal American magazine.*
  1801–1805: *Port folio.*
  1817: Carey, M. *Sporting magazine.*
  1818: *Farrier's magazine.*
  1819–1821: *The Western review.*
  1819–1834: *The American farmer.*
  1821–1822: *The Moral advocate.*
  1827: *Farmer's, mechanic's, manufacturer's and sports-man's magazine.*
  1829–1844: *American turf register and sporting magazine.*
  1830: *The Casket.*
  1830: Cincinnati Angling Club. *Proceedings.*
  1830–1833: *The Journal of health.*
  1831–1861: *The Spirit of the times.*
  1832–1836: *The People's magazine.*
  1833–1834: *New-York sporting magazine.*
  1833–1836: *The People's magazine.*
  1835–1836: *Gentleman's vade mecum.*
  1835–1836: *The United States sporting magazine.*
  1836: *Family magazine.*
  1837–1840: *Gentleman's magazine.*

Periodicals. *Continued:*

    1839: *The Whip.*
    1839–1840: *The Corsair.*
    1843: *The Southern sportsman.*
    1845–1860: *American turf register and racing and trotting calendar.*
    1851–1859: *The American veterinary journal.*
    1853: *New York clipper.*
    1854: *The Challenge.*
    1854: *New York monthly.*
    1854–1860: *California spirit of the times.*
    1856–1861: *Porter's Spirit of the times.*
    1858: *American racing calendar and trotting record.*
    1859: *Amherst express.* (*See* p. xvii.)
    1859–1902: *Wilkes' Spirit of the times.*
Physical education. *See also:* Exercise, Games, Gymnastics.
    1831: *A course of calisthenics for young ladies.*
    1831: Warren, John C.
    1834: Caldwell, Charles.
    1837: Comstock, John Lee.
    1855: Livermore, A.
    1859: Calthrop, S. R.
    1859: Grace, Charles William.
Pointer. *See also:* Dog, Hunting.
    1783–1792: *The Sportsman's companion.*
    1799: *A method of raising* . . .
Pugilism. *See:* Boxing.

Quail. *See also:* Game birds.
    1846–1853: Hawker, Peter.
Quoits.
    1839: Washington Social Gymnasium.

Raccoon: Songs.
    1830–1836: *Settin' on a rail.*
    1843: *The Book of a thousand songs.*
Racing. *See also:* Trotting.
    1785: Friends, Society of.
    1799: *General advertiser.*

Racing. *Continued:*

1803: Murray, John.
1809: M'Dowell, John.
1811: New Jersey.
1815: Worsham, John.
1819–1834: *The American farmer.*
1821: Waln, Robert.
1822: Egan, Pierce.
1823: Duncan, James.
1823: Purdy, Jr.
1823: Van Ranst, C. W.
1827: Depping, J. B.
1829–1844: *American turf register and sporting magazine.*
1830–1832: Gano, Daniel.
1831: Gano, D. *In:* Barnum, H. L.
1831: Union Race Course.
1831–1861: *The Spirit of the times.*
1833: Cox, William.
1833: Edgar, Patrick Nisbett.
1833: *The Olio.*
1833–1834: *New-York sporting magazine.*
1835–1836: *Gentleman's vade mecum.*
1835–1836: *The United States sporting magazine.*
1835–1859: Longstreet, Augustus Baldwin.
1837: *Horse-racing, and Christian principle and duty.*
1838: Surtees, Robert Smith. *Jorrock's jaunts and jollities.*
1840: Newdegate, C.
1843: Green, Jonathan H. *An exposure of the arts.*
1843: *The Southern sportsman.*
1844: Timbs, John.
1845: Green, Jonathan H. *The gambler's mirror.*
1845–1860: *American turf register and racing and trotting calendar.*
1845–1861: Sue, Eugene.
1847–1858: Porter, William Trotter. *A quarter race.*
1855: Hammett, Samuel Adams.
1856–1861: *Porter's Spirit of the times.*
1858: Thorpe, Thomas Bangs. *Scenes in Arkansaw.*
1858–1859: *American racing calendar and trotting record.*

1859–1902: *Wilkes' Spirit of the times.*

Racing: Associations and clubs.

    1803: Washington Jockey Club.

    1810: Massachusetts Society for Encouraging the Breed of Fine Horses.

    1823: New-York Association for the Improvement of the Breed of Horses.

    1831: Kentucky Association for the Improvement of the Breed of Horses.

    1835: Missouri Association for the Improvement of the Breed of Horses.

    1836: New York Jockey Club.

    1836: South Carolina Jockey Club.

    1838: Metairie Jockey Club.

    1857: Irving, John B.

    1859: Ashland Jockey Club.

Racing: Songs.

    1835: Blewitt, Jonathan.

Racquets.

    1811: Graydon, Alexander (1770).

    1845–1853: Racket Court Club.

    1848–1858: *Boy's own book of sports.*

Recreation. *See also:* Games.

    1785: Friends, Society of.

    1825: Henry, Thomas Charlton.

    1848: Wilson, John.

    1855: Beverley, Robert (1707).

Riding. *See also:* Horse.

    1771: Faulks, Mr.

    1776: Astley, Philip.

    1785: Pool, Mr.

    1809: *A Peep into the sports of youth.*

    1813–1828: Bunbury, Henry William.

    1828: Cowper, William.

    1830–1857: *The Young lady's book.*

    1833: Lebeaud.

    1837: Comstock, John Lee.

    1838: *The Juvenile forget me not.*

Riding. *Continued:*

    1839: *The Lady's book.*
    1839–1854: *The Young lady's equestrian manual.*
    1840–1843: Howitt, William.
    1840–1855: *Girl's book of healthful amusements.*
    1844–1847: Hershberger, H. R.
    1850–1856: Baucher, Francois.
    1851: Craige, Thomas.
    1852: Bristed, Charles Astor.
    1855: Beecher, Henry Ward.
    1855: *The Illustrated manners book.*
    1856: Cozzens, Frederick Swartwout.
    1857: Herbert, Henry William. *Horse and horsemanship.*
Riding: Songs.
    1820: Leibling.
    1840: Hooton, James.
    1845: Lyon, C. B.
    1853: Munck, Johann.
Rifles, shotguns, etc.
    1783–1792: *The Sportsman's companion.*
    1803: Pennsylvania. Commerce and Manufacturers Committee.
    1827–1828: *The American shooter's manual.*
    1846: Bosworth, N. A.
    1846–1853: Hawker, Peter.
    1848: Chapman, John Ratcliffe.
    1850: Clarke, F. H. & Co.
    1850–1857: Peel, Jonathan.
Rounders.
    1829–1859: Clarke, William.
    1847–1852: *The Boy's treasury of sports.*
Rowing.
    1833–1834: *The New York sporting magazine.*
    1836–1856: Walker, Donald.
    1838: Narraganset Boat Club.
    1850–1855: Frost, John.
    1852: Bristed, Charles Astor.
    1858: Putnam, J. D. R.
    1859: The Schuylkill Navy.

Rowing: Songs.
    1800–1825: Moore, Thomas.
    1823: Wiesenthal, T. V.
    1830: Stevenson, Sir John Andrew.
    1831: Jones.
    1834: Goodrich, Samuel Griswold.
    1834: Philadelphia Glee Association.
    1835–1842: English, Thomas Dunn.
    1836: Phillips, Jonas B.
    1837: Willis, J. H.
    1838: Clifton, William.
    1840: Power, Thomas.
    1846: Dodworth, Allen
    1847: Woodman, H. F.
    1849: Pike, Marshall Spring.
    1856: Turner, J. W.
    1856: University Boat Club.
    1857: Lisle, Estelle de.
    1859: Ross, H. P.

Sabbath observance.
    1762: Welles, Noah.
Sable.
    1843: Goodrich, Samuel Griswold.
    1857–1859: Hammond, Samuel H.
Saddlery.
    1836–1841: Hazen, Edward.
Salmon.
    1831: Cincinnati Angling Club.
    1832: Davy, Sir Humphrey.
    1848–1856: Lanman, Charles. *A tour of the river Saguenay.*
    1857: Nettle, Richard.
    1858: Herbert, Henry William. *Fishing with hook and line.*
Shark.
    1847–1848: Porter, William Trotter. *A quarter race.*
Shoeing. *See:* Horse: Shoeing.
Shooting. *See:* Rifles, shotguns, etc.
Skating.

301

Skating. *Continued:*

    1802–1830: *Youthful sports.*
    1809: *A Peep into the sports of youth.*
    1810: *Youthful amusements.*
    1818: *Winter. Old age.*
    1820: *Children's amusements.* (*See* p. xviii.)
    1827: Depping, J. B.
    1835: *Pretty stories.*
    1836–1856: Walker, Donald.
    1843: Maeder, James G.
    1845: *The Child's pictorial mentor.*
Sleighing.
    1852: Bristed, Charles Astor.
  Sleighing: Songs.
    1840: Field, J. T.
    1844: Barclay, B. S.
    1850: Muller, Julius E.
    1851: Brown, Francis H.
    1852: Sanford, R. B.
    1853: Sedgwick, A.
    1853: Wallace, William Vincent.
    1855: Engelbrecht, J. C.
    1856: Sangster, Charles.
    1856: Poppenberg's Band.
    1857–1859: Pierpont, James S.
Smoking. Songs.
    1836: Gear, J.
Songs.
    1843: *The Book of a thousand songs.*
  Songs: Archery.
    1836: Brown, Bartholomew.
  Songs: Bear.
    1853: Purves, William.
  Songs: Boar, Wild.
    1836: Moore, Thomas.
  Songs: Bowling.
    1845: Stewart, Adam.
  Songs: Buffalo.
    1848: Murray, Sir Charles Augustus.

Songs. *Continued:*

Songs: Chamois.
  1827: Rossini, Gioacchino Antonio.
Songs: Children's games.
  1850: Taylor, Jane.
Songs: Coaching.
  1832: *The Universal songster.*
Songs: Deer.
  1774: *The Royal American magazine.*
  1818–1821: Harrington.
  1820: Fitzsimons, E.
  1820: Philipps, Thomas.
  1822: Shield, William.
  1823: Farren, P.
  1827–1840: Weber, Carl Maria Friedrich Ernst von.
  1830: Lee, Alexander.
  1830: Van Dyke, Harry Stoe.
  1830: Williams, R. F.
  1833: Hewitt, John H.
  1834: Iucho, Wilhelm.
  1836: White, Edward L.
  1847: Schiller, Johann Christoph Friedrich von.
  1852: Munck, Johann.
  1854: Marshall, Leonard.
  1854: Pendleton, Mrs. A. V.
  1855: Reed, R. Rhodes.
  1855: Southgate, Fred.
  1856: Burnham, George P.
Songs: Dog.
  1843: Bailey, F. W. N.
  1853: Foster, Stephen Collins.
Songs: Fishing.
  1826: *The Memorial.*
  1835: Bailey, Johanna.
  1836: Ball, T.
  1840: A., S. A.
  1840: Russell, Henry.
  1854: Crosby, L. V. H.
  1856: Burnham, George P.

Songs: Fishing. *Continued:*

1854: Wallace, William Vincent.
1856: Jenks, Joseph William. (Henry Wadsworth Longfellow.)
Songs: Fox hunting.
1798: Hook, James. *Bright Phoebus.*
1803: Willson, Joseph.
1819: *Tally ho!*
1821–1825: Hook, James. *Diana.*
1830: Radcliffe, F. P.
1830: Rimbault, Stephen Francis.
1830–1842: Hyatt, George W.
1832: Imlah, John.
1835: Moxley, Alfred.
1840: Webbe, Samuel.
1854: H., W.
Songs: Game birds.
1854: Marshall, Leonard.
Songs: Gazelle.
1830: Moore, Thomas.
Songs: Gymnastics.
1844: Ordway, J. P.
Songs: Hare.
1815: Benham, Asahel.
Songs: Hunting.
1811: Scott, Sir Walter.
1820–1832: Woodworth, Samuel.
1828: *The Atlantic souvenir.*
1830: Hart, Joseph.
1831–1837: S., M.
1832: Ball, William.
1832: Proch, Heinrich.
1834: Benham, Asabel.
1834: Moschelles, I.
1836: Weber, Carl Maria Friedrich Ernst von.
1837: Hodson, G. A.
1839: Linley, George.
1841–1850: Morris, George P.
1842: Viel, Edmond.

Songs: Hunting. *Continued:*

1843: *The Book of a thousand songs.*
1856: Burnham, George P.
Songs: Mountaineering.
1844: Morris, George P.
Songs: Quoits.
1839: Washington Social Gymnasium.
Songs: Racoon.
1830–1836: Settin' on a rail.
1843: *The Book of a thousand songs.*
Songs: Racing.
1835: Blewitt, Jonathan.
Songs: Riding.
1820: Leibling.
1828: Cowper, William.
1840: Hooton, James.
1845: Lyon, C. B.
1853: Munck, Johann.
Songs: Rowing.
1800–1825: Moore, Thomas.
1823: Wiesenthal, T. V.
1830: Stevenson, Sir John Andrew.
1831: Jones.
1834: Goodrich, Samuel Griswold.
1834: Philadelphia Glee Association.
1835–1842: English, Thomas Dunn.
1836: Phillips, Jonas B.
1837: Willis, J. H.
1838: Clifton, William.
1840: Power, Thomas.
1847: Woodman, H. F.
1849: Pike, Marshall Spring.
1856: Turner, J. W.
1856: University Boat Club.
1857: Lisle, Estelle de.
1859: Ross, H. P.
Songs: Skating.
1837: Power, Thomas.
Songs: Sleighing.

Songs: Sleighing. *Continued:*

    1842: *Sledge quadrille.*
    1844: Barclay, B. S.
    1850: Muller, Julius E.
    1851: Brown, Francis H.
    1852: Sanford, R. B.
    1853: Sedgwick, A.
    1853: Wallace, William Vincent.
    1855: Engelbrecht, J. C.
    1856: Poppenberg's Band.
    1856: Sangster, Charles.
    1857–1859: Pierpont, James S.
Songs: Smoking.
    1836: Gear, Joseph.
Songs: Wolf.
    1835: Arnold, J.
Songs: Yachting.
    1838: Clifton, William.
Spaniel. *See also:* Dog.
    1783–1792: *The Sportsman's companion.*
Squirrel.
    1854: Winner, Septimus.
Stable management. *See:* Horse: Care, stable management.
Stool ball.
    1829–1839: Clarke, William.
    1847–1852: *The Boy's treasury of sports.*
Stud books. *See:* Horse: Stud books.
Swimming.
    1814: Bosworth, Newton.
    1814–1821: Franklin, Benjamin.
    1818: Coffin, John G.
    1818: Frost, John.
    1818–1826: Coffin, John G.
    1821: *The Art of swimming.*
    1836: Thomson, Edward.
    1841: Bosworth, Newton.
    1846: Bennet, James Arlington.
    1846–1849: *Orr's Book of swimming.*
    1849: *The Science of swimming as taught and practiced.*

Tapir.
    1855: Squier, Ephraim George.
Taxidermy.
    1829: Bullock, William.
Tennis, Court.
    1763: Massachusetts Bay Province.
    1772: Rush, Benjamin.
    1792–1822: Holcroft, Thomas.
    1796: Hoyle, Edmond.
    1796: New Jersey.
    1844: Timbs, John.
    1847: Paris, J. A.
Tiger. *See also:* Big game.
    1834: *Conversations of a father.*
    1858: Reid, Mayne.
Trapping. *See also:* Hunting, and names of animals: Beaver, etc.
    1815: *Eine Kurtzgefasste neue Sammlung.*
    1839–1843: Townsend, John K.
    1847: *The Hunters of Kentucky.*
    1847–1859: Coyner, David H.
    1849–1859: Ruxton, George F. A. *Life in the far West.*
    1850–1857: Simms, Jeptha Root.
    1857: Thompson, Daniel Pierce.
    1858: Robinson, John Hovey.
    1858–1859: Peters, DeWitt Clinton.
    1859: Hartley, Cecil B.
Trotting. *See also:* Racing.
    1813–1828: Bunbury, Henry William.
    1829–1844: *American turf register and sporting magazine.*
    1833–1834: *New-York sporting magazine.*
    1835–1836: *The United States sporting magazine.*
    1843–1859: Youatt, William.
    1845–1860: *American turf register and racing and trotting calendar.*
    1852: Bristed, Charles Astor.
    1855: Redhead, H. W.
    1858: *American racing calendar and trotting record.*
    1858: Williams, S. D.
Trout. *See also:* Fishing, Fishing, Fly.
    1833–1843: Smith, Jerome Van Crowinshield.

Trout. *Continued:*

    1837–1859: Walton, Isaac.

    1839: Willis, Nathaniel P.

    1842: Hawes, William Post.

    1844: Willis, Nathaniel Parker.

    1845: Lanman, Charles. *Letters.*

    1845–1857: Brown, John J.

    1847: Herbert, Henry William. *Trout fishing.*

    1848–1856: Lanman, Charles. *A tour of the river Saguenay.*

    1849–1853: Headley, Joel Tyler. *The Adirondack.*

    1850: Headley, Joel Tyler. *Letters.*

    1850: Lanman, Charles. *Haw-Ho-Noo.*

    1853: Prime, William Cowper. *The old home by the river.*

    1855: Beecher, Henry Ward.

    1855: *The Sportsman's portfolio.*

    1857: Garlick, Theodatus.

    1857: Nettle, Richard.

    1858: Herbert, Henry William. *Fishing with hook and line.*

Turkey, Wild.

    1845–1856: Bement, Caleb.

    1851–1857: Lewis, Elisha Jarett.

    1854: Thorpe, Thomas Bangs. *The hive of "The Bee-Hunter."*

Turtle.

    1834: *The People's magazine.*

    1855: Squier, Ephraim George.

Walking.

    1844: Elworth, Thomas.

  Walking: Songs.

    1839: Knaebel, S.

Wild fowl.

    1835: Davis, J.

    1841: Schreiner, William H.

    1847: Miller, Thomas.

    1851–1857: Lewis, Elisha Jarett.

    1853: Krider, John.

Wild fowl. *Continued:*

  1855: Beverley, Robert (1707).
  1858: Hammett, Samuel Adams.
  1859: Johnes, Merideth.
Wild horse. *See:* Horse, Wild.
Wild turkey. *See:* Turkey, Wild.
Wolf.
  1843: Hoffman, Charles Fenno.
  1851–1858: Webber, Charles Wilkins.
    Wolf: Songs.
  1835: Arnold, J.
Woodcock. *See also:* Game birds.
  1835: *Essays on various subjects.*
  1846–1853: Hawker, Peter.
  1853: Krider, John.
  1855: *The Sportsman's portfolio.*
  1857: Herbert, Henry William. *Sporting scenes.*
Wrestling.
  1820: Taylor, Joseph.
  1836–1856: Walker, Donald.

Yachting.
  1833–1834: *New-York sporting magazine.*
  1836–1856: Walker, Donald.
  1838: Clifton, William.
  1845: Houston, Matilda Charlotte (Jesse) Fraser.
  1854: Choules, Rev. John Overton.
  1854: *Swell life at sea.*
  1857: Stedman, Charles Ellery.
  1859: Dufferin and Ava, Lord.